Getting Down to Cases

Learning to Teach
with Case Studies

Getting Down to Cases

Learning to Teach with Case Studies

Selma Wassermann

Foreword by C. R. Christensen

Teachers College, Columbia University
New York and London

Published by Teachers College Press, 1234 Amsterdam Avenue
New York, NY 10027

The following cases originally appeared in slightly different versions:
Case 3.2, "My Friend Connie." Reprinted with permission of *Phi Delta Kappan,* December 1977 *59*(4):245–246.

Case 4.4, "Barry," from *Leaders in Education: Their Views on Controversial Issues,* Glenda F. Roberson and Mary A. Johnson, eds. Copyright © 1988, pp. 183–189, University Press of America, Inc. Reprinted by permission of the publisher.

Case 5.2, "Children working as Self-Motivated Learners? It Doesn't Work," in *Childhood Education,* 1989 *65*:201–205. Reprinted by permission of the Association for Childhood Education International, 11501 Georgia Ave., Suite 315, Wheaton, MD 20902.

Library of Congress Cataloging-in-Publication Data

Wassermann, Selma.
    Getting down to cases: learning to teach with case studies /
  Selma Wassermann; foreword by C. R. Christensen.
    p.   cm.
  Includes bibliographical references.
  ISBN 0-8077-3291-5
  1. Teachers—Training of. 2. Case method. 3. Teaching—Case studies. I. Title.
  LB1707.W37   1993
  370.71—dc20   93-23841

  ISBN 0-8077-3291-5 (pbk.)

Printed on acid-free paper
Manufactured in the United States of America`
99 98 97 96 95 94 93   7 6 5 4 3 2 1

Contents

Foreword

This unique and valuable book, a delight to read, provocative in questions raised and solutions proposed, is clearly must reading for teachers, teachers of teachers, and leaders of academic institutions, from high schools to university professional schools. *Getting Down to Cases: Learning to Teach with Cases Studies*, text and cases, is concerned with the challenge of how teachers can be better prepared in professional programs for the complexities of "real life" in the classroom.

Selma Wassermann brings new insights to old issues. Dissatisfaction with our education system seems to have been with us forever. Emerson, over 150 years ago, carped that we are "shut in schools for ten or fifteen years and come out with a belly full of words and do not know a thing." In 1915, John Dewey summed the challenge so succinctly when he noted, in *Experience in Education*:

> Why is it, in spite of the fact that teaching by pouring in, learning by a passive absorption, are universally condemned, that they are still so entrenched in practice? That education is not an affair of "telling" and being told, but an active and constructive process, is a principle almost as generally violated in practice as conceded in theory. Is not this deplorable situation due to the fact that the doctrine is itself merely told? It is preached; it is lectured; it is written about. But its enactment into practice requires that the school environment be equipped with agencies for doing, with tools and physical materials, to an extent rarely attained. It requires that methods of instruction and administration be modified to allow and to secure direct and continuous occupations with things.

Dewey's challenge, repeated by so many others—individual scholars as well as study commissions—remains largely unmet today.

Wassermann, however, in a disciplined and experimental mode, has been working away for over a decade at first-step solutions to Dewey's basic challenge. Her laboratories have been seminars conducted at the Faculty of Education, Simon Fraser University, as well as seminal experimental programs conducted at high schools throughout the province, a critical effort being the work done at secondary schools in Coquitlam and Cowichan school districts in British Columbia. That clinical research, and the resultant programs converting findings into practice, enable her to make a gift of considerable importance to all interested in improving the quality of the teaching-learning process throughout the academy.

What *Getting Down to Cases: Learning to Teach with Case Studies* does is to ask us to consider the adequacy of many, but certainly not all, teacher training programs. Are they preparing the novice teacher to deal with the reality of future classroom practice—how Connie deals with the tensions created by administrative directives conflicting with firmly held personal beliefs? What Barry's teacher might do as she tries to balance ways of helping him to learn math and yet maintain and build his almost nonexistent self-esteem? Or Mrs. Buscemi's difficulty in grading an underprivileged student's work when her evaluation will make the difference as to whether he gains, or does not gain, admission to a local community college? Can the essential attitudes, skills, and process knowledge needed to deal with these classroom problems/opportunities be lectured to—"poured into," to paraphrase Dewey—the preservice instructor? And the author further asks us to reflect on how in-service teachers actually learn on the job—how they deal with the complexities presented by students such as Adam and Barry.

The fundamental theses of this book are simple but powerful. Major improvements are needed in our preservice teacher education programs (implicitly also in in-service programs), and increased use of a case-based, discussion-oriented methodology as a primary, but not exclusive, pedagogical approach offers promise for substantial improvement over current efforts.

Chapter 1, "Shazam! You're a Teacher!" sends a message of concern, as well as hope, to preservice and novice instructors alike. Concerns—there are no neat and tidy "answers," no useful checklist of "solutions" (carefully copied from a principles of teaching textbook) to serve as a "security blanket" for the inevitable challenges and problems you will encounter in your future classroom practice. Much as your current instructors would like to ease your anxiousness about what to do when Jimmy refuses to write up an assigned paper, or when Susie simply won't stop whispering to Joanie, or when the tests don't arrive on time for the English quiz—they can't. It all depends! It depends, Wassermann reminds us, on having "intimate knowledge of the variables, the pushes and pulls and pressures and expectations of the event." It is the specifics of the particular event and the details of the context in which it occurs that govern what responsible action steps might be taken.

But also a message of hope—that teachers, novice and experienced, by mastering the basic clinical skills of observing, questioning, comparing, and intuiting can create personally appropriate ways of thinking about and acting on the problem of the moment. Wassermann labels this process "meaning-making."

"Making meaning of the events in the classroom," she notes, "is what competent teachers do from moment to moment every teaching day. We size-up a situation, reflect on what it means, and choose an appropriate action that depends on how we have interpreted the event. This is how *we teach ourselves* to understand 'what is happening; to determine the action to take.'" And teaching with and learning from cases is an excellent way of helping preservice and novice instructors to become competent classroom practitioners—master meaning makers.

Chapter 2, "'Hello, Ms. Chips'—Learning to Teach From Cases," overviews the benefits, and implicitly the risks, of changing from a lecture-knowledge transference mode, to a discussion skill-practice pedagogy. Teaching from cases, the author reminds us, enables a preservice student to increase his or her skills of questioning, listening, observing, and communicating ideas to others; it encourages reflection about "those complex acts known as teaching," to find ways of understanding how decisions are made in the classroom, to appreciate the complexity of the variables an instructor must consider before she or he chooses what action (if any) to take in the next few seconds; and, so important, it enables him or her to learn more about "self"—one's own pattern of beliefs and values and how they influence one's behavior in the classroom. The chapter, moreover, includes a wealth of practical suggestions for helping a preservice teacher to prepare for, and make the most of, a case discussion.

Learning from "Hello, Ms. Chips" does not end when your first re-reading is complete. Re-reading and reflection opens the door to a delightful "discovery"—that most, if not all of the benefits that accrue to the preservice student—the teacher to be—also accrue to the teacher of the moment who is guiding the seminar group through the case problem of the day. The result—a powerful synergism—gradually emerges: discussion leader and student of discussion learning simultaneously, interactively, and cooperatively leads to the almost inevitable outcome, first partnership, then the ultimate—the emergence of a learning community.

Case methods of teaching are increasingly being explored as a possible way of meeting what the philosopher A. N. Whitehead believed to be a major challenge of academia. "First hand knowledge" he noted, "is the ultimate basis of intellectual life. The second handedness of the learned world is the secret of its mediocrity—it is tame because it has never been scared by the facts." Case methodologies insist that learners, teachers, and students deal with first-hand knowledge—the written case as well as the emergent dialogue—by creating frames of thinking that enable them to apply knowledge to specific problems in a unique context.

I would define a teaching case as a partial, historical, clinical study of a predicament confronting (in this context) a teacher and/or an administrator, presented in a story mode with the "voices" of the key involved parties evident, that calls for an individual or group to take "action." A case should be "researched, designed, and crafted," as Abby J. Hansen reminds us, "to enable and encourage disciplined group dialogue and individual learning." Cases taught effectively are generative of an abundance of questions, a variety of next step options, and a multiplicity of wider issues that help link the discussion of the hour to prior and future dialogue.

Chapters 3, 4, and 5 of *Getting Down to Cases* share with the reader a "collection" of 26 cases developed by the author. The cases present a treasure trove of teaching-learning opportunities for all—they are the very best! They are rich in what Jerome Bruner calls "predicaments"—puzzles without neat and simple answers, packed with opportunities for "discovery rather than learning about it," a case method imperative. Despite inevitable stylistic differences—this "bank" of cases was developed over time, at different institutions, with an objective of exploring a spectrum of teaching challenges—each case will enable you to experience the learning of the whole in the particular; each case will provide you with a contained, bounded teaching instrument that encourages an expansive, even constructively explosive, learning opportunity. We are fortunate to be able to be granted their use.

Wassermann "bundles" her cases around three themes. Chapter 3, "The Teacher as Person," puts the spotlight on an individual teacher's "own needs, values, and expectations" and how they impact on her classroom practice. Chapter 4, "Teachers and Students," focuses on learners—the challenges that emerge when an instructor works with an individual, or groups of students. Chapter 5, "The Teacher and the Curriculum," examines the wider context of curriculum, instruction, and evaluation.

As one reviews the three modules as a totality, we note that the cases tend to be arrayed from the less complex, for example, Case 3.4, "I've Got a Problem," which highlights difficulties between a student teacher and his college supervisor—a common garden variety problem—to the more complex, for example, Case 5.3, "I'll Come Back When You're Teaching," where one's teaching plan of the day might end by posing the most fundamental questions of our vocation—who needs to learn, what, and how. The author also supports each case with a thought-provoking assemblage of teaching questions—questions tailored to exploit the special learning opportunities presented by a specific problem. And, as you review and compare all of Wassermann's carefully designed question sets, again uniformities appear. All are designed to help you strike an appropriate balance between "guiding the discussion" and "imposing lock step control." All tend to emphasize diagnosis and understanding first with action steps coming later. And many tend to conclude by raising wider issues that have a philosophic, ethical cast.

Another possible use of these cases, one of many, is as the basis for an independent study program. It has been done with success. The cases are so rich in "firing line detail"—how problems actually emerge in the give and take of classroom dialogue, how colleagues have thought about and worked through sensitive issues—that they inevitably offer new insights to dealing with many current problems. At the minimum, they prepare you to test out new ideas with a buddy over coffee—a much less threatening way of reviewing your proposed next step class experiment than speaking to a large group of colleagues. And, with a bit of luck, it may stimulate you to embark on a modest research effort— to write up a case of your own. Wassermann would be most enthusiastic about such a move.

Chapter 6 urges readers to consider "creating" a case based on a personal classroom experience: It introduces us to four author-colleagues who, having completed such a project, share their experiences with us, and then furnishes us with a detailed set of instructions on how to proceed with such a project. Substantial field experience has demonstrated that this is a powerful learning experience. Why?

First, developing the teaching instrument we call a case, gives one an in-depth appreciation of the intellectual challenge and artistic imperatives inherent in selecting a critical incident, gathering appropriate data, conducting multiple analyses, designing the flow-structure (to use Dr. Abby Hansen's words) of the case, writing up and reflecting upon multiple drafts, and providing aids for other instructors who might use this material. Completing such a project almost inevitably leaves teachers with increased respect for the case material they use in their daily practice and increased appreciation that a case is an intellectual work of art.

Second, creating one's own case about a classroom "happening" in which you played a key role enables you to see yourself, your strengths and weaknesses, with greater clarity—sometimes discomfort, sometimes pleasure. Impact comes from reading and re-reading the case. Did *I* do that? Say that to *him*? Wow! Listening then to a group of colleagues bring the power of their collective wisdom to bear on what you actually did in the situation, what you might have done, and what suggestions they might make to you (as a friend and colleague) about your future classroom teaching patterns provides an extraordinary self-learning circumstance.

Finally, in learning more about the complexity and challenges involved in *both* developing case *teaching instruments* as well as in *leading a case dialogue*, one's already substantial respect for this teaching-learning pedagogy will increase even more. You are onto something great.

Some years ago, Fred Hechinger, education editor of the *New York Times*, commented on the need for change with the academy:

> Education is the teachers you remember after you've forgotten the others. Changing the way schools are organized and introducing technol-

ogy to provide much of the instruction may increase the chances for serendipity to provide what is missing in schools, but the ultimate reform must come through the person of the teacher.

Wassermann, accepting Hechinger's diagnosis, asks schools of education to reconceive preservice teacher training programs, changing to a discussion pedagogy, and to begin using cases developed around the actual problems faced by instructors in their day-to-day classroom practice. Further, in *Getting Down to Cases*, she provides reader-practitioners with suggestions whereby they may develop their own bank of case materials and modify her format to meet better the needs of a particular school.

Her model, moreover, clearly has implications for the entire academy. We need more effective teachers everywhere in our educational system if we are to meet society's increasingly complex demands. A creative disturber, Wassermann has given us the concepts and materials to meet that challenge. We are in her debt.

C. Roland Christensen
University Professor, Emeritus
Harvard University

Preface

"If the situations [in the cases] were drawn from real life and not just concocted from someone's imagination, I believe they would have a lot more meaning," a student critic told me during a field test of some of the cases in this book. It may well be that truth is stranger than fiction. It may be hard to believe that an administration would dismiss a teacher like Connie on such spurious grounds; that a female college supervisor would "come on to" a male student teacher; that a teacher would allow her scantily clad photo to appear in a slick magazine. It may be hard to believe that a child's father could smear his genitals with lye; that a 9-year-old could shoot a classmate; that a teacher would be unable to help a child overcome his math disability. It may be hard to believe that children would resist and reject classroom freedoms; that a principal would usurp a teacher's decision-making prerogatives. In spite of issues in these cases that appear to be "concocted from someone's imagination," the truth is that all the cases are rooted in real events. While names, places, and contexts have been fictionalized to guard and respect the privacy of the individuals involved, all the cases are based in the real world of teachers, children, and schools.

The cases are not intended to present the "unhappy" faces of teaching; they are meant to provide pictures of life in schools, raising issues that beg for enlightened and informed examination. If, through studying these cases, teachers grow in their ability to see beyond the surface and feel ready to deal with deeper, more complex meanings, the cases will have served their purpose.

For their contributions to the case materials, there are many people to thank: Barb Burton, Hugh Blackman, John Richmond, and Brenda McNeill for allowing me to adapt material from their original cases; Michael Manley-Casimir, for the delicious title, "The Bared Breast"; Anita Plaxe and Teresa Saunders for the stories from their classrooms.

Mindy Ally, Maureen Adam, and Harold McAllister conducted numerous interviews that led to cases based upon critical incidents in the lives of beginning teachers. Joan Guido and her staff welcomed me into their school and shared their experiences generously. Steve Smith introduced me to the possibilities of student teachers who write their own cases.

There are others to thank: Lin Langley, Heather Hamilton, and Kelli Vogstead, those intrepid case teachers in the Faculty of Education at Simon Fraser University, who tried many of the cases and thus allowed for their "testing in the marketplace"; Linda Muttitt, who agreed to have her journal entry made public; Chris Christensen, for his inspiration and for showing me the joy of teaching and learning with cases; Susan Liddicoat, my good editor; and all my students at Simon Fraser University, who have been my best teachers in my ongoing search for making meaning of the educational process. To all, my deepest gratitude.

1 | Shazam! You're a Teacher!

Mary Dare Hitchcock taught Human Growth and Development, 3 credits, to sophomore students in the university where I was learning to be a teacher. She was a southern lady who spoke in the soft, drawn-out vowel tones of Geo-jah, and the musical cadences of her voice were sweet on my ears. What puzzled me most about her was how she managed to look so cool and unruffled on those beastly hot and humid days that insinuate themselves too early into the East Coast spring, while the rest of us, scraped from the mean streets of the city, were always sweating and grubby. Just looking at her made me feel less like a teacher. Did teachers never sweat? Did they never have a single hair out of place? Were they always as composed, self-assured, untouched by human experience as this teacher's demeanor would have me believe?

From the raised platform where she sat, elevated by position and attitude, she gave my class lessons in teaching. To be remembered, above all, she told us, was that children were different—physically, intellectually, emotionally, and socially different from one another. (If we learned the mnemonic P-I-E-S, that would surely help us to remember this important concept for the final exam. Dutifully, we copied P-I-E-S into our notebooks.) And because children are different in P-I-E-S ways, teachers must INDIVIDUALIZE THEIR INSTRUCTION. She spoke the words in capital letters. There could be no other acceptable way to teach.

Teaching to individual learning needs was a foreign idea to those of us who had spent the last twelve years in large, urban public schools, where as many as 35 children in a class were all instructed in exactly the same way, whatever our individual differences. In our school experiences, even going to the toilet was a group activity rather than an individual endeavor. If there were differences among us, they were neither acknowledged nor addressed. But in our desire to please Dr. Hitchcock and, of course, to pass the course, we took to heart what she said without question, without even mentioning the obvious and flagrant discrepancy between what she told us about individual differences and the way she taught. For as our professor sat on her platform, day after blah-blahing day, we

1

sat, too, in straight rows of tablet armchairs, listening, taking notes, and collecting our 3 credits' worth of human growth and development.

Needless to say, it was easy to learn the lessons in Dr. Hitchcock's class and to pass the course. It did not take much to remember P-I-E-S, and other such concepts, and to write about them with vigor on essays and final exams. Other courses in the education sequence did not vary from this format, in which scholarly professors lectured to students about what was important to know about teaching, and students listened, took notes, and returned, for the teachers' approval, their own words in different form. After 36 hours of education coursework I had amassed a huge repository of facts about teaching, which I fully expected would equip me for the challenges of classroom practice.

It should not come as a surprise that I would remember my first day of teaching as clearly as if I had gone down on the *Titanic*. Learning the "correct answers" had not only *not* equipped me for the complex and confusing world of the classroom, but even worse, had led me down the garden path. Implicit in what I had learned was that teaching was merely a matter of learning certain pieces of information about teaching. If I only knew what the "answers" were, I would be prepared to face the vast and overwhelming human dilemmas that make up life in classrooms. I, unfortunately, had been swindled. My training in learning the answers was as useless as yesterday's pizza. I was entering a profession in which there are few, if any, clear-cut answers, a profession that is riddled with ambiguity and moral dilemmas that would make Solomon weep. Even more of a handicap was that I became desperate in my search for the "answers"—certain that they were out there, somewhere, if only I could find them. So feverish was I in this quest that I was unable to perceive the real needs of the profession: how to use knowledge to deal effectively with the human dilemmas that teachers face from moment to moment on the job. Good teaching, I eventually learned, depends more on how teachers use knowledge to make intelligent meaning of complex classroom events than it does on knowing the "answers." These learned skills—the application of knowledge to practice—had been sadly omitted from my coursework.

Perhaps my education professors had assumed that knowledge, once acquired, would be easily applied to classroom practice, but it does not quite work that way. The application of knowledge to practice is a complex process that requires its own course of study. Aspiring writers who study verbs, adjectives, nouns, grammatical construction, and other language mechanisms will not become writers until they learn how to apply that knowledge to the art and craft of writing. Aspiring teachers who study P-I-E-S, learn that the "slow learner has an IQ range of 75 to 90 and is unable to think in abstractions," and memorize the four definitions of creativity and other fact-bytes from texts and/or lectures will not become teachers until they learn how to use that information intelligently in advancing student learning. The gap between *knowing* and *knowing how* must be bridged by a whole new set of skills that take the aspiring teacher from the world of information to learned applications.

My own teacher training had prepared me for a TV sitcom world of teaching, an artificial world in which situations are never very complicated and simple answers suffice to deal with whatever problem is dished out. Nothing in that TV sitcom world is ever ambiguous or uncertain. Kids never fall down and bruise their knees. They never poke each other with pencils. They never lose their lunches. They never have runny noses or wet their pants. Parents never make outrageous demands. Principals never intimidate. There are always enough books, chairs, desks, and other instructional materials to go around. Teachers are never tired, frustrated, or angry. There are no incidences of child abuse, no disappeared fathers, no drunken mothers. There are never any children who cannot learn, or will not learn, never any children who are hungry or emotionally ill. And in the TV sitcom land of certainty, there is always enough time for teachers to do everything the job of teaching requires. Should a more complex issue ever surface, not to worry. The matter is always massaged into a tidy little solution in a comfortable 30- or 60-minute package, less 10 or so minutes for commercial breaks.

No wonder my first day of teaching found me fumbling, bumbling, and limping through those five interminable hours of the school day. I was prepared for *The Brady Bunch* and what I got was *Hill Street Blues*. Kenny Henderson did not help my situation either. He kept following me around, telling me that his teacher last year never did things this way! At the end of that first day, I was very close to leaving that room, that school, that profession altogether. Who the heck wanted to be a teacher anyway! I could always earn my living making cabbage rolls, a profession in which I had at least some minimal competence.

In the years that followed, I found to my astonishment and consternation that what I had endured in making the transition from teacher education to teaching practice was not unique. It is very much the same for many entering the profession, a universally shared trauma. The ordeal of those first 100 days of teaching is the beginning teacher's initiation into the profession, the time during which "virgin" teachers face up to the bankruptcy of how little they know about the applications of concepts to the realities of the classroom. Struggling to survive, beginning teachers reach out for a lifeline and grab onto something that looks as if it is going to save them, to give them what they need to handle the demands of the job. When one is drowning and reaching, one does not spend a lot of time thinking carefully about the choices one is making. One simply grabs and holds on for dear life. Having thus grabbed, however, teachers find themselves on one of several pathways that influence their continued professional development.

One pathway on which some teachers find themselves keeps them on that relentless search for the "answers" to complex, death-defying classroom questions, angry with those "in the know" who do not provide them. These teachers are continually frustrated because inservice workshops and consultant "experts" repeatedly fail to provide them with precise cures for all their classroom ills. Survival on this pathway is dependent on the teacher's ability to assign blame for things that do not work to others.

Another pathway to survival is taken by those who have given up their quest and parachuted out of the profession into some more lucrative and less confounding job, like selling real estate or computer software. A third pathway to survival finds teachers shutting their eyes and their minds to the demands of the classroom, carrying out teaching in mechanical and mind-numbing ways. If it's 10 o'clock, it must be spelling. If it's October, the children are cutting out patterned paper pumpkins. Teaching methods are rarely subject to reflection or to consideration of cause and effect. Survival depends on following the prescripts of the teachers' manual as if it were a holy book, as if teaching were a religious ritual.

The most difficult survival pathway is taken by conscious choice. Teachers who choose this lifeline engage in a never-ending process of applying knowledge to practice and trying to make meaning out of the relationship between what they do and the impact of those actions on learners. In these classrooms, teachers constantly take risks in trying to make sense of what they see and hear, learning to use their own professional resources to interpret what is going on and making choices about what to do in each new situation. Teachers who choose this pathway accept that choices are not answers. They understand that while some choices lead to effective resolutions, other choices produce less-than-satisfying results. They understand that doing the "best you can" is often the best you can do; that the search for the right answers is illusory.

Why would teachers make a conscious choice of such a difficult pathway? Why would anyone choose a professional life in which everything they see and do is subject to the critical scrutiny of reflective practice? Is this professional survival? For teachers who have made such a choice, it is a matter of life and death, for to teach reflectively is to give life to students and to self, while any other route is professionally terminal. In taking the more arduous pathway, teachers continue to grow and learn on the job. One cannot grow professionally without risking. Without growth, one cannot hope to make a significant difference in the lives of children.

LIFE IN THE UNCERTAIN WORLD OF PROFESSIONAL DECISION MAKING: IT DEPENDS!

Arguably, the most frequently heard questions in education courses are variations on the theme "What do you do when . . . ?" These questions come from students who are searching desperately for help in finding the specific, practical, and real answer for a problem that is usually rooted in some hair-raising student–teaching experience. For example, What do you do when . . .

A child refuses to finish his work?
The principal insists that you do things her way?
A child keeps hitting and kicking the other kids?
A parent will not cooperate with you?
You have to give the tests?
You do not have enough time to help the child who needs special attention?
One child's behavior gets in the way of other children's learning?
A child is not ready to learn?

These "What do you do when . . ." questions come from the human drama of classroom life, a multilayered, multifaceted fabric of experience that must seem to beginning teachers like a crazyquilt. So many things happening all at the same moment, so many voices, so many actions, so many interactions. How do teachers find the threads in all the tangle? The following excerpt from Linda Muttitt's journal describes how this experienced and superb teacher perceives the classroom scene:

> Angry, Frustrated, Exhausted!
> This afternoon was a perfect example of one of those days when, as a teacher, I felt overwhelmed and bombarded with circumstances and decisions that pressed a greater and greater weight on the down side of the day. Kids were high, restless, wild. I was tired from the moment I got up this morning. All were conditions contributing to one of those moments when I felt FROZEN, PARALYZED to act effectively at a moment of crisis.
>
> In the computer room, three groups of children working on different things. Already there is separation, pressure to keep track, trusting in kids' ability to make choices that are intelligent and responsible.
>
> I'm trying to mark tests for reading skills, circulate among kids, be encouraging, keep track of the groups and times to rotate onto the next activity. Too many things are playing into my concentration.
>
> The computers break down. Kids' codes are not being received. Kids are demanding help, attention, changes, and their "fair" amount of time with the computers. Shawn says, "But if they've broken down, that's not fair, 'cause Groups 2 and 1 will have more time than us."
>
> I'm thinking (expletive deleted)! Why can't the computers just *work*! Feeling frustrated and somewhat inadequate at not knowing how to fix them.
>
> After several attempts, my concentration with one group on computers has already shown in the kids who are working on other tasks. They're getting noisier and fooling around.
>
> The computers get fixed and times are adjusted, so all kids can have equal time. I get fiercer with misbehaving kids. Things settle for a while as I travel

around the classroom to help individuals and still am trying to be encouraging. My fatigue is really playing havoc inside me. I feel like crying or screaming, or running away.

Then Chelsea comes up to me surrounded by a group of supporters and opponents. She's crying hysterically and two kids start talking to me at once. What's the problem?

A book! Tom believes it's his. Chelsea insists it's her brother's. They're looking to me. Other kids start talking at the same time. "I saw Chelsea's brother carrying the book." "I know it's Tom's because . . . etc."

I sit immobilized, sort of listening, but mostly swelling inside with anger and feelings of desperation.

This is no exaggeration. The day is full of moments like this. Looking at the overlays of that moment, caught in time, I can feel my chest tightening and it brings home a deeper awareness of how COMPLEX and stressful teaching is. I've wondered often how I can be tired by 9:05 A.M., when I arrived at school feeling energetic. Of course, this "picture" only touches on a few of the many other things happening at the moment, too. Other stresses, personal and professional, complicate each moment. (L. Muttitt, personal journal, 1984)

Considering that this is what good classrooms are like—rich with enough human drama to make for 100 years of soap opera—it is no wonder that teachers are eager to know what the "answers" are, to know what it is that they *should* be doing to deal with these human crises. The crises are real, and they are an integral part of the classroom scene. Teachers' concerns about them are also real, often heart-breaking. Such crises keep teachers awake at nights and, when they sleep, are the stuff of nightmares. It is normal that teachers should look for answers. Answers reduce anxieties. Crises elevate teachers' anxieties, and deciding on one's own what to do is a high-risk endeavor.

The bad news is that there are no simple answers to the "What do you do when . . ." questions that come out of classroom crises. Teachers should, in fact, be wary, if they hear that "this is *the* answer." For, as in life's other complex and complicated crises, the ways of dealing with classroom crises depend on the interrelationship of a large number of variables. That is why it is impossible for even a knowledgeable authority to give an answer without an insider's appreciation of what those variables are, the pushes and pulls and pressures and expectations and situational demands of the event, not to mention the considerable weight carried by the variable of individual human needs: the teacher's, the student's, and those of whoever else makes up the list of players. Intimate appreciation of a situation cannot come from outside or from outsiders. It can only come from those who are themselves deeply connected to the inner workings of the situation. Only those inside can know, with real authority, what the situation is really like. That is why the decision about the action to be taken must come from the insider. An outsider may, through thoughtful questioning, help an insider to perceive the situation more clearly, or perhaps to see the problem from fresh perspectives. An outsider may, through helpful, facilitative dialogue, offer encouragement and support for the insider's right to choose, or for the choice made. But outsiders, whatever their credentials or their authority, cannot put themselves completely and totally into the insider's skin and experience the situation from the insider's frame of reference. That is why external advice, suggestions, guidance, and the offer of answers may be singularly inappropriate. Outsiders are playing with only a partial deck. It is the insiders who have all the cards. That, however, does not make the insider's choice of what to do any easier. Nor does it erase the insider's longing for someone else to provide the solution.

Were a close personal friend to ask you, "What should I do? Should I leave my husband?" you would know that it is she who must find her own resolution to her dilemma. You would appreciate that you, having only information about a situation that was distorted through the frame of reference of the "wounded party," cannot know, from the outside, what the "right answer" to her question may be. Although her situation may be heart-wrenching and although you would like to help, you recognize that the best help you can give is to support her in the decision she will make. Should she leave her husband? Well, . . . it depends! It depends on so many factors that only she, the insider in the situation, can make such a choice.

What, then, should a teacher do if Phyllis does not finish her work? If Marvin's parents think he is spending too much time in the sandbox? If Pauli wets his pants? If Joe wanders around the room? If the principal is intimidating? If there are not enough textbooks? If Marilee bites the other kids? If the class is too noisy? If the districtwide tests do not measure what the students really know? How should teachers decide, in the face of the thousands of dilemmas that occur in the natural playing out of classroom life? Well, . . . it depends.

It depends on the child, on the situational demands of the classroom, on the expectations of teachers, administrators, parents, school boards; it depends on teachers' needs, their feelings, their internal pressures; it depends on school rules and regulations; it depends on psychological factors, like a teacher's control needs, fears of failure, need for approval, need to be in authority. It depends on the day, the hour, the month; whether it is early or late in the school year. It depends on the teacher's access to resources, both in and out of the classroom. It depends on the teacher's patience, level of frustration and stress, fatigue. It depends on what the teacher knows and, not least, on what the teacher believes about what is "right and good" in that situation. It depends, too, on the teacher's willingness to take a risk, to make a choice, to act. All of these (and other) variables tumble around, like bingo numbers in a wire box, and bear, with different weights, on the kind of choice to be made. That is why outsiders cannot say what to do. They are not sufficiently informed. They cannot put themselves completely into the teacher's shoes. They may, of course, offer suggestions. But, in the end, it is the teacher, alone, from his or her best professional judgment, who will make the decision. Of course, it is risky. Of course, teachers are often unsure. Of course, decisions mean taking chances. Of course, different teachers will choose different ways of dealing with the problem. But whoever said good teaching was a rose garden?

There are no easy roads to professional expertise, and if you have allowed yourself to believe that the classroom dilemmas described above reflect those "more troubled" classrooms where teachers are in danger of losing control, and where teacher competence is suspect, or where the group of students is "below average," you may be deluding yourself. Some people may have fantasies of "perfect" classrooms, where children are docile, compliant, all eager to learn; where they sit quietly and calmly; where teachers rule and teach with authority, and children obey and do as they are told. Some beginning teachers may, in fact, have such expectations. But the truth is that the best, most exciting, more learning-rich classrooms are precisely those in which things repeatedly go wrong, where crises arise from moment to moment, where the *mise-en-scène* is uneven, eventful, sometimes turbulent, and rarely calm. The ship that is becalmed goes nowhere. The classroom that is becalmed cannot offer the rich experiences that make learning truly meaningful. Therefore the best that teachers can hope for are the tools that allow them to perceive dilemmas with intelligence and sensitivity and to make thoughtful, informed decisions that guide their teaching actions. If you are concerned about your ability to teach in the ambiguous world of choosing appropriate problem-solving strategies, this book may offer some insights, some ideas to think about, and some useful tools. Courage! There *are* tools to help you navigate the murkey seas of uncertainty, so that you are not hopelessly adrift. These tools include learning to use the knowledge you possess to make meaning of what is happening in your classroom; learning to make teaching decisions that are appropriate to the meanings you have made; and learning to make evaluative judgments about the effectiveness of your decisions. These tools strengthen your ability to apply what you know to classroom practice.

With such tools, you grow in your awareness that while there are no easy, clear-cut answers in teaching, there are decisions that teachers make; that in the presence of confusing and ambiguous issues, teachers search for appropriate courses of action, rather than resolution; that decisions are for better or for worse; that even in the best of times teachers must choose between several less-than-good alternatives; that many life problems cannot be solved. With growth of awareness, it is entirely possible that you will teach with the kind of understanding and insight that will see you through not only the first 100 days, but a lifetime.

APPLYING KNOWLEDGE TO PRACTICE: MAKING MEANING FROM CLASSROOM EXPERIENCES

His hands and fingernails are encrusted with what looks like a two-week binge in the mudlot. His clothes are shabby hand-me-downs that are rolled up and tucked in to make a better fit. He is small for his 11 years, but stocky and tough from life on the streets. He is most successful in arithmetic computation. He says he is good with numbers because he has had a paper route for two years. His homework is almost never done. When he turns anything in, the paper looks as if it had been chewed up in a cement mixer. While he is able to decode the words of stories, his ability to comprehend what is below the surface of situations is hopelessly inadequate. To questions like, "What do you think is happening here, Rick?" he smiles, mouth open, and sits, without uttering a word. You can wait for 100 years for his answer, but he will outwait you, until, in frustration, you are forced to ask someone else. What is going on behind that face, that open-mouth smile? And what to do?

The superintendent of schools visited the school this week. He came into my classroom and looked around. "Well," he said, "it's not too noisy for all this activity." When he observed Mike working on pieces of a large puzzle, he said, "I know that this teaches children to think. But what else does it do?" At the doorway, when he was leaving, he told me that the best class he had seen that morning was the first grade where all the children were sitting in their seats, copying the text from the chalkboard. In that class, the children were really learning! What is he really saying to me? And how should I respond?

Mei Li follows me around all day long. I keep telling her to go back to her seat, to get down to work. But the next time I turn around, there she is. My shadow. Does the fact that she knows no English have anything to do with it? What does she want? What is she trying to tell me? And what do I do with her?

Abby comes up to my desk about 30 times a day. "Is this right?" "Am I doing it right?" "Can you help me with this?" "Do you like this?" She is supposedly a good student, and last year she had the highest grades in the class. What is going on here? And what should I do with her?

Laura's anger is suddenly surfacing, after weeks of highly conforming behavior. She is intolerant with other children, and her dogmatism and hostility make small-group activities impossible if she is in that group. There is a nagging quality to her demands, an insistence that they must be met. Otherwise, the others in the group are "not being fair."

Her group behavior is intolerable. What is going on here? How should I deal with her?

Joe was participating in a group discussion in which the children were talking about their personal experiences. He volunteered that the saddest day in his life was when he was taken to Juvenile Hall and placed on probation for breaking and entering. A discussion ensued in which several children told how they took things from drugstores and supermarkets. Joe then bragged about "ripping off" things and said he did this frequently. One girl asked, "What if your parents find out?" He replied that his mother knew and that she often sent him out to "rip off" something for her, like hair shampoo or nail polish. What is behind these revelations? And what to do?

Frank cannot read, cannot spell, cannot do number work, cannot sit still for more than two minutes. Yet the psychologist says he has "normal" intelligence. What is going on here? And how do I understand all of this so I can better help Frank?

Bradley cries when he gets a paper back that shows his work to be less than perfect. He seems unable to accept any criticism, no matter how gentle. Any helpful suggestion seems to him a reproach. His intelligence is clearly superior, but he is anxious and very tense about his academic work. His parents seem very supportive and open. So what is causing him to be so stressed? What is going on? And how should I respond to him?

Hari seems to be coming apart at the seams. He complains and wails bitterly about children who do not let him play, who "kick" him, who take his things, who bother him. His actions toward others are also provoking, but he cannot seem to understand this. Living with only his older brother cannot be very nurturing for him. It is impossible to get any accurate information about when his parents are coming from Iran, or if they are ever coming. What is going on with this family situation, and how is Hari's behavior a reflection of it? And what to do with this troubled boy?

The tests upset the children badly. Afterwards they took out their frustration on me. "If you had done a better job of teaching us," they told me, "we would have done better!" What's behind these statements? And how should I respond?

Choosing books and spending time reading is something like six raccoons attacking the garbage: pandemonium. Very few children know how to choose a book. Very few children appear to enjoy reading. What is going on here? And how do I handle this?

In learning to apply knowledge to practice, we need to go beyond what we see and hear, to draw out understanding in and around what is happening. Applying knowledge involves more than merely adding up the pieces of what is seen and heard. It requires that we make meaning from experience, to figure out: What does this mean? An example of how Peter Mayle (1991) made meaning of his postman's unusual behavior is described in his delightful book, *A Year in Provence*. The postman, who normally deposited the mail in the box at the end of the driveway, this time came directly into the house waving a large envelope and proceeded to the bar. Mayle was puzzled. The postman had never brought mail up to the house and was never given to such informality. After the postman had consumed two glasses of pastis he indirectly revealed the real reason for his visit.

> "I have brought you the official post office calendar," said the postman. "It shows all the saints' days and there are some agreeable pictures of young ladies." He took the calendar from its envelope and leafed through the pages until he found a photograph of a girl wearing a pair of coconut shells.
> "*Voila!*"
> I told him that he was most kind to think of us, and thanked him.
> "It's free," he said. "Or, you can buy it if you want to."
> He winked again, and I finally understood the purpose of his visit. He was collecting his Christmas tip, but since it would be undignified simply to arrive at the front door with an outstretched hand, we had to observe the ritual of the calendar. (pp. 194-195)

Mayle had to look beyond the actual event itself, to interpret the postman's behavior within the context of the time of year. Once he put the pieces together, and understood, he was able to respond appropriately.

Making meaning of the events in classrooms is what we teachers do, from moment to moment, every teaching day. We "size up" a situation, reflect on what it means, and choose an appropriate action that depends upon how we have interpreted the event. That is how we teach ourselves to understand "what is happening." Understanding allows us to determine the action to take.

The Lens of Personal Reference

One of the conundrums in making meaning from experience lies in the way each of us filters what we see and hear through our built-in lens of personal reference. Our developmental histories shape us and shape how we view the world.

- Does Abby need more structure? Or is her behavior symptomatic of wrestling with the challenges of self-direction? How should it be interpreted?
- Is the superintendent subtly being disapproving of your classroom? Should his ideas of "good teaching" influence what you do? How do you see it?

- Is Rick "experientially limited"? Is he just slacking off? What is going on behind that open-mouth grin?
- Is Joe showing off? Does his mother really encourage him to steal? What is going on here?
- Is Bradley hung up on perfectionism? Does he need to be perfect in order to be accepted? Are the parents more than they seem, their supportive responses a facade? How are these data to be interpreted?
- Is Hari's brother abusing him at home? Are his parents ever coming? How is his behavior symptomatic of life at home? What is really happening in this family, and how is it affecting Hari's behavior in school?

Learning to "make meaning" depends, as the Indian Medicine Man said, "on where you sit on the medicine wheel." Meaning making is influenced not only by where a teacher sits, but by other factors such as time, physical and emotional states, knowledge, values, biases, and also by the other key players in the scenario.

From the less complex (What is the superintendent telling me about his views on good teaching?) to matters of much greater complexity (What is behind Bradley's anxieties?), teachers engage in a continual process of making meaning from classroom experience. And while it is demonstrably clear that there are few, if any, clear-cut answers in meaning making and that interpretations may vary widely, meaning making in or outside of teaching is not so open and so flexible that *all* interpretations are equally good.

Interpretations of meaning are more appropriate when certain criteria are met; they are less appropriate when these criteria have been ignored. And since choice of action follows from interpretation, we are better served when interpretation is "more appropriate," since to act out of a less appropriate or misinterpretation causes us to behave like fools.

Applying Critical Analysis to Meaning Making

Making more appropriate meaning from classroom experience is an exercise in the higher-order-thinking operation of interpreting data. The data are part and parcel of the experience. What skills are in play when we "read" those data and try to understand what they are telling us? And what safeguards can be built in, so that we may avoid going far beyond the data in making our interpretations?

- *Observing* is one of the skills used in making meaning. What is seen in this event? What is the context? Who are the players? What is happening? What, in the data observed, can be said to be true? What can be assumed to be true, with some degree of certainty? Observing is also done by listening. What is being said? By whom? To whom? How is it being said? What feelings are being expressed by the speaker? How do you know? What feelings are being generated in the others? How do you know? What, from what you have heard, can be said to be true? What can be assumed to be true, with some degree of certainty? While knowledge informs observing, observing requires that knowledge be selectively applied in discerning and apprehending what is seen and heard.

• *Comparing* is another tool used in the process of making meaning. How is this experience similar to others? What are the significant differences? Are the differences substantive, thus preventing us from drawing the same conclusions from both situations? What assumptions have been made in making the comparison? To what extent do the data support the assumptions? As with observing, knowledge by itself is not enough to make thoughtful comparisons. Comparisons are informed by the selective application of knowledge.

• *Extracting the main idea* depends on the ability to zero in on what the data are revealing. Extracting is more difficult than observing and comparing, since it is dependent on the ability to put pieces together in a new configuration, whereas in observing and comparing we are mostly examining the pieces. How do the pieces fit together? Which pieces fit? Which are the key pieces (the central ideas)? Which seem to be subsidiary? Which seem to be less than relevant? When the pieces are put together, what picture emerges? Is the picture consistent with the data? To what extent do the data support the new configuration? What assumptions have been made? To what extent are the assumptions warranted? In extracting what are perceived as the central issues, there will, of course, be some variance. Different people putting different pieces together will find different meanings. While a range of differences may be tolerated, there is a point beyond which the interpretation flies too far away from what the data allow and lands in the unsupportable territory of "having gone too far beyond the data." Extracting the main idea is a challenging task, but significant meaning may not be made unless the ability to do so is well developed.

• *Intuiting* is also used in making meaning, and while this is not a comfortable mode of operation for everybody, those who do it recognize that they operate in the murky waters of "hunches" and "guesses" and "reading into" the data what is not actually observed but is strongly felt to be true. Those who would intuit from data often guard their responses with words of caution, indicating a lack of certainty. For example: "It seems to me that this is the case" or "I have a hunch that she may be upset." The qualifiers indicate that caution is in order. Intuitors may be correct in their hunches, but they know well enough that their surmises are not data and must be treated with caution.

• *Application of facts and principles* requires finding ways of putting what we know into practice. With this skill, principles, rules, generalizations, concepts, ideas that have been learned are applied to the situation now faced by the teacher. What knowledge is applicable to this situation? Is this knowledge relevant to the situation? Are there adequate data to help our understanding? Does more information need to be gathered? The follow-up actions to application of facts and principles require thoughtful and nondefensive examination of the effectiveness of what has been done. Has the knowledge been applied in ways that enable student learning? What data are being used to determine the effectiveness of the action? What applications might have been more effective? How has the situation been misinterpreted? What other knowledge might have been used more effectively?

These several and various skills applied to the process of making meaning are not carried out in any particular sequence. No logical, sequential progression is followed. It is, however, helpful to know that at least part of each of these skills has been applied to the meaning making if the teacher is to draw relevant meaning from the experience. It is too easy to disregard the critical task of analysis, to leap into the quagmire of assumption, generalization, personal bias, dogmatism, in which significant meanings are grossly distorted and become utterly useless or, even worse, lead to actions that are entirely inappropriate. ("Oh, Abby. She's just a troublemaker. What she needs is good discipline." Or "Rick? He's just stupid. Look at his home life. What can you expect?")

When critical analysis of experience is in process, and data are examined by observation, comparison, extraction of meaning, and intuiting, through a frame of reference of what one knows, this allows for the generation of a "working hypothesis," which leads, in turn, to the choice of a particular course of action. The more meaning making is rooted in such intelligent analysis, the more sound the hypothesis is likely to be and the more reasoned, and reasonable, the decision about what action is to be taken. That is the goal of meaning making. It enables us to act in reasonable, intelligent, and appropriate ways, in ways that are consistent with the meaning of the experience. For example, the tests upset the children badly. They want to blame the teacher for their frustration. The teacher begins to see this in a larger perspective—the wish to attribute blame to others in order to avoid looking at personal inadequacy. The teacher could take this personally and be defensive, going on the attack. Or the teacher could try to empathize with their frustration and facilitate a discussion of their feelings, their frustrations, their anger. The latter action is more challenging for a teacher, and likely more stressful, but at least it would give teacher and students a chance at ventilating the bad feelings. It would also likely give all the players a chance to examine the test and the students' responses to it from other perspectives.

Caution: Mental Traps in Meaning Making

There are some dangerous bends and curves on the pathway to intelligent meaning making, and one way to avoid them is to know what they are. The dangers lie not so much in our misperception of the experience but in the way those misperceptions allow us to respond. Misperceptions invariably lead to misguided, inappropriate, even "stupid" choices, and hence actions, which we may live to regret.

Some of the common mental traps that constrain thinking, and thereby constrain our ability to make intelligent meaning from experience, are: making assumptions that are unrecognized and are offered as truths; making generalizations that allow us to leap from single events to universal statements; seeing situations in extremes, as absolutes; being rigid, inflexible, and dogmatic with respect to an interpretation; presenting personal bias as hard data; and acting impulsively, without regard to the data. In your attempts to understand complex situations, be careful to take these precautions during the meaning-making process:

1. *Look for assumptions.* In taking this precaution, ask yourself: What assumptions have I made? What data, if any, have I used in making those assumptions? What allows me to make such an assumption? Where did the assumption come from? Why do I think this may be true?
2. *Be cautious about generalizations.* In taking this precaution, ask yourself: How many examples are there in the data that permit me to make this generalization? How have I exaggerated in making the generalization? How have I used labels or slogans that indicate a generalization is being made? How have I used a single example to draw a conclusion that embraces everyone? How have I gone far beyond what the data allow in stating what I believe to be true?
3. *Avoid seeing things in extremes.* In taking this precaution, ask yourself: How, in any interpretation, have I drawn the picture in terms of only "blacks and whites"? How have I used words that point to extreme positions, such as *everybody, nobody, the only, the best,* and so forth? How have I allowed my black-and-white perspective to prevent me from observing the shades of gray?
4. *Be alert for dogmatism and closed-mindedness.* In taking this precaution, ask yourself: Where have I been certain, where evidence is lacking? Where have I been sure, when caution is called for? Where have I been unyielding, when the evidence is contradictory? Why do I need to feel I am right, in a situation that is clearly ambiguous?
5. *Discern personal bias.* In taking this precaution, ask yourself: Where have I expressed my opinion and allowed it to substitute for fact? What words, labels, and slogans have I used that reveal my own value judgments? Where have I expressed my preferences? What is there about the situation that "hooks" my personal bias?
6. *Take the time to think.* In taking this precaution, ask yourself: Have I acted impulsively, without taking the time to gather the relevant data? Have I

stopped to consider what is really happening here? Have I examined several potential courses of action and their consequences? Does the action I am considering mesh with the kind of problem this is?

What does all of this have to do with your professional development as a teacher? How is the process of meaning making related to the overpowering quest for answers that drives student behavior throughout most teacher-training programs?

Of all the professions, teaching is the one that is most full of surprises. Teaching is the profession in which the constant is change. Being a teacher means accepting that things never go as you think they will. It means being prepared for the inevitability of the unexpected. It means that no matter how well you prepare, no matter how clearly you set your course of action, at least one thing, small or large, will occur or fail to occur, which demands a rethinking, a redirection, a new plan. Good teaching means being able to think on your feet, to make the most of what each new situation presents. It means embracing change. It means being able to take the knowledge that you have accumulated and use it, to your and the students' advantage. That is why the accumulation of a body of knowledge by itself is not enough. Good teaching means using knowledge in the continual process of problem solving and decision making. Good teaching demands that teachers observe, listen, apprehend, intuit, and extract meaning from the untold numbers of experiences that occur in every classroom. It demands that teachers act in ways that appropriately reflect the meanings that they have made. It demands that teachers carry on this process of meaning making, followed by appropriate action, throughout each school day and throughout the school year. There is no respite from this process, for it is the essence of teaching. Perhaps that is why teachers are so fatigued at the end of each school day, and so desperately in need of R&R holidays. The risks of meaning making and choosing appropriate action is challenging and exhausting. It is, however, made somewhat easier as we grow in these skills and learn to trust ourselves in the meaning-making process; in our ability to discover, to apprehend, to extract; and in our confidence that the action we are taking is appropriate to the meaning we have made.

THE TENSION BETWEEN THE NEED FOR ANSWERS
AND THE AMBIGUITY OF MEANING MAKING

Having "answers" for all the problems of teaching makes for a secure feeling. Not knowing for certain, having to interpret each classroom event, trying to understand what is going on, and risking action—all of these are very anxiety-provoking. Make no mistake about it. It feels good to know what the answers are. It is stressful to have to take the risks involved in applying knowledge to practice, where answers are rarely clear, where the meaning you make is your own, and where the best answer is often, "It depends."

The human organism needs to resolve ambiguity; when closure can be brought, there is a distinct physiological "sigh," a palpable physical relief. It is no wonder that the right answers tempt us so sorely. They bring us peace of mind, comfort, and freedom from stress. It is understandable that life on the professional pathway of meaning making is uncomfortable and unsettling. Even intrepid teachers whose professional activities reflect this orientation often wish for the relief that right answers bring. But yearning for answers is not the same as embracing them unquestioningly when they are offered.

While the need for closure and the ambiguity of meaning making is bound to create tension, that tension is mitigated by the acceptance of the need for, as well as the uncertainties and risks in, meaning making. Eventually, as teachers gain skill in meaning making, and as they gain confidence in themselves as meaning makers, interpreting becomes less risky, less uncertain, less ambiguous. Teachers understand more readily. They put pieces together and see beyond them, to the big picture, more clearly. When that occurs, tension is reduced and levels of tolerance for ambiguity increase. The burden of such learning means never again being able to accept simple answers to complex problems; it means the development of habits of thinking that go far beyond the classroom and extend to every life circumstance. It means behaving maturely and wisely in dealing with the far-reaching choices of modern society. Such skills come only from experience—the one commodity that is in very short supply in beginning teachers. There are no shortcuts to experience, no ways around learning on the job. To accept that fact of life is yet one more step on the pathway of professional growth.

As a beginning teacher, it is natural that you look to "answers" to help you feel more secure, more informed, more confident to teach; to "cures" for the insecurities that lack of experience brings. But more than Band-Aids are needed to see you through those first 100 days of teaching, and answers will not ensure that you grow to become the very best teacher you can be. For that to happen, you will have to take on the challenge of giving up the security of certainty and stepping gingerly into the risky world of meaning making, where you are on your own, trying to apply what you know in the process of interpreting the hundreds of events that make up your teaching day. Such a step is not for the faint-hearted, but no coward ever got the Great Teacher Award. The happy news is that learning to make meaning comes much easier after the first thousand times, that is, with experience. The happier news is that you begin to distrust certainty, as you should, and become increasingly comfortable in the world of ambiguity. The happiest news is that you learn to trust yourself in that ambiguous world, trusting your intelligence, skill, and competence as a meaning maker.

REFERENCES AND RELATED READINGS

Berlak, Ann, and Berlak, Harold. 1981. *Dilemmas of Schooling.* New York: Methuen.
Chase, Stuart. 1956. *Guides to Straight Thinking.* New York: Harper & Row.
Dewey, John. 1980. *The Quest for Certainty.* New York: Perigree. (Original work published 1929)
Lortie, Dan. 1975. *Schoolteacher.* Chicago: University of Chicago Press.
Jersild, Arthur. 1955. *When Teachers Face Themselves.* New York: Teachers College Press.
Mayle, Peter. 1991. *A Year in Provence.* New York: Viking.
Raths, Louis E.; Wassermann, Selma; Jonas, Arthur; and Rothstein, Arnold. 1986. *Teaching for Thinking: Theory, Strategies, and Activities for the Classroom.* New York: Teachers College Press.
Schön, Donald. 1983. *The Reflective Practitioner.* New York: Basic Books.
Schön, Donald. 1987. *Educating the Reflective Practitioner.* San Francisco: Jossey-Bass.
Schön, Donald. 1991. *The Reflective Turn.* New York: Teachers College Press.
Strike, Kenneth, and Soltis, Jonas. 1985. *The Ethics of Teaching.* New York: Teachers College Press.

2 | "Hello, Ms. Chips"—Learning to Teach from Cases

The teacher glanced across the room and observed with satisfaction the serious engagement of each of the six study groups working on the case materials. The case of Barry, the boy who could not number, was the right choice to begin this General Methods of Education course (Chapter 4, case 4.4). No student appeared uninterested or indifferent to the issues in the case. The students within the groups were vying with one another for "air time." Each seemed to have a point of view about this case that urgently demanded to be heard. Phil Roman tried to tune in to what was being said, but could not make out the details. He wanted to hear, but he was conscious that his presence in or near the study groups would cause the discussion to "play to the teacher," and he preferred the students to feel free to make up their own minds. An experienced case method teacher, Professor Philip Roman knew when it was more important to stay on the edges of the room and to wait until he debriefed the case to hear what the students had to say.

When, after 45 minutes, he called time, the groups rearranged their tablet armchairs into a circle and waited to see what would happen next. Phil Roman looked around the circle, met the eyes of his students, and in a voice rich with invitation, asked, "Well, tell me, what do you see as the significant issues in this case?" Tentatively, two hands went up in the air; in a few minutes there would be two dozen.

The students approached the issues with the great certainty of sophomores. They *knew* what Barry's difficulty was. He just needed to learn his math from relating it to sports. He could add and subtract basketball scores, couldn't he? He could multiply and divide to compute baseball averages. His teacher? She was a turkey! What's more, what she did was stupid. Of course, Barry *had* to have known what she had done, and that would further undermine his confidence in himself. She was also lazy. Instead of trying to find ways to help him, she took the easy way out. She should be fired for unethical behavior.

Phil Roman had heard it all before, the way students new to studying cases began their analyses—missing the critical points of the case, applying glib solutions, reducing what was complex to its most simplistic forms, attributing motives where none were in evidence, making inferences that went far beyond the available data, and being so sure of themselves that it was unnerving.

But what Professor Roman also knew was that after a semester of learning with cases, there would be profound change in the quality of students' thinking and in the way they perceived and dealt with the critical issues of teaching. Learning to teach with cases increased students' abilities to be more thoughtful, to understand complex issues, to be more analytical, to make more informed decisions. Glibness and superficiality in thinking would evolve to mature and reasoned wisdom.

WHAT'S IN IT FOR ME?

A student whose judgment evolves from intransigence, impulsivity, and confusion to that of thoughtful reflection about the issues does not make this paradigm shift in a day, or a week, or even a month of learning. This is a cumulative process in which the need for a quick solution is gradually exchanged for the more enlightened skills of suspended judgment, the ability to see many sides of a question, insight into the feelings of others, clearer thinking about the key issues in complex situations, and the ability to arrive at decisions based on data. This evolutionary process occurs via learning with cases, as students develop "habits of thinking"—the tools that enable critical analysis. These habits are formed as the mind is stretched and challenged to compare, to observe, to suggest hypotheses, to interpret data, to choose, to select actions that are appropriate to particular problems, to examine alternatives, to appreciate others' points of view. These habits are naturally cultivated through learning with cases.

Old habits of thinking are not easily shed. It is less taxing to body and mind to respond to critical issues in superficial or knee-jerk ways; more difficult to dig down deeply, reflect, consider, evaluate. Yet do we dare ask less of ourselves as professionals? Would we want teachers to be otherwise? The payoffs that such new habits of thinking offer may be well worth the effort.

Learning with Cases Promotes Professional Growth

Becoming more analytical and reflective. Case method teaching requires your active, mental engagement in the case material. This active engagement of the mind gives you practice in the higher-order mental functions of comparing, observing, analyzing, and interpreting data as well as evaluating, hypothesizing, and examining assumptions. The more you practice and sharpen these higher-order functions, the more skilled you are likely to become. These habits are further strengthened in the study groups, in which you learn to question each others' assumptions, challenge ideas that seem inconsistent or irrational, and present alternate points of view for consideration. Case method teaching creates a climate for thoughtful reflection as well as putting you into positions where you are called on to engage actively in thinking.

This is quite different from sitting back and listening to the teacher's lecture, a passive enterprise that may or may not engage the mind and more often allows you to disengage from active thinking. While the lecture mode *may* create a climate for thoughtful reflection, there is no requirement that you do, in fact, actively engage in thinking about what is being presented. Consequently, "what a student learns is not always what a professor teaches, and what a professor teaches is not always what a student learns" (Ewing, 1990, p. 13).

The more a person actively engages in skiing, the more accomplished a skier that person is likely to become. One cannot become an accomplished performer without active engagement. The more you actively engage in the analysis of cases, the more accomplished you become at case analysis. It should also be noted that both skiing skills and analytic skills are considerably advanced through reflection on performance; in the latter instance, it is the small-group discussion of the study questions and the large-group debriefing conducted by the teacher that allow for ongoing reflection and the further strengthening of analytic and reflective skills.

Why should you work hard for these achievements? Isn't teaching just a matter of following the teachers' manual and sticking to the curriculum guidelines provided by the school board?

Anyone who has spent any time in a classroom will know how great are the demands and pressures of teaching. Teaching, far from being a matter of applying simple rules that cover all situations, consists of a variety of complex acts that are responsive to complex events. Although teachers may have seen similar situations in previous teaching years, each new classroom event is new, because all the conditions surrounding that event are different. Just because strategy X worked with Maryanne last year does not necessarily mean that strategy X will work with Harlan this year. Each situation demands a new examination and, in most instances, a new set of strategies that reflect the new conditions. To apply strategies out of a handbook, without regard for the way *this* situation is different from the last one, is to follow mindlessly what is written by others who are not in direct contact with the situation.

A professional teacher knows how to respond to each unique situation, based on a careful assessment of what the situation requires. To do this well requires the ability to make a thoughtful analysis of the situation and to speculate on which teaching strategies are more likely to be effective. Such skills differentiate the capital-T Teacher from the small-t teachers who operate at the other end of the spectrum (Wassermann, 1986).

Understanding the decision-making process. Learning how others choose helps you to become more aware of how you choose. There is, perhaps, no more pervasive activity in the life of a teacher than decision making. From the moment teachers enter their classrooms, they are bombarded with choices to make.

> Mrs. Howe, I forgot my lunch.
> Teacher, Bryan is hitting me.
> Mr. Logan, I couldn't figure out this math homework.
> Can I change my seat? I don't want to sit next to Devi.
> Teacher, Danielle is crying.
> He ripped my book.
> My mother wants to talk to you.

Sometimes the choices are overt. "May I sharpen my pencil?" or "What should I do?" demands a choice be made with respect to action. More often, the choices are covert. "Teacher, Danielle is crying," or "He ripped my book" may or may not require action, so the first choice is whether or not to intervene; the second is about the nature of the action to be taken.

Each decision a teacher makes, each action taken or avoided, is an act that forms part of the "hidden curriculum"—those forces that teach more to students than all the subjects combined. Children learn much about good and bad, about values, about caring, about respect, about humanity and human-ness from watching how their teachers choose to act. This, however, is only one of the reasons for raising teachers' consciousness about their decision-making processes.

Equally important is the toll that decision making takes on a teacher. Imagine a job in which more than 5,000 decisions have to be made rapidly, conscientiously, and responsibly every day. No wonder teachers are so tired at three o'clock. No wonder they are exhausted on Friday afternoons. No wonder they need a week at Christmas and another at Easter for R&R. The demands of choosing, of deciding what to do, are difficult enough; but when the choices are far from clear, when the situations demand action, and where the teacher is uncertain—such is the stuff of increased stress and emotional turmoil.

Teachers are helped in the difficult tasks of choosing by becoming more conscious of their own decision-making processes. When teachers are clear about what they believe and what they value, choices are easier to make. When teachers are aware that they are being called upon to choose, they are more likely to use informed judgment in making those choices. As teachers become both more aware of their own decision-making processes and more secure in themselves as decision makers, they are strengthened in their courage to take the risks involved in choosing. They are empowered as decision makers, and their classrooms benefit from those strengths.

In some teacher-education courses, students rarely get the opportunity to choose. It is the teacher who makes most of the significant choices. Even more, rarely do students get opportunities to examine how others choose or to scrutinize their own decision-making procedures. Learning with cases, however, thrusts you into confounding situations in which the protagonists face every imaginable dilemma found in classrooms. You learn how these teachers have made their choices; you learn how to examine those choices analytically; you learn to reflect on how *you* would choose, given a similar situation. The art of decision making is examined and practiced, and you are continually challenged to choose for yourself. In that process, you learn about the values you hold that guide your choices. As values become clearer, choice inevitably becomes more informed. Learning with cases strengthens you as a decision maker.

Examining your beliefs and values. Listen to a group of education students describe their experiences with their own teachers, and you will hear stories about those teachers who were heroic, who inspired and thrilled, who truly made a difference in their lives. You will also hear stories that are tragic, that repel and offend—of teachers who have left scars that endure into adulthood. In almost everyone's history, there is one great teacher, still revered, and at least one "dragon," still despised.

It is not likely that people enter the teaching profession with the express purpose of hurting children. This is an unimaginable thought. Yet it cannot be denied that some teacher behaviors are less than conducive to student learning and other behaviors are downright toxic. Where is the line drawn between professional acts that encourage and those that discourage learning? How do teachers grow to understand the intimate relationship between how they choose to act and the impact of those actions on the hearts and minds of their students?

One valuable way of knowing is through clarity of beliefs and values. Louis Raths, who generated a "theory of values," has written that the large group of people who operate out of clear value structures "seem to deal with life in consistent and purposeful ways . . . they appear to know what they want and how to work for it; . . . they operate constructively within society." Such persons are characterized as "positive, purposeful, enthusiastic and proud" (Raths, Harmin, & Simon, 1978, p. 5).

At the other end of the values continuum, Raths writes, are persons who do not seem to be clear about how to relate to persons and events in their lives. Among these people, there is much personal confusion. They seem more inconsistent, more confused, more irrational.

Teachers who are clear about the beliefs and values they hold about the way children should be treated are far less likely to choose actions that are abusive, irrational, or disrespectful. Their "values clarity" forces them to be ever watchful and mindful of their own actions and allows them to bring their actions into ever-closer harmony with their beliefs. Teachers who are unclear about what beliefs they cherish—who have never addressed the question, "What is important to me?"—are less likely to perceive their behaviors clearly and far less likely to choose consistently. Words and deeds of teachers in this group would be quite discrepant.

While we might wish that students' personally held values and beliefs would undergo intense scrutiny in teacher-education programs, the likelihood that clearer values emerge from traditional lecture courses is remote. One does not become clear about what one believes from listening to the beliefs and values of others. "The pace and complexity of life has so exacerbated the problem of deciding what is good and what is right and what is worthy and what is desirable," Raths has written, that it is "increasingly bewildering, even overwhelming, to decide what is worth valuing" (Raths et al., 1978, p. 7).

For greater clarity of values to emerge, we must struggle to wrest our own values from a vast array of options. Values that actually inform one's choices in intelligent and consistent ways are not likely to emerge any other way. Such "wresting of values" involves repeated active engagement in the tasks of reflection on choice, choosing, determining what is important, and behaving. Such tasks are the very essence of learning with cases.

Listening to others' ideas. A high school student who had experienced case method teaching in her eleventh-grade social studies class offered the following insight: "The case study method in the classroom allows you to listen to other points of view, consider them and then form an analysis of the issue using these other points of view. A better understanding and examination of the issue is possible." Another student from the same class wrote, "I have learned how to listen to other people and to understand that there are many different interpretations of one topic." A third offered, "In hearing others' opinions and ideas, I myself had more to think about and was forced to look at the issues in a different way, and then decide where I stood" (Adam, 1992b).

As these (and other) students point out, the opportunity to hear the views of others in the study groups and during the debriefing of the case allows you to move from narrower, personal views toward a larger perspective. You learn to see that there are many sides to an issue, depending on one's perspective; and as a variety of views are shared, minds open and new data are taken in and evaluated. The process helps you to transcend egoism and ethnocentricity and dogmatism, to move toward open-mindedness and a greater tolerance for diversity of opinion.

Listening to the ideas of colleagues and fellow students is more than just interesting. It teaches us about who we are, about what we stand for, about where we are coming from. We learn to listen, really listen, to others, to apprehend what they are saying, and to evaluate how it fits with our own views. A student wrote, "I listen to others better now before I respond. I respond to what they say, and not form my next sentence in my mind before I've heard everything they have to say" (Adam, 1992b). Such responses are inevitable consequences of learning with cases. Learning to appreciate the views of others and learning to listen are but two more of the many positive benefits of learning with cases.

Strengthening your problem-solving abilities. Teaching, which is riddled with decision-making dilemmas, is also burdened by the need to face and to create solutions to vast numbers of problems.

> How shall I help Barry learn his math?
> How can I motivate Julie to read more?
> How can I help Mrs. Davidson understand that she is putting too much pressure on William?
> How shall I create interest in this social studies topic?
> What materials will I need to create an appealing science center?
> How will I organize this school play?
> How can I help children extract the most meaning from our field trip to the bird sanctuary?
> What is a good plan for promoting students' higher-order thinking?
> What is a good way to individualize my math program so that it is more suited to individual learning needs?

It is a given in teaching that no two classes are ever the same. They may be in the same school, they may even be called by the same number (e.g., fourth grade). Yet the makeup of each group of children however similar, (e.g., all aged 8 to 9) and the interactive dynamics within the group are so different that each requires teaching strategies that are particularly relevant for *that* group. A teacher may teach fourth grade for 15 years and find that each year the approaches demanded, the curriculum studied, and the special needs of individual children require entirely new and different problem-solving procedures from the year before.

Creative teachers who teach the same grade for many years will shun "doing the same things." There will be new curriculum material to include, based on recent world or local events; new strategies to use, based on recent education coursework or staff development experiences; and new ideas that yearn to be incorporated into classroom life—so that teaching is ever fresh, ever challenging; so that classrooms are living, zestful, rich places to learn.

How do you learn to embrace the new, to spin new classroom experiences from the elegant threads of your ideas? If you have watched this process of creating curriculum experiences for children, you will have seen in it the skills of problem solving that evolve from the idea stage to classroom applications.

"I want to develop a science center for my third-grade students," says Devi Patel, to her mentor teacher, "but science is definitely not my strong subject. Can we brainstorm this together?" The two sit down and begin to generate questions.

> What objectives do you have for this science work? What do you hope will happen as a consequence of children's involvement in the center?
> On what "big ideas" in science would the center be built? What concepts would be examined?
> What materials would be essential? Where could they be obtained?
> What children's science books would be useful? Where might these be found?
> What teacher text(s) would give guidance?
> How would children's investigations with the science materials be promoted?
> How should the children be oriented to this new way of learning science?
> What organizational strategies need to be used to allow for different groups to use the science center at different times?
> What housekeeping rules need to be established?
> What group work rules are required?
> What teacher strategies need to be used to help children extract meaning from their science investigations?
> How will I know they are learning? What indicators will I take as evidence that learning of significance has occurred?
> How will I assess this, in relation to my objectives?

As the questions are raised, answers begin to form and the new curriculum design begins to take shape. The questions and the answers come from the creative and fertile minds of the two teachers. While they draw on previous reading and coursework, they must reconstruct knowledge and reframe it in new ways to solve the new problem of the science center. In the process, the teachers use previous knowledge and apply it to a new situation. Such generative thinking is, of course, risky. The teachers are inventing something new, something that has not been done before. They are pulling from their mental resources the ways and the means to put this curriculum into operation. They teach themselves to use what they know in new and different ways.

This is a messy endeavor, but nothing creative ever emerged without the mess that is an integral part of the creative act. This is also an endeavor with no built-in guarantees of success. Devi Patel will try it out and will learn much about how to make it better from observing her plan in action. As she puts her plan into operation, and learns from what she does, she advances the richness of curriculum experiences for her children 10 paces.

How do you learn to be a creative problem solver? How do you learn to apply knowledge to new situations? How do you learn to be confident about taking the risks that are involved in trying anything new?

Many students come into teacher-education programs already possessing some of these skills. Others learn them in courses that provide experience, practice, and reflection on creative problem solving and applying knowledge to new situations. Case method teaching is one way in which you may grow to become a more creative problem solver, since every case presents not one but several problems to be solved. Every case requires that you use what you know and apply that to the new situation of the case. Every case demands generative thinking. Learning with cases strengthens these skills and gives you greater resources to face the problems that life in the classroom offers.

Learning with Cases Promotes Personal Development

Increasing your autonomy. It has been said that teaching is one of the loneliest jobs. Teachers work in isolation—unlike physicians, for example, who normally work in teams, confer regularly on cases, have frequent opportunities to see one another at work, and make input to one another's medical performance; or attorneys, whose performance is subject to ongoing public scrutiny. Behind closed doors, teachers have the privacy to teach as they choose, without the public or collegial scrutiny that is part of the life of other professionals. But for that privacy teachers pay a great price. Freed from scrutiny, they are also cut off from the collegial support and the professional consultation of teammates in decision making. Where in medicine, "difficult cases" are habitually examined through the lenses of several specialists in consultation, the teacher who might benefit from similar consultation must seek that out in extraordinary ways. Most decisions teachers make are made alone, without benefit of consultation and without the burden of public or professional surveillance. This is not to say that teachers never consult, nor that they are never exposed to another's examination. It is to say, however, that such events are not an everyday occurrence in a teacher's life.

If teachers are, for the most part, left alone to do their jobs, what strengths would they need in order to do their work more effectively? What personal and professional characteristics would enable them to make those countless decisions on their own?

Arguably, personal autonomy must rank high on the list. If teachers operate, to a very great extent, on their own, then being able to rely on oneself in all matters, but particularly when the going gets rough, would be an immeasurable asset. The ability to think on one's feet, to intervene appropriately, to create new schemes, to find the resources needed to say and do what is required in the pressure-cooker of classroom life certainly requires confidence in self and the ability to function on one's own merits. It would not do for a teacher who faced a critical classroom incident that called for an immediate response to say, "Pardon me, boys and girls. Before I can tell you what I think, I must find out what Mrs. Abernathy would do in a similar situation." An effective teacher may not lean heavily on the advice and guidance of others for everyday classroom problems. The effective teacher must act autonomously, self-reliantly, and with confidence in the decisions being made.

Learning with cases promotes personal and professional autonomy. Cases require you to develop your own ideas, to evaluate situations as you see them, to make a decision based on how you see the issues being resolved. The study-group discussions offer a safe forum in which you and your fellow students, acting collegially, critically analyze one anothers' ideas in a climate of trust that is also professionally productive. With each case studied, you become more skilled, more resourceful, more analytical, and more informed. You also become more confident about expressing your ideas and more secure in what you want to say. As one case study student wrote, "I have never been a talkative person until I came to this class. Now, I speak freely and am able to express my thoughts and feelings about the issues" (Adam, 1992a, p. 69). Learning via the case method is a natural habitat for promoting increased student autonomy and self-confidence.

Controlling your own learning. More and more is being written about empowerment and how school experiences empower or disempower students. Glasser's (1986) "control theory" suggests that the need for power is genetically programmed and that it is that need for power that drives student learning. "If students do not feel they have any power in their academic classes, they will not work in school. The same could be said for teachers" (p. 27). Glasser also writes that when needs for power are severely frustrated in class, students feel unimportant and angry.

In *Serious Players in the Primary Classroom* (Wassermann, 1990), I have also described a "power theory" in which the basic human need for power-to drives human behavior. "Persons with a well-developed sense of power-to are adults who are able to be in charge of their lives" (p. 6). Power-to needs are fed when people are able to make choices for themselves, when they are given options in situations that genuinely matter. When people are given options, when they are allowed to choose, when the choices they make are respected, they grow to believe in themselves. They learn that they "can do." They learn that they have the power to make changes and that they have control over their environment. People who see themselves as having such control are empowered.

When choices are taken away, when the power to choose is exercised by others in their behalf, people become frustrated and angry. They learn that they cannot be trusted to decide for themselves. They learn to doubt themselves. Over a period of time, they may become quite submissive, depending on others "to do" for them. They have become disempowered.

School situations in which students have options, in which they may exercise control over what they do and how they do it, increase students' sense of power-to. School situations that reduce students' options, and in which they have little or no control of what they do or how they do it, since every action is regulated and circumscribed by the teacher's power-to, decrease students' sense of power.

Learning with cases allows us great control over what we do and how we do it. There is considerable freedom to think one's own thoughts, in a climate that is encouraging and safe. There is freedom to make one's own choices, to decide for oneself, "This is what I think she should do." In small-group discussions and in the debriefing that follows, respect for all points of view is an integral condition of case method teaching. Such methodology serves to empower learners. Learning with cases teaches us that we can be in charge of what happens, that we have control over what we do and how we do it. Ultimately such learning feeds our satisfactions as learners as well as our sense of "can do."

Communicating more effectively. In Adam's (1992a) study of 27 eleventh-grade students who were taught with the case method in their social studies class, she asked the students to respond anonymously to a questionnaire in which one of the questions was, "How has your ability to communicate your ideas been affected by the case study process?" (p. 70). Twenty-three students indicated that there had been substantial change. The four who responded that there was little or no change also wrote that they had already perceived themselves as high functioners in this skill area before they entered this class.

The students' comments are revealing. They demonstrate not only how case method teaching increased their ability to communicate their ideas, but how this actually occurred.

> You are more willing to speak out, knowing that others will.
>
> When I first came into class, I was very shy and did not want to say anything, because I was afraid of what others would think of me. But now, if I have something to say, I can. I know that I will not be judged for it.
>
> When you are asked your opinion, it makes you think. This makes it easier for you to communicate your ideas.
>
> I have to make everyone in my group understand exactly my point of view, whether they agree with it or not.
>
> Everyone spoke out, so it made it easier for me.
>
> Case method teaching gives the students an atmosphere and surrounding where they feel comfortable. This increased my ability to communicate and understand other people's points of view, which is critical out in the "real world."

You feel a little nervous to speak at first. No one wants to be the first speaker, but once the discussion has started, the class really gets into the work. By the middle of the semester, people felt very comfortable sitting down and talking about issues. This also helped people to communicate out of class. They learn how to explain themselves (Adam 1992b).

Communication of ideas, as these students note, is a two-way, not a one-way process. It involves the ability not only to express one's own ideas in a way that is comprehensible to others but also to think through the ideas, so that they make sense. It also involves the ability to listen to the ideas of others, to discern what is being said, and to understand the messages being spoken. Based on that understanding, an appropriate response can be formulated. As these students have attested, case method teaching provides the experiences from which such communication skills grow. For teachers, who must be skillful communicators with students, colleagues, administrators, parents, and the public at large, such skills are a decided advantage.

Cultivating your curiosity. One argument that has been lodged against learning with cases is that students are not going to be thoroughly grounded in the knowledge they need to understand the subject. For example, given a finite number of hours for a particular course means that if the bulk of the time is given over to case method teaching, less time is available for the teacher to provide students with the information they need to pass the course. One teacher voiced the complaint that without such information dispensing by the teacher, students' study groups are likely to become "exchanges of ignorance." The data that have been gathered on case method teaching in a variety of contexts reveal that this is far from true (Adam, 1992a; Christensen & Hansen, 1987; Christensen, Garvin, & Sweet, 1990; Ewing, 1990). In fact, what actually occurs with respect to increased knowledge is the opposite of what such naysayers claim. Students actually gather substantially more knowledge as they learn with cases. This is how it works.

The case always presents a dilemma, a thorny situation for which there are no clear answers. The case becomes a puzzle, and because none of us is comfortable with the terrible burden of "not knowing" that a puzzle presents, we become compelled to know more. Cases, by their very nature, drive us to find the information we need to arrive at more informed decisions. They are natural motivators that spur the need to know.

Studying the case of "It's Up to You, Mrs. Buscemi" (Chapter 5, case 5.4), for example, is likely to spur more interest in learning about how teachers might evaluate students' work in general math. Is averaging test scores the only way? Are there alternatives? Is it true that there is no subjectivity in evaluating math? What role should affirmative action play in the teacher's decision? Curiosity about these and other questions related to the case leads to additional discourse, not only with fellow students but also with resource teachers. There are books and articles to be read that provide additional information. All the information gathered becomes purposeful data because of the "need to know." The dilemmas in the case drive that need, and the information gathered is significant and meaningful because it sheds further light on the issues in the case.

This process of gathering information when it is needed makes that information more relevant, more meaningful. It is considerably different from having the information dispensed before it is seen as relevant to any situation. "Learn this, for someday you may find it important" is not a convincing argument for retention. That is now replaced by "I've just got to find out more about better ways to evaluate in math and how affirmative action impacts on my decision." For these reasons, data gathered through a need to know are more effectively retained and remembered, whereas information stored for some possible future need quickly evaporates once the real need to know (e.g., the final exam) has passed.

The students polled in the Adam study had this to say on the question of how cases stimulate interest in further learning:

> I've always hated textbooks and notes. Learning with cases has been far more valuable to me. I've looked forward to coming to class because it felt like we didn't have to do any work, although mentally we were doing much more and remembering much more.
>
> I have now noticed myself *not* being satisfied with one idea or one answer. I have the drive to gather as much information as possible and then make my own conclusion.
>
> I am more interested in learning about the topics than I ever was before, because the discussion made me more curious.
>
> Now I want to know more. Before, it really didn't matter.
>
> In this course, I have great interest in learning. You *want* to learn. When we are taught with a textbook, it is boring and you don't want to be there.
>
> It is the first time I ever wanted to learn and couldn't wait to get to class.
>
> Before this class, I wasn't very keen on learning. Now, I am eager to learn as much as possible.
>
> I think that if all my classes were taught in this way, I would have a very high GPA Learning is less boring. I have *learned,* not memorized (Adam, 1992a, p. 75).

Living with ambiguity. Dilemmas never die. They stay alive in your mind. You continue to wrestle with them for a long time.

Walking across campus, two education students were talking about their programs. "Ed Psych," said one "I've had it. It's toast."

"Yeah." said the other. "All that cramming for the final exam and what's left? Nada. What's all of that really got to do with teaching, anyway?"

A common complaint from education students, whose courses cover massive amounts of information to be memorized for the final exam, is that they do not see the relevance of the material they learn. Another complaint is that once the material has been learned and the exam passed, the facts are quickly forgotten. Instead of courses building up a cumulative repository of knowledge that can be applied to teaching practice, the information for each course seems to vanish after the exam. The mind, now emptied, makes room for the material of the subsequent course to replace what has melted away. At the end of the program, students who face practice teaching do so with little or no idea of the significance of the material studied for the practice of teaching.

Students who learn with cases have a different perspective about what they have studied. Many claim that the cases resonate; they continue to "play in the mind" long after the actual class is over. One student said, two years after she studied the case of Barry (Chapter 4, case 4.4), that she is still thinking about the issues in the case, still pondering about more effective resolutions. One of the eleventh-grade students from Adam's (1992b) study was more passionate in her response: "We talked and talked about the case [one in Bickerton et al., 1991, pp. 53-56] for weeks after we studied it in class, and I know I'll still be thinking about that case in 25 years."

Is this a positive attribute of learning with cases? If the truth be told, it is arduous to bear the burden of thinking about issues, of examining them from different perspectives, of keeping them alive in the mind. Some students might prefer to have the mind emptied, vacuumed out, freed from the affliction of unresolved dilemmas that compel further thinking. Yet if thinking as a process is valued, and if thinking about issues in order to further students' understanding of the complexities of teaching practice is what education is for, then learning with cases would appear to meet these goals in very substantive ways.

Understanding the complexities of teaching. Through the process of learning with cases, you are able to make meaning of the wonderful, terrible, joyous, and frustrating world of the classroom.

In an education program that consists of courses in which dissemination of vast amounts of information is the chief emphasis, students graduate "thinking about subjects as lengthy lists of facts with little or no consideration given to relationships among principles and concepts learned" (Gross, 1992, p. 3). The National Center for Research on Teacher Learning found that courses that do make a difference in the preparation of future teachers are those that require "students to reason about the subject, to argue about alternative explanations for what they encounter, and to test their ideas and those of others. Such academic interaction tends to improve students' understanding of important concepts in the subject matter and, along with that, their ability to explain concepts" (Gross, 1992, p. 3).

Imagine for a moment this scenario: A woman has a terrible pain in her chest, and it is alarming. She makes an appointment to see the doctor, who looks briefly at her face and concludes, "It's just gas; probably something you ate." And with that, she is summarily dismissed with a bottle of antacid tablets.

Imagine for another moment this scenario: This is the fifth day in a row that Bertha has not finished her seatwork. The teacher approaches her, chastizing: "Bertha, you haven't finished your work again! You are just being lazy. You'll have to stay after school today to get it done. There's no excuse for laziness in this class."

Leaping to conclusions, assigning blame, attributing motives, using labels as a convenient way to group people, places, or things—all avoid the requirement of thoughtful examination. Doctors or lawyers or teachers or any other professionals who fail to examine situations in their complexity, who have facile "answers" to difficult problems, or who are certain when they need to be circumspect fail to function as true professionals. Their dogmatic certainty is an indicator of their lack of ability to make informed analyses and interpretations of data. We would not choose a doctor who made medical diagnoses based on unfounded assumptions. Our respect for teachers who tend to glib pronouncements is similarly shaken.

Highly functioning professionals, whatever their profession, do not shirk from venturing into situations that are confusing messes to try to make sense of what is happening (Schön, 1983, p. 42). Schön calls this territory "the swampy lowlands" in which professionals deliberately involve themselves in messy, but crucially important, problems. From this involvement, we learn to find the deeper meanings that lay buried beneath the surface of what is easily seen. This process of meaning making increases our understanding of life in classrooms. We are no longer satisfied with surface or facile solutions to difficult problems. We have committed ourselves to a deeper quest: the search for understanding.

Cases, by their very nature, take students into the swampy lowlands of classroom practice. They are, as you will see, messy, since they show life in classrooms from real teachers' perspectives, as it actually exists. No issue in a case is pure, or clean, or uncontaminated by numbers of other factors that bear on that issue. Every issue demands examination from many perspectives. And just when you thought you had it all figured out, a fellow student proposes a brand-new theory that shoots your own theory right down. You learn about the complexities of classroom life, and you grow in your appreciation for those complexities. You begin to find value not in facts, not in glib answers, but in meanings. You begin to understand, really understand, what teaching is about.

It is a teacher's ability to understand deeper meanings that allows for richer, more intelligent diagnosis and, subsequently, more effective teaching strategies. The teacher who acts at this level elevates teaching to art.

MAKING THE MOST OF LEARNING WITH CASES

Your teacher distributes the first case and asks that the students read it prior to the next class, in which small study groups will examine the questions appended to the case, to be followed by the teacher's debriefing the case with the whole class. What do you need to do to prepare yourself for these adventures? How do you "study" a case? What do you need to bring to the study groups and to the debriefing that will allow you to make the most of these learning experiences?

Preparing

It is a very good idea to have read the case before going into class. This reading should consist of more than just knowing the story. Your analysis of the case material is helped by asking yourself certain important questions. You may prefer to make notes directly on the case, or in a notebook, to focus your thinking during the discussion. In making your analysis of the case, ask yourself:

1. What do I see as the key issues in this case? Have I identified the *key* issues?
2. Who are the key players? What roles are they playing? How are they performing in those roles?
3. How do the players interact with one another? Is this important in this case?
4. How would I describe the behavior of the players? What seems to be motivating the behavior? What examples from the case support my ideas?
5. What do I think the key player should do (should have done)? What data support my position?
6. What would I do in a similar circumstance? What values do I hold that inform my choice?
7. What meaning do I take away from this case?

Next, examine the study questions. Think about your responses to each. If you are unsure of your response, go back to the case and see if there are data that help you to respond.

Some students find it productive to create an out-of-class study group to discuss the study questions before the in-class study group. Students who discuss the case and case questions in advance will doubtless have an advantage during in-class study sessions and more likelihood of understanding the case issues for the debriefing.

Working in Study Groups

The study groups in class provide you with a forum that is both safe and provocative. Working with fellow students on the study questions is more comfortable for most individuals than is a full-class discussion led by the teacher. It is also provocative, since it is your chance to present your ideas to the critical scrutiny of others and to listen to others' perspectives on the same issues. In good study groups, the discussion is rich, alive, pregnant with opportunity to think, examine, and explore.

You can do much to transform your group into a rich forum of inquiry by applying a few rules of critical thinking. While these rules may be difficult at first, the more you use them, the more skilled you will become.

1. *Open your mind.* Come to the groups with the attitude that others may have some ideas that are as important as yours. Listen respectfully to others' points of view. When you ask questions, ask them "neutrally" to gather information, not to condemn or try to persuade otherwise. Free yourself from the desire to judge what others say as good or bad, right or wrong. This absence of judgment is one of the factors that contributes to the feelings of safety in group discussion. When others present views that are different from yours, try to understand how they are seeing the issue. Open your mind to alternate views. If you come to the group with the attitude that your and only your view is "correct," your mind is closed and therefore shut to any deeper examination. Closed-mindedness is a sure way to diminish the effective functioning of a study group.

2. *Suspend your judgment.* Rather than coming to the group with an already framed conclusion, writ in stone, hold off. Try to see your conclusions as tentative. Be cautious in areas where there are insufficient data. Try to gather as much data, from listening and fully appreciating the perspectives of others, before you decide.

3. *Trust your judgment.* After hearing many views, and after listening to others' ideas, form your own view about the case. Try not to be persuaded by the most vocal group member, or by the one who argues well. Use others' views to inform your own, but have faith in what you think and in your own ideas. Trust your own judgment to decide for yourself.

4. *Be cautious about your assumptions.* Assumptions made about people or events are like mind-traps. We think we *know* why Connie chose to defy her

administrator. Yet the data in the case are ambiguous; we cannot know for sure. When assumptions are made without good evidence to support them, analyses are weakened and conclusions are likely to be faulty. Where data are absent, or unclear, or ambiguous, be cautious about the assumptions you are making. If you venture toward making an assumption, avoid stating it as fact (e.g., "I know why she did that; she thinks she's too good for this small town"). Instead, frame the assumption with caution, tentatively, to suggest uncertainty. That signals that you are out on a limb and prepared to have your position reexamined.

5. *Take a risk.* You may have an idea or a theory that seems to you to be "off the wall." You may think the idea is too silly to present to the others. Take a risk. Volunteer your idea. Your intuitive hunch may be both perceptive and innovative. You may have shed new light on a complex issue. To shirk from presenting an innovative or risky idea may mean the loss of a truly insightful theory. It is only when a person takes risks that original and refreshing new ideas may be revealed.

6. *Be actively involved.* A good study group is only as good as the dialogue. Students who say, "I was actively involved by listening," not only prevent others from learning what they think but also limit their own opportunities to have their ideas tested in the open marketplace. All participants in the study group lose if even one member chooses not to be actively involved in presenting ideas. Active involvement means you are "in there"—learning to present your ideas, learning to take risks, learning to communicate, learning to hold your own. The rewards for active involvement are many, and the losses incurred from noninvolvement affect everyone.

Participating in the Whole-Class Discussion

It is safer to apply the rules of study-group participation in small-group forum and much more difficult to do the same during the whole-class debriefing. But the same rules apply if the whole-class discussion is to be productive. How do you overcome the obstacles of shyness, of fear of looking stupid, of anxiety about "being wrong"? The first time you speak will be the hardest. After that, it gets a bit easier. Remember Paul Winchell's (1954) advice to budding ventriloquists: Don't get impatient with yourself. Don't get discouraged. Don't ever give up.

Following the Need to Know More

A well-written case drives the need to know more. Each case will present you with dilemmas and issues that defy easy resolutions. In formulating your own views, it is always helpful to find out what the "experts" say, and what data, if any, can be found in the research on the issues. The more resources inform your thinking, the more are your views informed.

For example, as you study the case of The Bared Breast (Chapter 3, case 3.3), you will likely want to know if there are state, city, or board of education laws that protect a teacher's right to privacy, and what is meant, in that school district, by a "breach of professional ethics." You may want to seek out other cases with similar issues that have gone to court. You may want to know what your own rights are, with respect to your behavior outside of class, and what constraints are placed on that behavior. Being informed about the issues helps you to understand more about the case as well as about your own rights as a teacher.

As another example, as you study the case of "I Need You to Tell Me What to Do!" (Chapter 4, case 4.1), you will want to learn more about how children use their behavior to express their feelings and about what feelings Bobby might be expressing in his actions. You will likely want to read more about the relationship between thinking and behavior, as well as about instructional strategies that are helpful in working with children like Bobby. As you do this related reading, your views on the issues in the case become more informed, and you grow to understand more about children and behavior and more effective teaching practices. Learning with cases is an important way for you to grow as an informed, knowledgeable teacher.

Enjoying Yourself

Students who have learned with cases claim that this is a more enjoyable way to learn. "I can't wait to get to class," is a frequently heard comment. "You don't even feel that you are learning—but actually, you are learning much more," is another. Being actively involved, working with provocative case material, having a chance to express your ideas and hear those of others—these are all enjoyable facets of learning with cases. So when you begin to experience the pleasure of learning with cases, don't fret. Learning does not have to be full of pain to be productive. Relax, enjoy it, and be confident that what you are doing will have profound payoffs for you as a teacher.

REFERENCES AND RELATED READINGS

Adam, Maureen. 1992a. *The Responses of Eleventh Graders to Use of the Case Method of Instruction in Social Studies.* Unpublished Master's thesis, Faculty of Education, Simon Fraser University, Vancouver, British Columbia.

Adam, Maureen. 1992b. [Unpublished raw data from study].

Bickerton, Laura; Chambers, Rich; Dart, George; Fukui, Steve; Gluska, Joe; McNeill, Brenda; Odermatt, Paul; and Wassermann, Selma. 1991. *Cases for Teaching in the Secondary School.* Coquitlam, British Columbia: CaseWorks.

Christensen, C. Roland, & Hansen, Abby. 1987. *Teaching and the Case Method.* Boston: Harvard University Graduate School of Business.

Christensen, C. Roland; Garvin, David; and Sweet, Ann. 1990. *Education for Judgment.* Boston: Harvard University Graduate School of Business.

Ewing, David. 1990. *Inside the Harvard Business School.* New York: Random House.

Glasser, William. 1986. *Control Theory in the Classroom.* New York: Harper & Row.

Gross, Sandra. (ed.). 1992. *Findings on Learning to Teach.* East Lansing: National Center for Research on Teacher Learning, College of Education, Michigan State University.

Raths, Louis E.; Harmin, Merrill; and Simon, Sidney B. 1978. *Values and Teaching.* (2nd ed.). Columbus, OH: Merrill.

Schön, Donald. 1983. *The Reflective Practitioner.* New York: Basic Books.

Wassermann, Selma. 1990. *Serious Players in the Primary Classroom.* New York: Teachers College Press.

Wassermann, Selma. 1986. "How I Taught Myself How to Teach," in *Teaching and the Case Method,* ed. by C. Roland Christensen and Abby Hansen. Boston: Harvard University Graduate School of Business.

Winchell, Paul. 1954. *Ventriloquism for Fun and Profit.* Baltimore: Ottenheimer.

3 | CASES: The Teacher as Person

"Good teaching," the distinguished educator Arthur Combs (1978) once wrote, "is not a question of right methods or behaviors, but a problem-solving matter, having to do with the teacher's unique use of self as he/she finds appropriate solutions to carry out the teacher's own and society's purposes" (p. 558). The process of "personal becoming"—students' personal discoveries of how their beliefs are translated into classroom actions—is an important route in preparing effective teachers. Combs cautioned, "In a program for becoming, learning must be personal and experiential; mere acquisition of knowledge will not do. What is required is the development of a personal system of perceptions or beliefs to provide the new teacher with long-term goals and short-term guidelines for the moment-to-moment decisions of classroom interactions" (p. 559).

The cases in Chapter 3 are all centered on issues that call for examination of how teachers' own needs, values, and expectations bear on their educational decisions. These cases call for journeys into personal meanings, and careful study should allow for taking the next steps on the pathway of "personal becoming."

Each case is followed by a list of questions, with an additional question for those with classroom teaching experience denoted by a dagger.

3.1   I SO WANTED TO BE A GOOD TEACHER

She passed by the school board office twice before she spotted the driveway that led into the parking area. Was it nervousness that prevented her from finding the road the first time? Or was she just a klutz, dressed up in a teacher's suit? She parked her little red VW, a relic from better days, in one of the visitor's spots, gathered her papers, and pulled herself up to the full height of her newly achieved status: *certified teacher.*

As she walked down the carpeted corridor of the administrative wing of the building to the door marked Personnel, she felt like a first grader approaching the fire-breathing dragon. The knot in her stomach tightened like a fist.

Dr. Alan Marshall, Director of Personnel, greeted her warmly. "Sit down, Miss Ziti. I'm very pleased that you could meet with me this morning."

The warmth of his greeting did little to dispel her anxiety, and when she tried to respond to his greeting, her voice came from a throat so dry, the words felt like small dust motes that were blown into the air.

Alan Marshall's interview was brief. She had been told to expect complex questions on classroom management and teaching strategies, but his questions were so simple and direct that she could answer them with a minimum of sophisticated thinking. Yes, she had done her student teaching in a primary class-room, and yes, she felt she was ready to handle a class on her own. What else could she say? Certainly not the truth: "I'm terrified! I've never really handled a class for a long period on my own! I'm not sure of what a teacher has to do! I feel so . . . incompetent!"

As she searched his face for any sign that he might have picked up on her terror, her teacher-training program, every moment of it, passed through her mind, as if she were drowning. What were the key experiences? What had she actually learned about teaching? At this very moment, whatever it was she had learned had completely evaporated. She felt naked and incompetent. A fraud with a teaching certificate.

She must have said something right or else he must have been desperate for a new teacher. It was, after all, three weeks into the new school year. There was an opening at the River Road Elementary School, a primary classroom. The regular teacher had just left for maternity leave. She could begin on Monday.

"Yes, that's fine," she muttered, uncertain whether what she really wanted to do was run out of the office. She remembered thanking him for his time and for his confidence in her, and she remembered moving, like a zombie, past the desks of the secretaries and out to the safety of the parking lot.

"Whew! I've done it! I got the job! So what do I do now?"

She must have driven all the way home, because suddenly, she found her-self pulling into space #63 in the underground parking garage that tunneled under the suburban high-rise. But she couldn't remember the drive, or the traffic, or even if she had stopped at the traffic light at the corner of Lonsdale and First Streets. Is this what anxiety did? Did it give you instant amnesia?

As Marilyn Ziti rode up the elevator to the ninth floor, she vowed to get a grip on herself. "This is ridiculous," she talked to herself in the empty car. "I've got to get it together here." She remembered what her mentor teacher had told her about her nervousness during the first week of her teaching practicum: Nobody dies from her first days of teaching! "Oh, yeah?" she chuckled.

That evening, she treated herself to a celebratory dinner of Caesar salad, prime ribs of beef, baked potato with lots of sour cream and butter, and apple pie, the $12.99 take-out special from Tony's Rib House down the block. Cholesterol City, right? What the heck. If you were sailing on the *Titanic,* you might as well go first class. But she vowed that first thing Saturday morning she would take charge and get herself ready for Monday. Enough of these wild terrors. Nobody dies from her first day of teaching, right?

Armed with her second cup of coffee, the Saturday morning sun winking at the pile of papers and books on the carpet surrounding her, she settled down for some serious planning. Like any good student preparing for a test, she read through her pile of accumulated notes from her education classes. Here were all the answers she would need about teaching. In these notebooks and in her texts lay all the secrets of the profession. If she could only remember them, she would have a clear line to a passing performance:

"It is difficult for slow learners to think in abstractions, since their low IQ's of 75 to 90 prevent them from this kind of thinking."

"There are four definitions of creativity."

"When you organize curriculum, you should not think of it as 'set in stone,' but rather as a guide in the teaching–learning process."

"Educational objectives fall into three categories: (1) school objectives; (2) content or subject-matter objectives; and (3) teacher and child objectives."

"Evaluation is the process of gathering data about student progress, both formally and informally, in order to further pupil learning."

The ideas seemed familiar to her, but she took little comfort in the fact that she had once known them and been able to repeat them on tests to win high marks. What did any of them have to do with the reality of her, in front of 25 primary children, on Monday morning? She thrust the books and notebooks from her and reached for the coffee cup, wishing it was something considerably stronger.

With the worst weekend of her life behind her, she arrived at River Road School at 7:45 A.M.—early enough to meet the principal and walk on rubbery legs down the hall to her own classroom. There had been enough time to have her name put on the door, and she felt a thrill when she saw it—her room, her class, her children. The excitement of beginning to teach was running a close second to her anxiety and feelings of inadequacy. She wrote her name on the blackboard, in large primary letters—MISS MARILYN ZITI—and sat down at the desk.

Helen Cameron, the teacher who had just gone out on maternity leave and had started with the class from the first days of the school year, had left detailed instructions for the new teacher. The class was three weeks into the fall semester, and routines had already been established. As Marilyn looked at the teacher's plan, she saw how the reading groups were to be occupied, what seatwork was to be distributed, and what assignments were to be made in arithmetic. That about covered the morning until recess. Could she survive until recess? When the schoolbell rang, she felt faint.

The children buzzed into the room, noisily and purposefully hanging up their outer garments, and proceeded to their seats. They sat quietly, looking at her. She swallowed hard, looking at them.

"Good morning, boys and girls. I'm your new teacher, Miss Ziti. There's my name on the board. I hope we are going to have a very good year."

"It would help me very much to learn your names. So as I call the roll, please stand up and let me see you. Let me know, too, if I am saying your name correctly."

In retrospect, she thought that calling the roll was the best thing she did that morning. The children were quiet and she was in full control. After that, everything began to deteriorate. She tried to get the students into their reading groups, but a thousand small problems got in the way of her carrying out those procedures effectively. The more the operations broke down, the more disruptive behavior emerged. Pretty soon, she found herself shouting.

"Sit down, Walter!"

"This is the last time I'm going to speak to you, Judy."

"No, you may *not* go to the washroom now."

"Why are you coloring when you haven't finished your arithmetic yet?"

"It's too noisy in here. Be quiet everyone!"

The more she shouted, the more she felt she was losing it. She picked up the yardstick, in fury, and smacked it down on her desk. The children were startled and lapsed into silence. She hated what she had done and hated herself.

She somehow got through the rest of the day in a nightmare of tension and conflict. Her classroom felt like a battlefield, with a terrible power struggle going on in which she felt more and more the loss of control. She had the children get ready for home 10 minutes before three o'clock and didn't care about dismissing them early. She hated every one of them and if she wasn't going to be fired for total incompetence, she would very likely resign. If this was what teaching was like, if now, after working so hard to complete her training program successfully, she still had so much to learn about teaching, she would be better off selling real estate.

Study Questions

1. Working in your study groups, talk to one another about what each of you perceives as the important ideas in this case. Talk together about the feelings that this case provokes in you.

2. Marilyn Ziti wanted very much to be a good teacher. What, in your view, is a "good teacher"? What are some characteristics of a "good teacher"? Working together, make a list of the characteristics you believe are key.

3. As you read this case and as you draw from your own experiences, what do you believe got in the way of Ziti's performing competently in the classroom?

Working together, list what you perceive as the impediments to Ziti's competent functioning.

4. In this case, you will note that Ziti was able to successfully complete her education courses with good grades. Yet her performance in her training program did not seem to help her in the classroom. How do you explain this? What hypotheses can you suggest?

5. Some experienced teachers claim, "You only begin to learn to teach on the very first day you set foot in your own classroom and you never stop learning for as long as you are in the profession." How, in your opinion, may a teacher reconcile his or her needs to feel successful and competent in the face of such a claim?

6. How can Marilyn Ziti be helped to recognize and appreciate her professional growth needs without further undermining her feelings of self-worth? What are your thoughts on this?

7. If you had gone through training with Marilyn and she now called on you for help, what would you do?

8. If you found yourself in a situation like this, how would you help yourself?

†9. As an experienced teacher on this staff, what would you be prepared to do to help Marilyn? What assumptions have you made about the effectiveness of the strategies you have proposed?

3.2 MY FRIEND CONNIE

She's tall and angular and looks as if she were put together by Paul Klee in one of his more creative moments. Connie wound up in my education seminar group—it was just a crapshoot that the groups broke that way. She was gung-ho from the start, that is, after she'd registered her complaint about the difficulty she had in getting to campus by bus. At the beginning, I knew only that she was a tall, skinny, curly-headed, very enthusiastic student who didn't have a car and who felt comfortable enough to voice a complaint in the first class session.

As the semester made headway, I learned that Connie read *The New Yorker* like it was her Bible and had come west with her husband, Bill, via a short lifetime of touching bases in Montreal, Rochester, New York City, and a small village in France, not necessarily in that order. She was mad about the movies and had a passion for Life, with a capital L. What's more, whenever we had an intense discussion in seminar, which was a lot of the time, some idea or point would touch her, and she would respond with a snort that told me she had seized on a powerful insight and had been deeply affected by it.

In four months of classes Connie and I got to know each other better. I admired her sensitivity to the others in the group; her quick, sharp mind that easily grasped difficult concepts; her warmth and caring; her skill in doing the variety of course assignments. When the course ended, I knew that however our paths parted, we'd be friends for life.

The following semester, Connie did her 16-week student teaching practicum in a kindergarten class in the city. Her sponsor teacher, one of the most admired primary teachers in the district, said about her: "She's like having another teacher in the room. I never think of her as a student teacher." It was a happy alliance for both of them, and when it was over, it meant that Connie had completed her professional training and was blessed with the certificate that made it possible for her to enter the teaching profession. On a howly, rainy commencement day, Connie received the Claude E. Lewis Award in Education, a medal for "the student who attains the highest standing on completion of his or her professional work in the School of Education at Chinook University."

Without so much as a breather, she applied for and was hired to teach a first-grade class in a small town about 250 miles from the city, taking over for a teacher who was retiring at Christmastime. This meant pulling up roots and separating from Bill for half a year. When I asked Connie about it, she was awfully clear that this was precisely what she wanted to do: teach. And how could she know what life in a small town was like until she could experience it from within? She had visited the class in November, talked with the teacher she was replacing, and gathered some information about the children, the materials, the processes of classroom management, the interpersonal interactions, the classroom routines, the curriculum.

When Connie came back from her visit, she remarked that the children were wonderful. She also mentioned that the classroom was highly teacher directed and that the children were pretty compliant about following orders. She believed that she would have to work with them slowly, very slowly, to help them progress toward more self-directed behaviors. She seemed sensitive to the growth processes of children and clear about the direction she would take, helping students to take small steps in functioning in a more open type of classroom. This was her goal, a choice she had reflected upon, and it seemed to her to be a thoughtful and reasonable way to proceed. She was certain that she did not want to do anything that would cause stress for the children. As she described the situation, and her plans for change, I admired the respectful way in which she spoke about the retiring teacher. It would have been easy for her to condemn her methods, like so many new, young teachers do when they find teachers who work in ways more traditional than their current, more innovative educational training. But I never heard a trace of accusation or of condescension in her words or voice.

After her first month of teaching, Connie was visited by her principal for the purpose of evaluating her teaching performance. In her letter, she wrote that he had spent two hours in her classroom and one hour in consultation after school. While she was doing lots of things well, he reported, "her biggest fault was that she was unable to stick rigorously to her schedule." The principal was adamant that a new teacher must follow her plans without deviation. For example, if social studies was scheduled for 10:45 A.M., that is precisely when it should begin. This did not mean 10:50! Connie allowed the children to go from one activity to another too casually. Consequently, there was too much time lost, some "unnecessary" noise, and a falling behind schedule. Although Connie tried to persuade him that children, especially very young children, needed the freedom of movement that more flexible scheduling allows, he was certain that because the schedule was not rigorously kept, it was a sign of sloppy teaching; that good teaching was, in fact, a matter of promptness and diligence in keeping to the schedule. On this point, the principal and Connie seemed to be on different planets with respect to their educational beliefs about children's needs and teaching priorities. But Connie, in an attempt to reconcile herself with his mandate, told him that she would try to pay closer attention to keeping the schedule. She did not want to present herself to him as rigid, defensive, or unwilling to be sympathetic to his concerns. In response, he told her that this would be his main area of focus when he made his next observation.

In May, another letter arrived from Connie. She had been dismissed from her teaching position. Her words did not suggest depression; in fact, her spirits seemed good. She said it had been a good and valuable learning experience for her. Of course, she was disappointed, but she did not seem in despair over what had happened. She said, "I gave them the best I had, but it wasn't what they wanted. I feel bad about it of course, but I learned so much, particularly about myself."

When school was out in June, Connie came back to the city to get ready to go to New York for a holiday, during which she had hoped to saturate herself at the movies. We met for lunch, on a sunny Saturday afternoon, in a small bistro downtown. Connie was full of zip, and if there was a trace of diminished self-esteem, I did not see it. At that lunch, I heard the details of the story of Connie's failure as a teacher.

She had heeded the advice of the principal about sticking to her schedule and found it difficult. The needs of individual children seemed always to get in the way. Nonetheless, she kept trying, aware that here was a true conflict of educational values between what she believed was right and good for children and what the principal believed. To put children's needs aside in deference to the schedule seemed an invalidation of all she had grown to believe about children and education.

The recognition scene occurred in March, during her second evaluation visit. This time, the principal came accompanied by the superintendent of schools. They both stood, large and looming figures among the group of tots. This was a strictly no-nonsense visit, and Connie's job could be on the line.

She went into it with her eyes wide open, she said. She knew exactly what the schedule dictated: 9:30 A.M.—end of reading; begin work in math! Connie dismissed the group of children working with her and asked them to return to their seats and to take out their math materials. But 6-year-olds have other things on their minds. Several children lingered at Connie's side. "Mrs. Fairmore! Mrs. Fairmore!" They wanted, were eager to share some private thoughts and feelings with her. It is the kind of moment that is pivotal in the classroom, in which building blocks of respect, of interpersonal contact, of warmth, of caring, of the way in which humans relate to each other are laid. Connie looked up to see the stern, disapproving faces of the administrative team and, in that moment, made a decision that affirmed her beliefs and affected the rest of her life. With conscious, deliberate action, she turned to the little ones at her side, knelt down, embraced them, and said softly, "Yes, sweetheart, what is it you'd like to tell me?"

Study Questions

1. Working in your study groups, talk together about what you see as the significant issues in this case. Identify them.
2. How would you describe Connie as a teacher? What adjectives would you use to describe her? Classify your list of adjectives into "positive" and "negative" categories.
3. What is your view of these administrators' insistence on following the schedule as a primary requirement of good teaching? How do you explain the importance of this criterion of teaching effectiveness?
4. What, in your opinion, were the options open to Connie?
5. As you see it, what values underlay Connie's decision?
6. Is this a value worth losing your job over? What are your thoughts on it?
7. At what point should a teacher stop compromising his or her values and take a stand for what she believes? What are your thoughts on this?
8. What price might Connie have paid to keep her job? Would the job have been worth the price? Where do you stand on this issue?
†9. To what incident in your own experience does this case compare? What are some similarities in the two situations? What do you see as some significant differences? What were the costs to you in the decision you made?

3.3   THE BARED BREAST

What was she thinking when she let Jim pose her nude for his photography class assignment? She must have been crazy, or at least temporarily deranged in that moment that now threatened her whole career, if not her life. Her eyes returned, for the thousandth time that morning, to the headline in the local paper: BURNSIDE TEACHER SUSPENDED! Was this the end of her career in teaching? Was she

to be driven in shame from her students, the school, the community where she and Jim had made their home? Would this community brand her with the scarlet letter that she would wear for the rest of her life?

When Hilde Muller and her husband Jim had taken jobs as teachers in Burnside six years ago, they knew that this small, rural community was not exactly the San Francisco of the North. Primarily agricultural, about 60 miles from the large, urban center of the state, Burnside boasted more churches per capita than any other city in the territory. Politically conservative, Burnside residents took their Bible studies seriously, openly and vigorously rejecting, in their local newspaper and church sermons, the city life that bred loose morals. Hilde and Jim could have chosen to live in the city, commuting the 60 miles each way to their teaching jobs in Burnside, but they had decided to live in the community where they taught. In that way, not only would they save the time and the energy of a tiresome and expensive daily trip, but they would become true members of the Burnside community in every sense of the word. Living in Burnside was limited, they knew. There were no movies, no theater, no interesting restaurants other than Uncle Willy's—the "all you could eat" smorgasboard for $5.99, where you could take the family for a Sunday supper without fear of being corrupted by foreign foods. If Jim and Hilde felt the need for a cultural shot in the arm, they could easily make the trip to the city, which they did at least twice a month. Both Hilde and Jim were agreed that they could not really grow as teachers unless they enriched their lives with some exposure to real city life.

Six years of teaching in Burnside had been good years for Jim and Hilde. Hilde taught English at the Burnside Intermediate School. She liked the pupils. They were well behaved, polite. She never, in six years of teaching, had had a class where children were disrespectful. She knew from her friends and colleagues who taught in other communities that kids at this prepubescent age could be perfectly disgusting! But not in Burnside. She thought she was pretty lucky. Of course, the kinds of books she was expected to teach in seventh and eighth grades were a bit of a bore, but she could live with that. This was not a community that would take kindly to *Catcher in the Rye*, or even Steinbeck or Hemingway. Even *Goldilocks* had been turned out of the primary grades, because it "taught wickedness." Goldilocks, parents protested, had broken into the home of the bears, and young children were not to be exposed to such wicked behaviors.

Hilde had winced when the people of Burnside voted overwhelmingly to include creationist theory as part of the secondary school science curriculum. If Darwin had a place in the biology curriculum, people argued, then creationism must be given equal time. When the biology curriculum was thus revised, the news reached the city and townsfolk were mocked in the city press. But the people in the community took these condemnations as one more sign of the evil lurking behind the concrete facades of big-city life. While parents of primary chil-

dren were voting against *Goldilocks* and parents of high school students were voting for creationism, the curriculum of Hilde's Intermediate School seemed, so far, to have escaped notice. Jim Muller, who taught industrial arts at Burnside High, seemed also to have found a safe haven in his classes. There were no controversies, no moral dilemmas in a curriculum that consisted of wood and metal shop work.

Neither Hilde nor Jim was an active churchgoer, but they nonetheless settled into the neighborly community of Burnside, put some roots down, and felt very much a part of the town. Things could not have been sweeter . . . that is, until the bricks hit the fan.

Jim did not even need the credit for the course! He had enrolled in the photography workshop at the community college simply for his own pleasure. His teacher had encouraged him and told him that he had real talent as a photographer. What was it he said—that Jim had an "eye for visual composition"? Jim loved the photography course. He loved taking photos. When he got tired of landscape shots, he turned to people.

It was a rainy spring Sunday and Hilde was in her brown sweatsuit, sitting in the easy chair, marking students' papers. "If I read one more 'God Loves Me' essay, I think I may puke," she said, as Jim opened his third beer, his camera dangling from a strap around his neck. He glanced at her, eyes bright.

"How about taking a break and posing for me?" he said, grinning.

"Give me a break," Hilde answered brusquely. "I've got about 12 more papers in this batch before I can even think about dinner."

"Come on. A break is just what you need. It'll do you good. Besides, I need six more composed shots to complete the class portfolio for this week."

"Are you kidding? Me? Why would you want to submit my photo? Look at this face. Ugly. Look at these legs. Ugly. Look at this waistline. Fat. Fat and ugly. Uh, unnnh," she said. "No picture."

"Hilde," Jim said. "You're not ugly and you're not fat. You're nuts, is what you are. Let me promise you this. I'll take the photos and if you don't like them, you can toss them and no one will ever see them. I promise. Cross my heart."

Now, looking at the headline in the newspaper, Hilde could not even remember how she had let Jim persuade her not only to take her picture, but to pose in those black lace scanty panties and bra he had gotten her for Christmas. But he was right about one thing, though. She was not ugly or fat. The way Jim posed her, arranged the light and shadow, the way her hair fell down the side of her face, the picture was stunning. She could not believe it was her, Hilde Muller, teacher of English at Burnside Intermediate School. She could have been a model, or even a movie star!

They did not discuss it beyond that. Jim used her photo for his class assignment and got an A in the course. Encouraged by his success, he submitted the photo to a contest in *A-Line* magazine, where he took second prize. Along with

a check for $500, Jim's award-winning photo of Hilde was published on page 6 of *A-Line*.

Even after the picture's publication in *A-Line*, there was no response from the town of Burnside. Maybe nobody in Burnside read *A-Line*. The fur began to fly only when the caption under the photo, "Hilde M., age 34, teacher, Burnside," caught the eye of a reporter from the city tabloid, who, sniffing the chance of a bigger story, telephoned an inquiry to the school board. Hilde was immediately suspended for "inappropriate behavior." Jim was suspended a month later.

It did not help that 50 of her students staged a walkout in support of their teacher. Their claim that "she is a great teacher and what she does in private is her own business" failed to impress the school board authorities, and the students were served with a five-day suspension for *their* inappropriate behavior.

The State Teachers Association came to the defense of Hilde Muller when she pleaded her case before the school board. Muller claimed that the appearance of the photograph did not prevent her from being a good teacher. Also supporting Muller's claim was the public relations manager for the magazine, who argued that the photograph was a matter of freedom of expression with which no government should interfere. The school board was not persuaded and took the next step: the dismissal of both Hilde and Jim Muller.

The Mullers appealed their dismissal and a mediation board was set up, consisting of three selected professionals from outside the Burnside community: Judge Kuyk, a member of the state judiciary for 17 years; Dr. Franco Milano, the superintendent of the large-city school district in the state; and Arthur Kroll, a city councilman. The mediation board was charged to resolve the question of misconduct versus an individual's civil liberties. What rights do teachers have to carry on their private lives as they wish, without placing themselves in jeopardy of losing their jobs? To what extent is a teacher a public servant, under the scrutiny of the community in which he or she is employed? To what extent should such a community be in a position to dictate what a teacher may do outside the classroom?

The mediation board split 2–1 in their decision in favor of the Mullers. William Van Dam, the president of the Burnside board of education was apoplectic at the board's finding. He immediately called a press conference to announce that the Burnside board of education would press formal charges in a court of law against the Mullers. This case would not end with the exoneration of these vile people!

Study Questions

1. Working in your study groups, begin your discussion with an identification of what you consider to be the important issues in this case. List these, and rank them in order of importance to you.

2. A fundamental question raised by the Muller case is whether a teacher is free as an individual in the community to behave as any other person. To what extent should a teacher's behavior be circumscribed?

3. If restrictions are to be placed on a teacher's behavior in the community, to what other professional groups would such restrictions apply? What professional groups would be excluded?

4. One of the arguments advanced by Dr. Franco Milano, the city superintendent of schools who was part of the mediation board, is that a teacher is regarded by students and parents as a role model. If teachers are to be role models for students, what kinds of behaviors should be permitted in the community? What behaviors should be excluded? What other professionals are role models for children? How should their behaviors be legislated?

5. How does a teacher decide what behavior is appropriate for him or her in the community? Faced with this question, how would you decide?

6. What laws in your community, state, and country protect a teacher's rights in that community? What laws protect the rights of other citizens to behave, in their private lives, as they choose? In your view, what laws should exist to protect teachers' rights?

7. If you had been chosen to serve on the mediation board to decide the case of Hilde and Jim Muller, what principle would have guided your decision in favor of or against these teachers? To what other professional groups would this principle apply? What groups would be excluded?

†8. To what incident in your own experience or knowledge does this case about a teacher's private behavior relate? Describe the incident and discuss its resolution. Discuss the extent to which teachers' freedoms are limited by being a member of the teaching profession. What, do you suppose, are some "prices" that teachers pay for being members of the teaching profession?

3.4 "I'VE GOT A PROBLEM"

The coffee was thick and black and tasted like liquid Vaseline. He was already pouring his second cup when he began to tell me what was on his mind. At first, I couldn't make head nor tail of what he was saying. He seemed to be telling the story from inside out. But as I started to put the pieces together, I could hardly believe what I was hearing. "I've got a problem, Mike. A real problem. I don't know what to do."

I'd known A. J. Davis since we were freshmen. We were both anomalies in freshman English 101, where we stuck out like lumberjacks at the Queen's Ball—two beards in a room full of zits. A. J. was almost 30, and I was pushing 33. Our eyes met and asked each other the same question: What are we doing here? I

had already lived a full life as a cab driver in Chicago, had married and was raising a family of three kids, when I decided that life had better things to offer and
put in for a career change to teaching. A. J.'s story was more complicated. He
had flunked out of four different colleges by the time he was 21. Alcoholic and
on the skids, he woke up one morning in the gutter, with puke all over his shoes,
and headed for the blood donor's clinic, where he could trade a pint of blood
for the $5 that would buy him a quart of muscatel. But they weren't buying. His
blood was no longer of acceptable quality. He sat on the sidewalk outside the
clinic for what seemed to him to be a lifetime and finally got up, turned the
corner, and headed for the nearest AA center. When I met him, A. J. had been
sober for six years, still wrestling with the desire to drink, still vulnerable. "One
day at a time," he liked to tell me. And in his more cheerful moments, "One
more sober day for the kid," he'd smile with inner satisfaction.

Belmont State College was A. J.'s "one last" try at making it into a profession. A first-rate golfer, he had been able to earn a good living teaching and
coaching at a private club in Forest Hills, but with an IQ of about 180, he was
getting ready to take on something more challenging. A gifted but as yet unpublished writer, he thought he had a chance at success in teaching English. Maybe
he even had enough empathy to be able to help kids. For A. J., success at Belmont
State was going to make the difference between a career as a semipro golfer or as
an English teacher. If he could make it at State, he would know that he could
make it in teaching. The teacher education program at Belmont State became
his litmus paper test of "can do."

It didn't take very much effort for A. J. to pull A's in all his English classes.
His writing was powerful, poignant and had real class. Compared to the quality
of stuff turned in by the other freshmen, A. J. looked like Hemingway. His English
teachers loved him. I used to watch his face when we got our English papers
back—a small, slow smile would stretch across his mouth as he read the teacher's
usually laudatory comments. When I asked, he'd let me read some of his stuff,
but he never gave it to me to read without my asking. He was not showy, or
pushy, in that way, and he was very unaccustomed to being successful at anything. But when I read his stories, the pangs of envy burned deep. The guy could
write!

By the time we were juniors, we'd grown very close. My wife and I had him
down to dinner often, but he always came alone. He was still wary of attach-
ments, felt he needed a few more sober years before he could trust himself in a
relationship. There was no shortage of female attention, though. A. J. was tall
and muscular, and his face looked as if a million tragic stories had been etched
onto its landscape. Women followed him around as if a stick-on magnet had
been attached to his elbow. He enjoyed their attention, was always respectful
and courteous, but kept his distance. On the academic side of the picture, his
work in humanities subjects was consistently excellent, a little shaky in science

and math, but his GPA by the beginning of senior year was a healthy 3.0. He had made it this far and received a student teaching assignment at Hillside High, in nearby Farmington. We went to the student union building to celebrate. I had a beer and A. J. had ginger ale. We clinked our glasses together and toasted ourselves as seniors. We'd soon be teachers. We'd made it!

Student teaching in different high schools in different communities meant that we didn't see each other with the same regularity as in college. But we'd talk on the phone, and A. J. would come over regularly on Friday evenings for dinner with my family. We'd talk about our classes, the kids, our sponsor teachers, and it was clear that we'd both made the right choices. Teaching social studies was what I loved, and it was easy to tell that even from student teaching. A. J., too, had found what he'd been looking for. Listening to him talk about his classes, watching the fire in his eyes, it didn't take a Sherlock Holmes to see the picture. A. J. was a born teacher. This week our college supervisors were going to make their first visits, to "check us out," but we were confident that we were doing okay.

My own supervisory visit was unremarkable. Dr. Black, a well-known and well-liked professor from the Social Studies Department at the college, sat in on my Western Civilization class and talked with me for an hour afterwards. She gave me some pointers about resource material and about class discussion and I found her ideas helpful. It was a perfectly amicable visit, and I was particularly pleased when she told me that I was doing a good job. On Friday, when A. J. came over for dinner, I was anxious to hear how his visit had gone. His supervisor, Ms. Downs, was a new faculty member in the English Department, and she didn't have any history in the college that we knew about.

"Well, how did it go?" I asked as I took his jacket.

"I'm not sure," he said, his face twisted into a knot.

"What do you mean, man, you're not sure?" I blurted out.

"I'm just not sure. I think I'm doing something wrong, but I'm not sure just what it is."

"Look, A. J. I'm having trouble following you. Can you give me some examples?"

"That's just it, Mike. I can't give you any examples. And if you don't mind, I'd like to drop it, okay?"

He sucked on his ginger ale, but his brows arching down toward his nose told me the matter was far from dropped. Then he blew out his breath and said, "She's coming again on Tuesday."

"Tuesday?" I almost yelled. "She's supposed to give you some time between visits. That's the college plan for supervision. This is too soon for a second visit."

"I know," he said. "But she's coming Tuesday and I really need to do some careful planning here. This time, I've got to be sure that everything goes right."

I called A. J. on Monday night. He had spent the whole weekend thinking about and planning his lesson on the short story. The students would have read Yates's short story *Eleven Kinds of Loneliness*, and there would be a class discussion in which he would try to help them examine how the author used metaphor to enrich narrative power. He had strong questions prepared, and he had good examples to draw on. It sounded to me like a carefully thought-out lesson. The students were a good group. What could go wrong?

When the phone rang on Tuesday evening, I nearly fell over a chair in my rush to answer it. I didn't like the sound of his voice. "Can you come over? I've got to talk to someone. I'll make some coffee."

"I'll be there in 20 minutes." I grabbed my jacket and bolted out the door, as I yelled to Mary that I would be back later.

His face was gray under his beard and full of pain. "I think I'm in trouble, Mike."

"Well, what happened, for Pete's sake? What went wrong?"

"I just don't know; I don't even know," he shook his head, as if trying to sort out the pieces.

"Tell me what she said."

"Last week, she told me that my jacket was wrong. This was my beige sports jacket, you know? I didn't know what she meant by 'wrong' and I thought I was *supposed* to know, so I didn't ask. On Saturday, I bought a gray sports jacket, thinking that the color was more subdued. Today, she told me that I was wearing green socks, and that they were too loud. She also made other comments about my clothing, my shoes, my shirt, as if she was examining me for a job as a male model. She never said a single word about what I was doing in class."

"You mean all she talked about was your clothes?" I couldn't hide the disbelief in my voice. "What about your lesson? Your preparation? The way you worked with the students?"

He shook his head. "Nothing about any of that."

If I hadn't known any better, I would have thought this was a joke. I still couldn't take it seriously. "You mean that in all the time she was in your class, she couldn't take her eyes off your bod? Come on, man. Give me a break."

He didn't even laugh. "There's more," he almost choked it out. "She wants me to come to her apartment next Friday night, so that she can help me choose more appropriate clothes for teaching. What do I do now?"

Study Questions

1. What do you see as the central issues in this case? Try to make a summary statement of this case in about 50 words. Compare your summary statement with those of the others in your study group. What are some significant differences in what is being highlighted in the different summaries of the case?
2. How would you describe A. J. Davis? What adjectives would you use in cre-

ating a profile of this student? How would you classify your list of adjectives?

3. How would you describe Ms. Downs, the college supervisor? What adjectives would you use in creating a profile of this teacher? What assumptions have you made?

4. What do you see as the role of the college supervisor who makes a visit to a student teacher's class? How does A. J.'s description of Ms. Down's visit compare with your view of the college supervisor's role?

5. What is your diagnosis of what has occurred during the supervisory visit? What examples are you using as evidence to support your diagnosis? What assumptions have you made?

6. Based on your diagnosis, what advice should Mike give A. J.? How does the advice you are recommending "fit" in with your profile of A. J.? What do you see as some potential consequences of the action you are recommending? What do you see as some potential risks? What values are paramount in the action you are recommending?

7. What protections exist for the vulnerable student teacher who is not being treated appropriately by another professional who has some power over him or her? What are your thoughts on this issue?

†8. To what experience in your own student teaching (teaching) does this case relate? Talk about your own experience and how it was similar to/different from A. J.'s. Talk about the action you took and how the situation was resolved. In retrospect, what different action might you have taken?

3.5   ISN'T IT THE TEACHER'S JOB TO HELP CHILDREN?

Heidi closed the conference room door behind her and walked quickly down the brightly lit corridor, its walls cheerful with the primary colors of children's art, while the tears that she had been holding back for the last hour stung her eyes. By the time she reached the parking lot, her tears were a torrent of sorrow and confusion that ran down her cheeks and made large gray splotches on her neatly tailored white blouse. She knew that she could not drive now, that she would be unable to see the road. She had better sit in the car and wait until she calmed down. She would talk to her God, and she knew she would find comfort and solace there.

Heidi Trueman had wanted to be a teacher for as long as she could remember. When she was only 6, she was already gathering neighborhood children in her backyard, playing school and instructing them in lessons modeled on her own school experiences. As a 6-year-old teacher, she did not have to face the dilemma of the separation of church and state, and she cheerfully combined lessons from both her secular and church school classes. The children she taught never seemed to mind. They were glad for the organized activity that mitigated the humdrum of the long summer days. And there were always cookies and lemonade for snacks.

For Heidi, Christianity, unlike teaching, was not a conscious choice. It was rather something she felt born to—a part of her that she would be lost without. Being a Christian was so much a part of her that Heidi felt it identified her. Christianity guided her everyday actions and was thoroughly integrated into her day-to-day life. When Heidi had applied to the teacher-education program at Eastern State College, she was confident that her GPA plus the required letters of recommendation from her teachers and church leaders would assure her acceptance. She also had what she thought was the key to acceptance: her great yearning to be a teacher. More than anything, she wanted to help children, to help them learn, and to help them find God, as she had.

Four people sat on the interviewing committee, and although they had introduced themselves, Heidi did not know who they were and what their functions were at the college. She did know that these two men and two women held her future in their hands. It would be up to them to decide on her application. She knew, however, that God was with her. He always was.

Dr. Thornhill put her at ease and asked her to tell about why she thought she wanted to be a teacher. Heidi had no trouble with the question.

"I've always wanted to be a teacher," she smiled brightly, her enthusiasm spreading to her cheeks and her eyes. "Ever since I can remember, I've always wanted to help children. My belief in God is so important to me, it has a profound effect on my life. God makes my life better. I want to incorporate that belief into my teaching and bring that to my students. I want to teach them what they need to know and what will help them and what God can do for them. Of course, I know I must do this like a professional and go only as far as the regulations permit me to go."

Heidi thought she saw Dr. Thornhill shift uneasily in his chair as he glanced across the table to meet his colleagues' eyes. There was an uneasy silence, and Heidi wondered if she had gone too far, had been, perhaps, too enthusiastic.

"My dear," Dr. Evans approached her kindly. "Do you know that in this country, we have agreed to the separation of church and state? This means that public classrooms may not be places where teachers can promote their religious beliefs."

Heidi had expected the question. "I realize that is the law, Dr. Evans. I also know that the Pledge of Allegiance does recognize that this is 'one nation, under God,' so that God is not entirely absent from the classroom. I know, too, that in many public schools children are allowed to celebrate the joyous occasion of Christ's birth. I believe that I can reconcile my own beliefs without stepping over the boundaries."

When Heidi left the interview room, she smiled to herself. She felt she had handled the questions carefully, intelligently, and without apology. She thought, too, that she had presented a fair view of her own position, without compromising her beliefs. One week later, when she received notification of her acceptance into the teacher-education program at Eastern State, she knew that God had been with her.

The program at Eastern State consisted of a series of courses in education subjects that provided a foundation for further studies in methodology. The foundations courses included an introduction to education, educational psychology, social and philosophical foundations, and the history of education. The methods courses included work in the elementary curriculum areas of mathematics, social studies, language arts and science, as well as a course in art and another in music. The two years of education coursework was then capped off with two semesters of student teaching. While Heidi was mildly interested in the coursework, she was counting the semesters until she could begin actual work with children. Knowing that the senior year would give her that opportunity, she felt even more motivated to do well in the education courses, to demonstrate, without equivocation, that she was the "right stuff."

When Heidi's first student teaching assignment came, by letter, to her home, she could barely open the envelope. Her hands were trembling with excitement. She had asked for a primary assignment because she felt that primary graders would be more open to her teaching and more receptive to the kind of help she wanted to give. Her heart drummed in her chest, her eagerness almost overpowering.

The letter was so formal, so impersonal, to contain a message of such importance.

Dear Miss Trueman:

   For your first student teaching practicum, you have been assigned to Miss Paulette D'Angelo's third-grade class at Grandview School in Cambria Heights. Please report directly to the principal, Mr. Thomas Hood, on Thursday, September 9, at 8:00 AM.

   Mrs. Bonnie Reid has been assigned as your college supervisor. She will contact you about arranging classroom visits. Please telephone my office if you have any questions regarding this assignment.

   Yours sincerely,

   Janet Frost
   Director of Student Placements

The first morning of school, Heidi dressed carefully. She wanted to be sure she looked like a teacher should look—white blouse, tailored skirt, low-heeled, comfortable shoes, her hair neatly groomed and pulled back behind her ears. She was ready.

Mr. Hood, the principal of Grandview School, greeted her warmly and wished her a successful practicum. He seemed full of fun and made a few jokes, perhaps, she thought, to try to put her at her ease. But she was not at all nervous. When Mr. Hood took her upstairs to meet Miss D'Angelo, she knew that she had been waiting for this moment all her life.

Paulette D'Angelo told Heidi that she had been teaching for 11 years and that she loved it. She had had a student teacher from Eastern State College before, and she would try to do her best to help Heidi and to give her the opportunity to grow. Paulette had gone to some pains to create a space for Heidi in the classroom—a table where she could keep her books and materials, and half of the tiny teacher's closet to store her outer clothing and her personal belongings. Paulette also pressed upon Heidi the importance of being on time and of regular attendance, but Heidi thought to herself that Paulette need not worry on that score. Heidi would gladly have come on Saturdays, too, if she had been asked.

"What did you want me to do today, Miss D'Angelo?" Heidi asked, hoping that she would be able to do more than just sit and watch all day.

"Oh, Heidi, please call me Paulette. Miss D'Angelo makes me feel 20 years older. Well, today, I thought you should have a chance to introduce yourself to the children so that they can get to know you. Then, I'll ask you to be on the alert to see which children are having any difficulty with their work. When you see a child raise his or her hand, please go over to help. I think we'll start you off by giving you an opportunity to work with children individually. In that way, you can learn who the children are, as well as get practice in instruction. After a few weeks, we'll get you to do some planning for lessons with small groups, and then with the whole class. This is only the fourth day of school, so things are still a bit new for everybody. You might have a lot of calls for help."

"That's fine with me, Miss D' . . . I mean, Paulette. I think I can do that. I'd be really pleased to try. And I hope you'll tell me when you see me doing something wrong. I want to learn from you. I want to be a very good teacher."

At precisely 8:45, the school bell rang and moments later, 23 bright young faces filled the room with their childish enthusiasms, hung up their outer garments, sat down in their seats, and got ready for the business of the day. When they had settled down, Paulette D'Angelo immediately got to the first item on the agenda.

"Boys and girls, we are going to have a new teacher helping us out in this class. Her name is Heidi Trueman. I hope you will be very nice and polite to her as you all are to me. I'm going to ask her to tell you something about herself, so you can get to know her better."

Heidi beamed as 23 pairs of eyes shifted in her direction. "Boys and girls, I'm very happy to be here in your classroom. I hope to be able to help you all. I thank God for bringing me to this classroom."

Heidi sat down, a bit breathless, and watched the children's eyes drift back to Paulette D'Angelo. She was too excited to see the look of concern furrow Paulette's forehead.

Several days later, Paulette overheard Heidi talking to Jaime Santiago, a troubled boy who was having a lot of difficulty with his schoolwork. Jaime was crying. "Nobody likes me," he said. "There's no reason for me to come to school anymore." Heidi responded, "That's not true, Jaime. I love you and so does God." Paulette beckoned Heidi over to the corner of the room.

"Did I go too far, Paulette?" Heidi wanted to know. "I didn't know what else to say to him. I wanted so badly to help him, to know that he is loved."

"I know, Heidi. I know that your intention is to help. But you must be careful not to overstep your bounds. If word gets out to parents, for example, or to the administration, that you are allowing your religious beliefs to intrude into your classroom work, you're headed for big trouble."

"I know that, Paulette. And I really do try to keep my religious beliefs out of school. But my Christian beliefs really affect everything I do. I want my Christianity to be a big part of my life, and teaching is also a big part of my life. The two can't help but get mixed together. But tell me this, Paulette. You're a Catholic. What's so wrong about telling Jaime that God loves him. That's true, isn't it? And doesn't that help Jaime to know that he is loved?"

"Look, Heidi. I don't make the rules. I'm just telling you what the rules are. I think you need to be careful."

The following week, Heidi was overhead counseling a sixth-grade girl during recess in the schoolyard. Heidi saw the girl, Martha, crying, and went over to help. Heidi said later that she thought that Martha was wrestling with feelings of guilt for having talked back to her teacher, and Heidi had told her that one way to help with guilt was to ask forgiveness from the person she had wronged, and from God. When Heidi told this to Martha, she took pains to walk with Martha out of the schoolyard, and off school property, so that she would not be in danger of crossing the line and going against the rules. Yet Heidi could not imagine why she should not tell Martha what she knew to be true and what she believed, deep in her heart, would help this troubled girl.

When Bonnie Reid came for her first supervisory visit in the third week of Heidi's practicum, she was confronted with a series of Heidi's indiscretions— examples of incidents in which Heidi had allowed her religious beliefs to impinge on her work with students. Bonnie sat in the back of the classroom observing Heidi read a story to the children, after which she engaged them in discussion about the story. Bonnie noted that Heidi's choice of story was appropriate and interesting, that the children listened respectfully, that Heidi's delivery was good, and that the classroom discussion was lively. Heidi seemed to have good classroom control, and the children seemed genuinely to like her. There was no incidence of Heidi's allowing her personal beliefs to infiltrate the lesson.

Bonnie nevertheless asked Heidi to meet with her in the conference room after school. She told Heidi of the concerns voiced by Paulette D'Angelo and cautioned Heidi about the possibility of parental reaction.

"Heidi, it's clear to me that you have a very nice way with these children and that you care about them very much. It's also clear to me that you have a great love of teaching. But Heidi, you just can't, I repeat, can't allow your religious beliefs to enter the classroom. If you continue to do this, you are in grave danger of being asked to withdraw from the program." Bonnie's eyes fixed on Heidi's face and did not waver. She kept her gaze steady, as if she were boring straight into Heidi's soul.

"I know what you are saying, Mrs. Reid. But believe me, I'm very confused. I thought that helping children was what was expected of teachers. I don't think I go overboard in allowing my beliefs to get into my teaching. I really think that there have been situations where I could have helped students a great deal more if I had told them about God and shared with them what I knew to be true, but I held back. This conflict puts me in a terrible dilemma. I know I could be helping more, but I'm holding back. And yet you say I'm going too far."

"Heidi," Bonnie Reid's voice was firm. "This is a warning to you. Please listen to me. You are overstepping your bounds and it must not happen again."

Heidi fought back the tears. Was this going to be a battle that she would have to fight all her life in the public school system? Would she be better off teaching in a Christian school? What was the matter with a system that prevented a teacher from using all the resources she had to help children? What about all those other teachers who hurt children—the mean, cruel ones? Why were they allowed to be a part of a system that had no room for God?

"I only want to help children, Mrs. Reid. Isn't that what a teacher is supposed to do?"

Study Questions

1. What seem to you to be the key issues in this case? Working in your study groups, list what appear to be the issues of significance. Then rank them in order of what you see as their importance.
2. From the data in the case, how would you describe Heidi Trueman? Working together, write a profile of Heidi, including information about how you see her as a teacher.
3. What is your response to the way Heidi helped Jaime Santiago? In your view, did Heidi go too far in allowing her religious beliefs to interfere with her actions on Jaime's behalf? What is too far? What are your ideas?
4. What is your response to the way Heidi helped Martha? In your view, did Heidi go too far in this incident? What is too far? What are your ideas?
5. To what extent can the classroom be a place where a teacher's personal beliefs

impinge on that teacher's classroom behavior? Which beliefs would be more acceptable? Which beliefs are unacceptable? What are your ideas about this?
6. What is your view about the position taken by Bonnie Reid? In your opinion, do you think she is being fair to Heidi? What data are you using to form your opinion about fairness?
7. Is there room in the public school system for a teacher like Heidi? What do you think?
†8. As you examine your own beliefs, which of them do you see "leaking out" into your classroom practice? To what extent do you see your students being subtly persuaded by your beliefs? How is this different from the case of Heidi Trueman?

3.6 "HOW CAN I MAKE A DIFFERENCE?"

He lay there on the gray tile floor, his blood forming a large dark inkblot pattern under his inert body. I could see his life ebbing away in front of my eyes as I stood there, paralyzed with fright and horror, unable to move or speak. I don't know how long I watched the blood leaking out of that small, frail shape that yesterday sat in my fourth-grade class, my eyes fixated on the tear in his abdomen wall and on the shattered tissue that used to be his intestines. Maybe seconds. Maybe hours. The sound of the sirens in the distance telegraphed the arrival of the paramedics, and their footsteps drumming staccato beats on that slick, polished floor brought me back to life.

"Step back, everybody. Please step back and give us room," the young Hispanic man with full beard ordered us, and we carefully shifted two or three steps away from Willie, lest that small movement break the slender thread that held his life in the balance and make a difference to whether he lived or died.

"Come on, guys, let us do our job here." Insistently, but not unkindly, the second paramedic moved into place, and both men lifted the small boy onto the stretcher, attached an IV drip to his arm, and made quick steps down the hall with their burden, toward the waiting ambulance. We teachers stood there, frozen with shock and disbelief, watching our fourth-grade pupil, gutshot, disappear into the ambulance and, heralded by the shriek of sirens, ride off down the streets of East New York.

Loreen Taylor, the principal of PS 157, was the first to speak. Loreen had grown up on the mean streets of this neighborhood and she knew, from her own life as well as from the stories of the children in her school, how very precarious was life in this neighborhood. Just walking to school meant running a gauntlet of obstacles that represented every kind of evil and danger: drug pushers on the corners, pimps and hookers, shootings, boarded-up buildings that were "shooting galleries," vacant lots overrun with garbage and rats the size of dachshunds. If Satan had invented a hell-on-earth for children, he must have put it here. Overcoming such obstacles to grow up with any chance at a successful, satisfying life should earn the winner a Nobel Prize for courage and perseverance. The chance of growing up at all was the more pregnant question. Handguns, sawed-off shotguns, and Uzis were as common as adolescent acne; the neighborhood was armed like a war zone. People carried guns to protect themselves from predators; criminals carried larger guns to take what they wanted. Everybody "carried."

Loreen herded us into the staff room and we sat in our usual places around the table where we normally gathered for lunch, where we tried so hard to make order from the chaos around us. Black humor was our primary tool for trying to stay sane, to keep our teaching lives in perspective. This time, however, no one spoke. I sat there, studying the pink fingernails in my dark hands, as if I was making a new medical discovery. My breath was coming in short bursts. I couldn't remember if I had breathed at all since I had heard the shot, run down the hall screaming, and seen Willie lying there. My Willie. With Lamar George standing over him, a magnum-44 in his hands, the smell of cordite in my nose.

"I know the police will be here shortly," Loreen spoke softly, awakening us to our responsibilities, "so we have to pull ourselves together and try to tell, as best as we can, just what happened here. When we're finished with the police, we'll have to decide about how we are going to tell Willie's grandmother. I don't know what will happen to Lamar. He's in the office now with Mr. Ortiz." Suddenly Loreen stopped talking, and I looked up from my fingernail study for the first time. Tears were falling down Loreen's face, onto her bright red shirt, and great sobs pierced the air. I went over to her and took her in my arms, and the two of us sobbed together, like children who had seen their worst nightmare come to life.

It was nearly 8:00 P.M. when I finally pulled into my driveway. The rains of early May had turned the garden very green, and in the last few moments of dusk, I could see the yellow roses starting to unfold for their first appearance. I loved that garden. It was my refuge from the ugliness and brutality of East New York and my therapy from teaching in a school where so many children were caught in traps of hopelessness. My wife, Roxanne, and I had been the first black family to move into this suburban neighborhood, across the New York City border, in Nassau County. While things were tense at first, we eventually settled into moderately agreeable relationships with our neighbors. We wanted to live in a community that was safe for us, and for our daughter, Alicia, a community where she could go to school without fear and get a real education. I had grown up in such a neighborhood and so had my wife, and we wanted the same for Alicia.

Yet when I chose my professional pathway, I made a deliberate and conscious choice to teach in an inner-city school. I felt a deep responsibility to children of color. I had something to give them, I thought. I could try to replace a little of what was absent from their bereft lives. I knew about the lack of "male role models" in many of these children's families and felt that my presence, my teaching, my caring, my encouragement might make a difference in some of their lives. Did I have a savior complex? Was I being hopelessly naive? Did I think I could endure, while so many of my friends and professional colleagues opted for schools in better neighborhoods, in the suburbs?

My good friend and buddy from college days, Mark Ewing, applied for and accepted a teaching position at Garden City Elementary School, and Mark was on my back at least once a week, trying to persuade me that I was nuts. "When are you going to leave that public disaster area?" Mark would ask, riding me, each time we spoke on the phone. It was not that Mark was unsympathetic to my situation. He just couldn't understand why I would want to stay on. As we compared everything about our different teaching situations, Mark seemed to have every advantage.

"How many in your class this year, Hobbsey?" he'd ask, knowing in advance that my class size could be larger than his by a third.

"Thirty-three this time, Marko." I played the game with him.

"Thirty-three? How 'bout twenty-four? With lots of space to move around in."

Mark not only had eight to ten fewer students in his classes each year. His classroom was spacious and well kept. The textbooks were up to date and new looking. There was science equipment in the cupboard, as well as art supplies for the most imaginative and creative projects, a well-equipped library, AV equipment that *worked!* You could come into his school building without having to pass through a metal detector; there were no police guards at the door or bars on the first floor windows. Garden City Elementary had all the latest equipment, a room full of computers, special teachers for gym, art, music, and one for enrichment programs for gifted pupils. And wonder of wonders, teachers had unlimited access to the photocopying machine and to whatever school supplies were needed. As he described it, Mark made Garden City Elementary sound like a learning paradise.

By contrast, we never had enough textbooks and what we did have tended to have a short shelf life. Kids at PS 157 treated books roughly; some just loved them to death, others treated them as objects of contempt. In an environment where human life was so cheap, how could books be cherished? Science equipment was in short supply, and art supplies—did the kids eat them? Whatever the board of education gave us in September was usually gone by January. If AV equipment broke down, it was months before it ever got repaired, that is, *if* it ever got repaired. School supplies were rationed like butter and eggs during World War II—and a photocopying machine? Locked up and guarded as if it were a rare antiquity, to be handled by only a very select few.

Instead of special teachers for art and gym and music, we had two part-time social workers connected to the school. We could easily have kept both of them busy on full-time schedules. And we had a part-time psychologist who was available every other Thursday—about as effective as spitting in the ocean.

The differences between Garden City Elementary and PS 157 were like those between the royal palace and the dungeon. Yet in spite of Mark's confrontations, his taunts, and his insistence that I was wasting my time trying to make a difference in the lives of my impoverished students, I had believed, truly believed, that PS 157 was where I was really needed. Where did I get those values from?

My father was the minister of the Baptist church in Yonkers and even as a very small boy, he was my hero. I never knew a kinder, more generous, more compassionate man. He rarely lectured to me about my social responsibilities— I think he just took it for granted that I would behave in socially responsible ways. "A man's got to put something back, Hobbsey," he'd tell me, when I saw him worn through with fatigue yet going off to see Mrs. Baron, whose husband had just been laid off. He never thought of himself first, always putting others' needs ahead of his own. We lived in a large stone house on a tree-lined street in a quiet, residential neighborhood, and my father was looked up to by every family on that block, black or white. I guess I thought I had the most perfect father that any boy could ever imagine.

I can't remember when I, Lee Jacobs Hobbs, decided to become a teacher. I knew I didn't want to go into the ministry, like my father, but I did know that I wanted to have a job where I would be able to "put something back." I liked working with kids at camp and I liked coaching basketball. I thought teaching would be fun.

During my sophomore year at NYU, I applied for and was admitted to the School of Education. That's when I met Mark. Mark was clear, from the very beginning, that he wanted no part of an inner-city school. "Look, man," he told me, "I *live* in the city and I think it's the most wonderful city on the planet earth. But I won't teach here. Too many problems in the city schools. You can't be a teacher. All your energies are dissipated by having to deal with crises. I know, man. My mother teaches at PS 72, in Queens. Now that's a good school by city standards. But even there, it's no match for the suburbs."

"But you've got to give something back, man," I told him, with my father's passion. "If none of us will take a job in the city, if we all head out to the 'burbs, who will be left to teach the children of the city?"

"Not me, boyo." he looked into my face, his eyes flashing. "We're talking about my life here, man. I want to be able to get up in the morning and be happy that it's a school day. I need to work in a place that's respectable, and where I feel respected."

Two years later, Mark and I were still arguing. He hadn't persuaded me to consider teaching in the suburbs and I hadn't persuaded him to "put something back" by taking a job in the city. He applied for Garden City Elementary and I took and passed the New York City License #I Exam and was appointed to PS 157 in Brooklyn.

I put my key in the lock and turned the knob. The living room was softly lit, and I could smell the remains of dinner lingering like a memory of a happy time lost. Roxanne, my wife of 11 years, came out of her study to greet me. She put her arms around me and I rested my head on her shoulder, feeling my wounds.

"You hungry, hon?" she whispered in my ear, and I shook my head. The lump in my throat felt like a granite boulder, and I knew I wouldn't eat again until someone was able to extract it.

"Come on and sit here and tell me what happened." Rox, the mother of my child, my solace and my comfort, took my hands into her hands and moved me toward the soft, spacious couch. "What happened, Hobbsey? Can you talk about it?"

My tongue began to come unglued, as I found the comfort of her face, her eyes telling me that it was all right to acknowledge that feelings could be larger than a body could hold. Tears once again came spilling down my cheeks, and the words came out in short, inarticulate bursts.

"He died on the way to the hospital. Willie Turk. You remember him. That skinny kid who never had his homework done. Looked like the dog chewed it up, only he didn't have a dog. Didn't have a chance. Didn't ever have a chance." I heard my voice getting louder. Was I screaming? I couldn't tell.

"Lamar George, boy from the fifth grade, just blew him away. Just like that. For nothing. For stepping on his new shoes. Pulls this gun, this big magnum, out of his pocket, and blew a hole right through him. Blood all over Lamar. Blood all over the walls, the floor. Pieces of Willie splattered on the walls, like it was confetti." I put my head in my hands and sobbed, big gasping sobs, that racked my entire body. Roxanne held me, waited, until I began again.

"Was I kidding myself to think it would never come to this?" I asked her. "Did I think that PS 157 would somehow be exempt? That God gave us special protection? Ninety thousand kids carry guns to school. That's a lot of kids with guns. Did I think that just because we had a metal detector that we were safe? Here I am going along, making like I'm a teacher, teaching reading and arithmetic, giving homework, marking papers, and there are the kids, armed to the teeth. Two thousand kids killed and wounded by guns last year. Why did I think we could be the school that would be untouched by that violence?"

Roxanne cupped my face with her hands and looked deeply into my eyes. "Honey, listen to me. The work you've been doing at that school has been so important. You're teaching those kids more than reading and arithmetic. You're teaching them to have pride in themselves, to believe in themselves, to feel they have a chance at something better in their lives. I know it hasn't been easy and that it's been an uphill struggle. But what you're doing, it counts for something. Don't let this day, this terrible tragedy let you lose sight of that."

"Oh yeah?" I answered, mouth twisted in anger. "Tell that to Willie Turk. How can one teacher make any difference? Look at the facts and use a little logic. Look at the neighborhood, the pimps, the drugs, the poverty, the violence, the utter hopelessness of the lives around these children, and then tell me that one teacher can make a difference. Look at what they go home to. If I manage to help them gain a shred of self-respect, that melts away on the way home from school. And what about the cost to me? I'm exhausted from giving so much of myself. Just exhausted. There's nothing left I have to give, Rox. I see what I do and then I see the gains vanish. I feel as if I'm never really gaining. I'm just creating a holding action, just keeping some of them from slipping further back. That's not teaching. I don't know what it is, but it's not teaching."

She wouldn't let it alone. "You're exhausted, Hobbsey. You're angry and you're hurting. You'll feel differently when you've had a hot bath and a good sleep. The children need you. Don't even think of giving up on them."

"It's no good, Rox. I'm beaten. As long as I live, I'll be seeing Willie lying there on that gray floor, with blood all around him. God, I didn't know there could be so much blood. I'll see him every time I go down that hall. I'll see him in my dreams. His death is a constant reminder that my classroom is a terminal ward for children. How can I make a difference against those odds? It's arrogant and presumptuous of me to think so."

The ringing telephone broke the silence that hung in the air, and I knew that it would be Mark calling.

Study Questions

1. What do you see as the important issues in this case? List them and talk together about which issues you believe to be key.
2. How would you describe Lee Jacobs Hobbs? Talk together about what you see as his distinguishing characteristics. In one paragraph, write a descriptive profile of this teacher.
3. Based on the data in the case, how would you describe the learning situation at PS 157? How would you describe the learning conditions at Garden City Elementary? What, in your view, explains the differences in conditions at these two schools?
4. What kinds of attributes are required in a teacher who chooses to teach in a school like PS 157? What data support your ideas that these attributes are important?

5. What do you see as a teacher's potential to make a difference in the lives of the children at PS 157? To what extent is it possible to make a difference? What are your views on it?
6. What do you consider "making a difference"? How do you know if a difference has been made? How can you tell?
7. How does a teacher maintain a positive outlook in a school where conditions for learning are less than favorable? How does this work?
8. What should Lee Jacobs Hobbs do? What advice would you give him? What would you do if you were in his shoes?
9. Given the fact that teaching conditions are less than satisfactory and that the children's learning needs are extreme; given that positive gains may be small, or even invisible; given that the best that can be done is a "holding action" to keep some children from slipping further back—is teaching at a school like PS 157 worth it? What are your thoughts about it?
†10. Under what circumstances have you questioned whether you were making a difference in the lives of the children in your class? What were the circumstances? Where did the doubts come from? What data were you using to determine success?

3.7 "I CAN'T HANDLE IT ANYMORE"

The principal's voice cracked out of the intercom like pieces of broken glass and shattered the stillness of the conference room. "Ms. Pelikan, would you please phone home. Your daughter just called, and she needs a ride."

Wendy Pelikan looked across the table at me, and slowly put her head down in the cradle of her arms. "I can't handle it anymore, John. I just can't handle it."

Wendy Pelikan came into the Fourth Street School like a ray of sunshine, and I took an immediate fancy to her. Fourth Street School, a relic of pre–World War II days, looked like the ghost of schools past. An old red brick building with high ceilings and long dark corridors, it was a school ready for an old-age pension but kept in service because it was functional and it was there. It was not a bad place to work, though. The principal, whether by intention or neglect, stayed out of the teachers' way, leaving us to do our jobs in the best ways we knew how. The parents, mostly newly arrived immigrants from diverse ethnic groups, cherished the school as a place where their children would be assimilated into the culture of their adopted country. The children, most of them wrestling with English as a new language, were like English as a second language children everywhere: a bit fearful of talking, a bit shy, a bit aggressive, a bit confused, happy to be in school, reluctant to be away from their homes and parents—not very different from children in other schools, in other cities, in other states or provinces. The 40 teachers on the staff, all with years of experience, ran the gamut from highly traditional and authoritarian to the more open-classroom types, who encouraged freedom of choice and thought group work and noise were an integral part of classroom life. My own classroom falls in the latter group, and maybe that's why I took so quickly to Wendy. She and I embraced the same educational values and we seemed to be cut from the same cloth.

She came in September, transferred by choice from a school on the more affluent west side of the city. Hers was the first new face on the staff since teaching jobs got tight, about six years ago. At first glance, she looked younger than the rest of us, but it might have been due to her youthful style and her exuberance for teaching. She walked down those ancient corridors with a bounce that the school hadn't seen in 20 years. It was fun just to have her around. Of course, it didn't hurt that her eyes were bright blue sapphires that could have sold at Birks Jewelry store for $5,000 apiece, and that her smile could melt the heart of a dragon.

Wendy's fourth-grade class was just across the hall from mine. We very quickly turned to each other to talk about kids, about curriculum, about all those complicated aspects of a teacher's life that make the job so tough, so challenging, so exciting. Pretty soon, we thought about team teaching. How could we function as teaching partners, to the best advantage of both groups of students? Each afternoon, we spent time planning together, developing curriculum materials and examining potentially more effective ways of dealing with individual children. Working with her, I felt renewed as a teacher and constantly challenged. She told me that my partnership with her was significant in her own professional growth as a teacher. What a team!

I watched her work with envy and admiration. She was one of those natural teachers, instinctively tuned into kids, that experience was just helping to polish. Her enthusiasm was catching, and she gave of herself and her time as if both were unlimited resources. Her energy and her ability to bounce back from disappointments were a source of profound wonder to me. How did she do it? How did she keep up the pace?

I knew what went into her teaching. She spent many after-school hours preparing materials, keeping a journal of her own reflections, writing helpful comments in her students' journals, and thinking about and preparing work for individual students. She ran the kind of classroom that required great behind-the-scenes preparation to make it work smoothly. I marveled at her ability to make her classroom the dynamic, exciting, vitally alive place it was. If I had kids, I'd want them to learn in such a room. Naturally, her students adored her. The respect she gave them helped them to build their self-respect. She challenged them to take risks, to make thoughtful and reflective decisions, to strive for excellence. There couldn't have been a better learning environment for newly arrived immigrant children. To me, she was the model of the master teacher.

In January, the midpoint of the school year, we were just sitting down to our after-school planning session when she told me that she had just enrolled in an evening class to upgrade her Teaching Credential. Wendy was separated from her husband, and she carried the burden and the costs of raising her three children almost entirely on her own. She needed the course credits to apply toward a salary increase. She was barely making ends meet, and now that her children were old enough to participate in after-school activities, she couldn't afford new soccer uniforms, shoes, skates, and the hundreds of "little" expenses that cut into the family budget like a surgeon's scalpel removing unwanted tissue.

I looked at her in shock. "How are you going to manage?" My voice squeaked out of my throat as I tried to hide my concern for her. She looked back at me, and for the first time, those sapphire-blue eyes were moist. "John, I just don't know. But somehow, I'll just have to. We need the money, John." That was all there was to it. She was a big girl, and I had to respect the decision she was making for herself.

As our daily planning meetings progressed into spring, I watched her visible symptoms of stress increase. If she was putting in as much time on assignments for her course as her own standards of excellence required, where was the time coming from? I knew that in addition to all the extra hours she put into teaching—and now studying for exams, reading, and writing essays—she also was a devoted mother. There were meals to prepare, laundry and marketing to do, and that never-ending requirement of all parents: chauffeuring the kids to and from a variety of extracurricular activities after school and on weekends. Could she be sleeping more than four hours a night? I couldn't see how.

She banged the door in haste, coming into the conference room about 15 minutes late. "Sorry, John," she said without looking at me, as she got her books out. "I just had a phone call from Won Lee's mother. She wanted me to know that he broke his leg and she needs some work for him to do at home. I told her I'd try to get it together this afternoon and stop by on my way home. I've got to stop off at the market, too, because I promised the kids that tonight, for a change, I'd cook a real dinner. We've been living on pizza for the past five days and it's getting pretty boring. I need at least four more hours in a day, John. It's beginning to wear me down."

I saw her chin come perilously close to her chest and the tears begin to tumble down her cheeks, making wet spots on her tailored yellow shirt. As I looked at her face, I let myself see what I had been afraid to see before—the lines of tiredness around her eyes and mouth, the dark areas suggesting sleep deficits, the bent shoulders. Suddenly she looked 100 years old to me. What a moment for the principal to let her know that there was yet one more task to crowd into her day: "Ms. Pelikan, would you please phone home. Your daughter just called, and she needs a ride."

Study Questions

1. Working in your groups, talk together about what you see as the "big ideas" in this case.
2. What do you see as the key events that led to Wendy's stress?
3. What is stress? How does it occur? What are its symptoms? What are your thoughts on it?
4. Why do you suppose people (teachers) take on more than they can comfortably handle? How do you explain it? What are your ideas?
5. What decisions do you see Wendy Pelikan having made that contributed substantially to the increased stress in her life? How did these decisions increase her stress? How does this work?
6. What might she have done differently? What assumptions have you made in suggesting alternate choices?
7. What are some ways in which teachers might deal more effectively with the stresses in their lives? What are your ideas?
8. How should John respond to Wendy? What principles of psychology are you using to inform your choice of an appropriate response? What is Wendy likely to say in return?
9. Some teachers see teaching as a job and are able to put the job behind them when the teaching day is over. Others see teaching as a profession in which a great deal of their post-teaching day is taken up with related professional activities. What is your view of teaching? What do you see as the implications of that view for your professional growth? Your classroom practices? The amount of time you plan to devote to the task of teaching?
†10. What factors contribute to your increased stress in teaching? What strategies do you have for identifying the stressors? What strategies do you have for taking steps to alleviate the stress?

3.8   THE TEACHER NEXT DOOR: TO TELL OR NOT TO TELL?

"You stupid boy!" she shouted. "You can't do anything right. You are utterly worthless. Get to your seat and don't let me hear another word out of you for the rest of the day."

The words echoed across the hallway, bouncing off the concrete walls and into Yuko's heart. "There she goes again," Yuko thought. "I wonder who the poor kid is this time." In her mind's eye she could envision the scene in the classroom across the hall: Mrs. Friedken standing in the front of the room, eyes bulging and veins popping out of her forehead, ranting and raving; the children cowed; the child singled out for public humiliation in torment, slinking to his seat, hoping that he might become invisible.

What would keep a teacher like Mrs. Friedken at her job, if she so conspicuously hated teaching, hated school, hated kids? Yuko could not understand it. And how was it possible that a school system closed its eyes to what was happening in Mrs. Friedken's class? Was it possible, Yuko thought, that no one actually knew?

Yuko picked up the book, smiled to the children sitting clustered around her on the carpet, and began reading. "This is the story of the *Shrinking of Treehorn*. It's rather a long story, so get quite comfy and settle in." Reading the story would help to ease the pain in her heart.

Yuko Itami was thrilled when she was appointed to teach second grade in the vast urban district of Los Angeles. All her life, she had wanted to be a teacher. Even when she was small, she would corral all the neighborhood kids into her backyard to "play school." Growing up, she never had a moment's hesitation when relatives asked her what her plans were for the future. "I'm going to State College," she told them, "because I'm going to be a teacher."

Unlike many of the other students, who voiced bitter complaints about their education coursework, Yuko always found something of value, no matter what course she was in. If you wanted to be a teacher, she believed, you had to know a lot, and keep your mind open to learning. Yuko did her student teaching practicum in an elementary school in east Los Angeles. Even though the neighborhood was considered tough, and many children came from dysfunctional families, Yuko found that she could easily love them all. To her, each child was special. Sometimes she felt that the more troubled a child appeared, the more he or she needed the loving and nurturing affection she could give. It did not take long for Yuko to become the children's favorite teacher. They knew she cared about them, and they loved her furiously in return.

When Yuko applied to teach in the greater Los Angeles school district, the personnel officer asked her how she felt about teaching in east Los Angeles. "I'll be happy to work with children wherever you send me," she said, without a trace of guile. "Children are children," she added. By the end of the interview, her assignment to Baker Heights School was confirmed.

Baker Heights was an older school, a red brick anomaly in the la-la land of palm trees and orange crush signs that looked like they had been designed for a movie set. Opening the heavy metal door to the main hallway, Yuko was gripped by the smell of chalk and old gym shoes, overlaid by the still pungent aroma of last June's cafeteria special, spaghetti and meatballs. What was it about old schools, Yuko wondered, that they held their smells forever?

Carmen Estevan had been the principal of Baker Heights for six years. She welcomed Yuko warmly and told her briefly about the school's history. Forty years ago, the neighborhood had been largely white and working class. As times changed, so did the neighborhood. The working-class families moved to the suburbs of San Fernando Valley and Orange County, and the neighborhood was now populated by the poor, disenfranchised "underclass"—the children of many ethnic backgrounds, but largely African-American and Hispanic. Carmen did not try to gloss over the kind of job that Yuko was being asked to do.

"You have to recognize, Yuko, that our children need more, much more, than subject-matter learning. Of course, they need to learn to read and write, and that is still the primary function of a school. But many of our children come from deep wellsprings of hopelessness. This school can build their hopes for what a future can give them. This school can build their confidence in themselves, their self-respect. This school can be their lifeline. I want a teacher who understands that, Yuko, and one who is willing to commit to that kind of challenge."

Yuko felt her eyes fill with tears, so great was her desire to join with Carmen Estevan in the good work that she was describing. "Yes," she said quietly. "Yes, I want to be part of this staff."

From the very first days of school, Yuko was already making inroads with her second-grade pupils. Her cheerfulness, her open caring for every one of them, her soft voice, and her pleasure in who they were and what they did were in evidence in everything she said and did. Her clear belief in their ability to learn was also an important factor in the children's growing beliefs in themselves.

"You don't know that word, Jorge? Come on over to me and I'll help you figure it out." She put her arm around the small boy with the dark curly hair, and heads together, they would work through the page in the reader. When Jorge came away from that teaching moment, he was one step further along toward becoming an independent reader.

In Yuko Itami's classroom, children always seemed to be busy, productive, engaged. There were many art projects: making masks, painting, clay, working with wood. She also included at least one movement education experience in each school day. Sometimes it was dancing; sometimes movement to music; sometimes stretching. In her social studies work, children took walking trips with her around the neighborhood. They looked at houses, at architecture, at stores, at streets, at traffic, at animals. Children made pictures of what they saw, or built constructions with papier-mâché or wood, or wrote stories and poems, or did a combination of these activities, in an attempt to know the neighborhood better. Even though some thought the neighborhood bleak, Yuko was able to help the children find some beauty, too.

On one occasion, Yuko arranged for a bus trip to the beach. Although it was less than an hour's drive to the beautiful Pacific shore, many of her students had never seen the ocean. Yuko was determined that she would continue to expand the horizons of her children, to show them the limitless opportunities of the world. When they returned to class, they wrote stories and poems and drew pictures that were then collated into "Our Beach Book," which became part of the class's library collection.

Whenever a child came to her in difficulty with his or her learning, she managed to convey such profound belief in that child's ability to learn that the student could not help but come away feeling empowered. By spring of that school year, every child in her class had learned to read and write. Some were still struggling with numbers, but she was confident that by June, most, if not all, children would be successful in that subject as well. On the few occasions when Carmen Estevan stopped by at Yuko's door, she never ceased to smile at what she saw in the classroom. On one occasion she said, "Yuko, you are a born teacher. I bless my lucky stars for the day you came to this school." To Yuko, there was no greater compliment.

If only she could have shut her classroom door, and pretended not to know what was going on across the hall, Yuko would have felt like Cinderella at the ball. In her own classroom, with her own children, she had everything she had ever wanted. But no matter how hard she tried, she could not blot out the ugly sounds that came from the classroom across the hall.

Stella Friedken was at least 30 years older than Yuko. She had been a teacher many years ago, in the New York City school system, and then left teaching to raise a family. Now, with her two children grown, and widowed by the sudden death of her husband, she had decided to return to teaching. Her knowledge of Spanish was an important asset in securing a position in southern California, and now, at age 52, Mrs. Friedken found herself back in the classroom. From all appearances, she did not look happy there.

The few occasions when Yuko talked to Stella Friedken in the staff room revealed some of her ideas about teaching and some of her attitudes about her children. It was clear that Mrs. Friedken was a strict disciplinarian. Although most primary classrooms tended to have children sit together in small groups, Stella had her children sit in rows. "No talking" was a rule that was strictly enforced. Children who did not finish their seatwork were made to stay in at recess or lunch, or lost privileges. Sometimes they were made to "write lines"— 100 times of "I will not talk in class." Even more to Yuko's distaste was that Stella Friedken taught a third-grade class—children so young, tender, and malleable that they had very few resources for dealing with Mrs. Friedken's authoritarian rules. Worst of all, however, was the manner in which Yuko overheard Stella Friedken talking to her children. Perhaps, Yuko thought, she believed that insulting and humiliating children was the way to "keep them in line." Yuko wished she could shut out the sound of Stella Friedken's voice, but it was impossible not to hear her. She called the children names, like "worthless" and "stupid."

She insulted and humiliated them. She made them cry. She punished them for the most minor infractions. Yuko felt that she taught by terrorizing the students. She seemed indifferent to their pain and suffering, as if she looked beyond them, never at their faces.

One day during lunchtime, one of the third-grade boys had just been released from his noon-hour penalty and was heading out the door. He stopped for a moment, lingering at the doorway of Yuko's classroom, looking in. How could he not be jarred by the differences in the classroom landscapes, between his own stern, barren environment and Yuko's room, rich with children's art, colorful, full of treasures that beckoned, a bit like a playland?

"Oh, hello there, Ben." Yuko had known this boy from one of their lunchroom encounters. "Can I help you?"

The boy's large brown eyes sought her out. "I wish I could be in your class," he said sorrowfully; then he raced quickly down the corridor, lest his wicked revelation be overheard and he be changed into a frog.

Yuko watched the boy disappear down the dark hallway and bit on the end of her pencil. She remembered the message Carmen Estevan had given her when she first came to Baker Heights School—that this school was *more* than just a school; it was a lifeline for many of the children. Stella Friedken was not a lifeline. She was, Yuko felt, a toxic influence. The kind of teacher who, intentionally or not, was destroying the hearts and souls of the children in her class.

What could Yuko do? It did not seem either prudent or effective to confront Stella directly. What would she say? "I think you are a hurtful person, poisoning children"? That would hardly help. Even if she politely suggested that maybe Mrs. Friedken should change her ways, that was not likely to do any good, either. She would certainly be perceived as arrogant. Where did she come off telling another teacher what to do? And on top of it, this was Yuko's first year of teaching and Stella was a senior teacher.

But what about the principal? Was it possible that Carmen Estevan failed to notice what was happening in the room across the hall? Surely Mrs. Estevan saw the unadorned walls, the desks in rows, the military-like discipline, the barrenness of the curriculum—workbook exercises, all day, every day, never a song, never a smile, never a game. Didn't Mrs. Estevan hear what Stella Friedken was saying to children? "You stupid, worthless child" was certainly far from the standard of empowering children.

Maybe it was possible that Carmen Estevan did not know. In that case, was it Yuko's responsibility to tell the principal what *she* knew? And how did a first-year teacher get the courage to do that? Do you just knock at the principal's door and announce, "I want to report a teacher on grounds of malpractice?" Would the principal appreciate her ratting on a fellow teacher? Was it considered ethical to tell? And if she did tell, was *she* opening herself up to charges of unethical behavior? Why wasn't there a course in her teacher training that addressed such problems with colleagues? Where did her own values lie? And how did her feelings for children enter into the equation?

When her own class returned from lunch, Yuko's mind was once more occupied with the demands of her own children, crowding out further thoughts of the teacher across the hall. Keeping Stella Friedken out of her mind was one way to deal with the problem. For the rest of the term, she closed her eyes and ears and put all her energies and concentration on the delicious and delightful children in her own class.

With June came all the end-of-year duties and assignments. School records had to be brought up to date, books counted and returned to storage, science and art equipment packed away. The warm desert wind was not conducive to deep thinking, and Yuko's class spent their last days of school reading and writing stories, playing games, and finishing their art projects. The school was not air-conditioned, and exerting too much energy made everyone even warmer and more uncomfortable. Mostly they were rounding out the jagged edges and waiting until the last bell signaled summer holidays.

Yuko reflected on how very far her children had come. All the children could read and write, some with considerable fluency. All had learned to number, although some were still a bit shaky. Even more important to Yuko, though, was that the children had become such a supportive and nurturing group. This could only happen, Yuko felt, when each member of the group felt prized and cared about. She was not sure exactly how she had done it, but the children had developed faith in themselves as people and as learners. She was overwhelmed with pride in what they had accomplished together. From a starting place like this, their further gains in third grade were virtually insured.

As Yuko was putting the last notes down on the children's permanent records, Carmen Estevan appeared at the door.

"Hi, Carmen. Come on in. I've just finished the record cards. Whew! What a job!"

Carmen Estevan did not respond to Yuko's statement, nor did she look her in the eyes. "I thought I'd better tell you this now, Yuko. I think you should know that your children will go to Stella Friedken's third-grade class in September."

Yuko felt as if she had been thrown down a deep, dark well, and her heart pounded with anxiety. The two women faced each other, the hot June sun making a white shaft of light between them.

Study Questions

1. What do you see as the critical issues in this case? List them, and then put them in what you believe is the order of their importance.
2. What kind of a teacher is Yuko Itami? What do you see as her strengths?

What do you see as her limitations? Write a profile that would describe her to a school that was considering hiring her.

3. What kind of teacher is Stella Friedken? What hypotheses can you suggest that might explain her teaching behavior?

4. What kind of principal is Carmen Estevan? What hypotheses can you suggest that might explain her lack of response to Stella Friedken's teaching?

5. How, in your view, does a teacher help children to become empowered? What kinds of teaching strategies may be used to bring about the kind of results seen in Yuko Itami's class? What are your ideas on it? What data do you have to support your ideas?

6. Should Yuko have talked to Carmen Estevan about Stella Friedken earlier in the school year? What ideas do you have about that? What do you see as some potential consequences of that action?

7. What should Yuko say to Carmen now? What values do you hold that support your position? What do you see as some potential consequences of that action?

†8. Talk about a situation in your own teaching or student teaching experience in which you had a dilemma about the ethics of a colleague's actions. What actions did you take in response to the situation? In retrospect, what might you have done instead?

3.9   WHY CAN'T THINGS STAY AS THEY ARE?

The staff room was noisy and the tension elevated as the principal took his seat at the far end of the long table. He glanced around the room without smiling, nodding acknowledgment to individual staff members, and waited for the din of voices to fade. As 26 pairs of eyes turned in his direction, he opened the meeting by saying, "Thanks very much for coming today. I know that this is short notice, but I felt that this new business could not wait until the next regular meeting to be discussed."

Roslyn Varon whispered a comment into Janet Tigard's ear that made Janet smile. Neil Horvath nudged Art Metzger with his elbow. Julie Wilson whispered under her breath, to no one in particular, "This is it, folks."

Claus Braverman, the principal of Sherwood Forest Elementary School, fingered the sheaf of papers on the table in front of him. This was hard for him, and he had considered various ways of approaching it. In the end, he had decided that his best option was to lay the cards directly on the table and respond thoughtfully to what came next. This was, after all, not of his own doing; he was not the person responsible for the new policy statements about goals and objectives and about school reforms coming from the school board office. He had not even been a member of the Committee to Restructure Schools that had been meeting for the last two years and had put together these plans for how schools in the district were to change to meet the challenges of the twenty-first century. He was just the guy in the hot seat, the one on whom the responsibilities for implementation fell, who had to see to it that the changes were going to be made in his school.

"As you all know," he began, "the Committee to Restructure Schools took its plans for school improvement to the school board meeting last night. I was there, so I can tell you from personal experience that the meeting was lengthy and heated. The proposed changes were not unanimously endorsed. But they were supported by the majority of the board, with only two dissenting votes. There was, however, unanimous agreement among the board members and the public that we needed to make major changes in our school programs to help prepare children to live productively and responsibly in the next century."

Braverman had everyone's attention now. The teachers were told that the plans for change were inevitable. How they would be implemented in each school in this district, however, was the principal's decision. That meant Claus Braverman had some options with respect to how the school went about planning for change and what some of the timelines were going to be for those changes to be put into effect. It also meant that he and the staff were to be involved in developing specific strategies for change.

Braverman had brought with him copies of the new goal and objective statements, including those changes that were required to be implemented by the end of the school year. He distributed copies to each staff member, saying, "I think it would be a good idea if each of you read through the policy statements and became familiar with the goals and objectives part. Then, I suggest we focus the rest of this afternoon's discussion on how we, as a staff, might most comfortably, and with a minimum of disruption to children, move to make these changes in our classroom programs. With respect to the restructuring changes mandated by the board—that's on pages three and four of the document—I'd like to leave that part for a subsequent meeting. But you should take notice that the plan calls for an ungraded primary program, an intermediate program that will incorporate those grades now defined as four through eight, and a graduation program that will include grades nine through twelve. But that latter program is not our immediate concern. Now, won't you take a few minutes and read through pages one and two of the proposal?"

The room fell silent, except for the rustle of papers, as teachers read through the policy statements that had become, as of last evening, school board policy:

Policy Statement for School Restructuring

The primary goal of our school programs is to prepare children to live as "educated citizens" in the twenty-first century. This means that school programs will be dedicated to enabling learners to develop their individual potential and to helping them develop the knowledge, skills, and attitudes required to live productively in the world of the future.

Educated citizens are:

Thoughtful, critical thinkers

Creative, flexible, self-initiating, and have a positive sense of self

Capable of choosing responsibly and wisely

Skilled and have the ability to make positive contributions to our society

Cooperative, respectful of others, tolerant of differences, and principled

To meet these goals, classroom practice should emphasize the following:

1. Students' active participation in the learning process
2. Learning activities that are reflective of individual differences
3. Learning activities that encourage student discussions with one another in the examination of subject-related issues
4. Evaluation practices that are learner-focused and provide for self-evaluation and meeting individual learning needs
5. Student assessment that encourages informed choices and allows for examination of student work over a period of time

"I'll begin by taking your questions. Then, I hope we can proceed to suggestions for what we do next to get these ideas into your day-to-day classroom lives. Yes, Effie?"

Effie Thibadeau, a veteran kindergarten teacher two years from retirement, made the first of what was going to be a stream of negative remarks. "You know, Claus, I've been at Sherwood Forest longer than anybody here." Effie liked to begin her comments at staff meetings by directing everyone's attention to both her seniority and her senior position on the staff. "I've seen recommendations for change come and go. I was here 20 years ago when all the children were going to learn to read with the Initial Teaching Alphabet. That bombed out quickly and those plans hit the dust. Who here has even *heard* of the Initial Teaching Alphabet! I was here 10 years ago when Madeline Hunter's direct instruction plans were laid on for all elementary teachers in the district. That, too, came and went. Now here's another new plan. I predict this too will die in two or three years' time. So why should we either get excited about it, or even interested in putting it into operation? I'm getting too old for this, Claus. If I'm going to be asked to make changes in what I'm doing in my kindergarten, just for the sake of some committee that's never even been in my classroom, I'm going to take early retirement. The heck with it."

Braverman had anticipated that Effie would be among the first of the teachers to speak against what needed to be done. Effie was an extremely conservative and traditional teacher who had taught very much the same way today as she had when she first became a teacher. The kindergarten equipment might be more modern, but Effie's teaching style was strictly medieval. Claus would be glad to raise a glass at her retirement dinner. He was tired of teachers like Effie, who were so stuck in their ways and so unwilling and unready to meet the changing demands of the profession and of society. He nevertheless responded to her concerns without malice. "Why am I not surprised at your response, Effie?" he said with a smile. "And I do take your point about other changes that have come and gone. But there's something in the air in this district and in this land that suggests that these school reforms are not going to be as fleeting as what was done in the past."

Several other teachers voiced questions about the policy statements, which Braverman fielded. As Braverman read the teachers' faces, however, he saw that his responses did not seem to alleviate their concerns. Their troubled looks indicated that his answers had not satisfied them.

Ruth Anne Potter was new to the Sherwood Forest staff. She had come in October, fresh from her teacher-training program, to replace Bernice Chadwick, who had been transferred to the district office. Ruth Anne was young, inexperienced, and very anxious. She was easily intimidated and rarely spoke at staff meetings. But this was one of the exceptions.

"I hope you won't think it's silly for me to ask this, Mr. Braverman, but I'd like to get some clarification on some of these points." Her voice sounded like cracking ice, but she pressed on in acknowledgment of Claus Braverman's suggestion that she continue.

"As I look at some of these goals and objectives, I'm wondering how what I do in the classroom is going to be any different. I mean, look at what the first statement says: Children should be thoughtful, critical thinkers. Look at the third: Children should be capable of choosing responsibly and wisely. Well, that's exactly what I believe in and exactly what I'm doing in my classroom. So how am I supposed to change? Isn't this what we've all been doing all the time? How is this going to be different?"

Braverman smiled weakly at Ruth Anne and thought about what a good response to her question might be. He decided to be tactful, rather than confrontational. "I take your point, Ruth Anne. I guess the answer to your question is, 'How can we do more, and maybe a better job of what we've been doing all along.'"

Ruth Anne, impressed with her courage to voice her opinion, smiled and sat back in her chair. The principal, it seemed to her, had just given her his tacit approval to continue to do just as she had done all term. She would not have to worry about changing what she did in the classroom to accommodate to the new school board policy. She was safe!

At 4:30, Claus Braverman signaled that they ought to bring the meeting to a close and continue the discussion the following Monday. There were major issues at stake here, and these issues would not be resolved in a day. It would be a better idea if the staff continued to think about them, and to keep the discussion ongoing, until some specific plans could be made.

The tension in the staff room had not diminished, and the pitch and intensity of small-group discussions revealed that nothing had, as yet, been resolved. Neil and Art exchanged glances as Neil said, "All you need to get teachers in a lather is to talk about the need for change! Tell me, buddy, what is it about change that scares teachers to death? Are we the only professional group that hasn't changed what we do in our professional practices in 60 years? I mean, look at Fredda Fonebone. Teaching third grade in 1932. And look at, dare I mention the name, teaching third grade down the hall today, and you tell me, buddy: Is there any difference to speak of?" Art smiled at his teaching buddy, knowing immediately what he was talking about. The two of them, with their open-classroom practices and integrated curricula, were the iconoclasts of the school, out of step with the rest of the staff. They, more than the other teachers, saw the new school board's policies as hopeful and exciting—a plan that sanctioned much of what they had been advocating and doing for years. What the new policies would bring, in the form of major changes to Sherwood Forest School, was impossible to predict. They both feared that teacher resistance in the district would be pitched against district policy and that, in the end, the teachers would somehow win out. Teachers who were afraid of change would find ways to subvert the new plans, and finally the plans would be abandoned in despair. They had seen such forces operating before.

After chatting individually with several of his staff, Claus Braverman picked up his books and the extra copies of the new policy statements and left the staffroom, heading back to his office. In his own heart of hearts, he cheered the new proposals for bringing what he considered much-needed change to the schools. The children in these classrooms would be entering the job market in the twenty-first century. The skills they would need were going to be different. The world would be far more complex, the population increased significantly, the nature of jobs and work changed dramatically. Unless teachers were prepared to face the changing needs of society and to help children become equipped to live in that uncertain future, schools would indeed become obsolete. Already, existing technology had far outpaced the individual classroom teacher's ability to present curriculum in meaningful, exciting, and knowledgeable ways. How could teachers justify spending endless hours drilling the multiplication tables, when pocket calculators cost $4.95 and were in each child's pencil case?

His eye caught the last glimpse of Ruth Anne Potter's blue scarf as she pushed through the exit door to the parking lot. Ah, Ruth Anne, he mused to himself, thinking about what she had said about what she was doing in her classroom. He was hard put not to smile at the discrepancy between what she *thought* she was doing and what she was actually doing. Her anxiety about having to change was palpable; he could almost smell her fear.

As he walked past her first-grade classroom, he could see evidence of her program, even in the absence of any living being. Desks in rows, so that children were isolated from one another and could not talk or work cooperatively together; red-and-white Valentines, all cut from the same pattern, all virtually identical, on the bulletin board. If there was independent thinking going on in this classroom, he'd eat his knife and fork. If children were learning to make their own decisions, he'd eat his spoon, too.

He recalled with distress the three times he had spent an hour in Ruth Anne's class in the last three months. They were painful visits for an administrator who believed in children's thinking, creativity, and independent decision making, but he thought it was a good idea to give Ruth Anne some space. She was new, anxious, and very inexperienced. He hoped that given time, and a climate in which change was encouraged and supported, she would grow professionally, take some risks, break out of the narrow and restrictive educational practices she was using.

Ruth Anne was a teacher who liked to be in control of all classroom decisions. "Let's open our books for reading now," she'd say, and when children responded obediently, she thought that was involving them actively in learning. When she asked, "Now, would you like the story of *The Little Engine That Could* or *The Boy and the Flute*?" she believed that was allowing the children to be independent decision makers.

All of Ruth Anne's worksheets required children to give single, correct answers, which she then graded as "right or wrong." Ruth Anne thought that asking children to determine the right answers to such questions as "What color was the wagon?"—was an activity that required children to think.

In her classroom discussions, she also relied heavily on interactions that called for children to give the single correct answers to her lower-order questions. "How many cupcakes did mother bake?" and "What was Tom's sister's name?" were the kinds of questions she emphasized in her teaching, and when children could respond by recall of simple facts, she thought she was providing for individual differences.

To Claus Braverman, teachers like Ruth Anne were preparing children to live in the past. She was teaching obedience, conformity, and passivity, rather than thoughtfulness, creativity, flexibility, and independent decision making. And in all of that, the big irony was that Ruth Anne thought she was doing all the right things. She would not have to change her ways. She was already doing all that the new policy statements required!

Claus Braverman opened his office door, put down his books and papers, sat down in his swivel chair, and put his face in his hands. Whatever he was going to do with Ruth Anne, that job would not be easy.

Study Questions

1. What do you see as the significant issues in this case? Talk together, and make a list of those issues in the order that you consider to be their importance.
2. What is your impression of Ruth Anne Potter? Talk together and develop a profile of her, as a teacher, based upon the data in the case. What do you see as her teaching strengths? What do you see as her teaching weaknesses?
3. What is there about educational change that makes teachers so uncomfortable? What are your thoughts on it?
4. What strategies might be used in a school to help teachers accommodate to the change process being advocated in this school board policy? Explain your reasons for thinking that those strategies would be appropriate.
5. Where do you stand on the new school policies being proposed for this district? In what ways do your own educational beliefs concur with/conflict with what is being proposed? Where do your educational beliefs come from?
6. How should Claus Braverman help Ruth Anne Potter to grow as a classroom teacher? What strategies might he use that would be both respectful to Ruth Anne as well as professionally helpful? How do you see those strategies as being appropriate to the kind of teacher/person Ruth Anne is, given the data about her in the case?
7. What kinds of changes should schools be making to prepare children better for life in the twenty-first century? Where do your ideas about school reform come from? What do you see as impediments to such change?
8. If you were in Ruth Anne's place—that is, being faced with having to make radical changes in what you are doing in your classroom and being somewhat intimidated by the new program—what kinds of help would you like to have?
†9. What is your response to administrative requests to change your teaching practices? Where, in your view, is the line drawn between administrative policy and teaching autonomy?

RELATED READINGS

Ashton-Warner, Sylvia. 1963. *Teacher*. New York: Simon & Schuster.
Berlak, Ann, and Berlak, Harold. 1981. *Dilemmas of Schooling*. New York: Methuen.
Bruckerhoff, Charles E. 1991. *Between Classes*. New York: Teachers College Press.
Cohen, Rosetta Marantz. 1991. *A Lifetime of Teaching*. New York: Teachers College Press.

Combs, Arthur. "Teacher Education: The Person in the Process." *Educational Leadership*. April 1978, pp. 558–561.

Conroy, Frank. 1972. *The Water Is Wide*. Boston: Houghton Mifflin.

Dennison, George. 1969. *The Lives of Children: The Story of the First Street School*. New York: Random House.

Freedman, Samuel G. 1990. *Small Victories*. New York: HarperCollins.

Glover, Mary K. 1992. *Two Years: A Teacher's Memoir*. Portsmouth, NH: Heinemann.

Goodlad, John; Soder, Roger; and Sirotnak, Kenneth. (Ed.). 1990. *Moral Dimensions of Teaching*. San Francisco: Jossey-Bass.

Goodson, Ivor F. 1992. *Studying Teachers' Lives*. New York: Teachers College Press.

Grossman, Pamela L. 1990. *The Making of a Teacher*. New York: Teachers College Press.

Hamachek, Don. 1971. *Encounters with the Self*. New York: Holt, Rinehart & Winston.

Herndon, James. 1968. *The Way It Spozed to Be*. New York: Simon & Schuster.

Jackson, Philip. 1986. *The Practice of Teaching*. New York: Teachers College Press.

Jersild, Arthur. 1955. *When Teachers Face Themselves*. New York: Teachers College Press.

Kidder, Tracy. 1989. *Among Schoolchildren*. Boston: Houghton Mifflin.

Lieberman, Anne, and Miller, Lynne. 1992. *Teachers—Their World and Their Work*. New York: Teachers College Press.

Lortie, Dan. 1975. *Schoolteacher*. Chicago: University of Chicago Press.

Louden, William. 1991. *Understanding Teaching*. New York: Teachers College Press.

McDonald, Joseph P. 1992. *Teaching: Making Sense of an Uncertain Craft*. New York: Teachers College Press.

Ohanian, Susan. 1992. *Garbage Pizza, Patchwork Quilts and Math Magic*. New York: Freeman.

Owen, David. 1981. *High School*. New York: Viking.

Perrone, Vito. 1991. *A Letter to Teachers*. San Francisco: Jossey-Bass.

Rubin, Louis D. Jr. (Ed.). 1987. *An Apple for My Teacher: Twelve Authors Tell About Teachers Who Made the Difference*. Chapel Hill, NC: Algonquin Books.

Shaw, George Bernard. 1946. *Pygmalion*. London: Penguin.

Spark, Muriel. 1962. *The Prime of Miss Jean Brodie*. London: Penguin.

Wassermann, Selma. 1990. "How I Taught Myself to Teach," in Christensen, C. Roland, with Hansen, Abby, *Teaching and the Case Method* (pp. 175–183). Boston: Harvard University Graduate School of Business.

Yee, Sylvia Mei-Ling. 1990. *Careers in the Classroom*. New York: Teachers College Press.

4 | CASES: Teachers and Students

"What do you do about a child who . . . ?" is the most frequently heard question from teachers anxiously seeking more effective methods of working with individual children. Children's classroom behavior is often puzzling, exasperating, and exhausting, and acting-out behavior may drive teachers to the very limits of their endurance. Yet behavior is the way that most children send messages to others about how they feel.

If we adults could, perhaps, learn to read and interpret these behaviors more knowledgeably and with greater insight, we might have a better chance of understanding what the child is "telling" us behaviorally and, consequently, choose better and more effective ways of helping. Although not all children's problems are fixable—that is, within the sphere of influence of teachers and schools—there are many more children who might be helped if we could learn to free ourselves from facile judgments and apply greater wisdom in reading and interpreting behavior.

The cases in this chapter deal with aspects of pupil behavior that range across a wide variety of contemporary classroom "problems." The cases should challenge thinking about behavior, promote understanding about data gathering and hypothesis generating, and, in general, provide for deeper awareness of classroom behavior and effective treatment.

Each case is followed by a list of questions, with additional questions for those with classroom teaching experience denoted by a dagger.

4.1 "I NEED YOU TO TELL ME WHAT TO DO!"

When I saw his name on the class list, I felt a cold hand reach into my solar plexus and squeeze. "No," I cried to nobody. "Not Bobby Miller. Not Bobby Miller."

It wasn't that he was the worst kid in the school. There were probably others that I hadn't heard about who were his match in at least some ways. But I had been hearing about Bobby since he was a first grader. Even at the tender age of 6, he was already head and shoulders taller than the other kids. Taller and stronger did not necessarily lead to bullying, but in Bobby's case, he managed to use his physical attributes most effectively to intimidate and push other kids around. He wore physical aggressiveness like a badge of honor. If he was going to be bigger than all the other kids, then why not make the most of it? That was not quite the end of the story about Bobby Miller, either. I had heard all of it in the staff room over the years:

"His work habits are poor."
"He's got an attitude!"
"He doesn't apply himself."
"I have to be after him constantly to get to his work."
"He wanders around the room and disturbs the rest of the class."
"He likes to push other children around."
"His work isn't as good as it should be."
"He just isn't trying!"

Coming into the sixth grade, Bobby was reaching for 5' 8," and he had me by a good two inches. "Lucky I'm tall," I grimaced. What if I had been short, like my friend Lee Roberts who taught the sixth grade class across the hall? A grim-reaper laugh came from the back of my throat, and I wondered if I pulled Bobby just because I was a tall teacher? Lots of luck, Maggie.

But why wouldn't I find Bobby Miller on my class list? I was a senior teacher on the Winslow School staff, with 11 good years of teaching behind me. I was considered a good teacher—no, that's being too modest. I was a very good teacher, and I knew that about myself, too. I was self confident, tough-minded, *and* had a graduate degree. Surely, I'd be able to handle Bobby Miller. Maybe I could even do something good for him! So why the knot in the pit of my stomach? Oh well, nobody's perfect.

I used the last days of the summer holiday to do some housecleaning in my classroom, putting up the plants, hanging a few of my favorite posters— Picasso's *Gertrude Stein*, Kathe Kollwitz's *Mother and Child*, Van Gogh's *Sunflowers*, Monet's *Water Lilies*—to bring a little life and color to the dull beige walls. In my interminable war with the custodian, I reshaped his neatly arranged rows of desks and chairs into groups of four, set up the library corner with about 150 titles borrowed from an enthusiastic school librarian, and installed a scrap of tattered carpet for the floor, a few floor cushions, and one ratty easy chair, a remnant from a Salvation Army excavation sale. I was grimy, hot, and tired when I finished moving furniture around, and I thought twice about going down to the office to check Bobby's cumulative records before I left for home. Yeah, I know, this could cause me to prejudge him and maybe it wasn't such a hot idea. But from all that I already knew, hadn't I already prejudged him? Wasn't the verdict already in on Bobby Miller? Maybe I could find a trace of something positive? Now that would be something!

The general office was quiet, with that ghostly silence that precedes the *Sturm und Drang* of the first days of school. Alice, the school secretary, and I exchanged pleasantries about the summer holidays, and then I asked her for Bobby Miller's file. She looked at me, her eyes kind and knowing. "So it's your turn," she said affectionately. I shrugged and bit the bottom of my lip. Alice pulled a slim red folder from the filing cabinet and handed it to me over the counter. I lifted my distance glasses to the top of my head so that I could read the fine print. Not much there for six years of cumulative work. I was particularly anxious to see his most recent records and shuffled the papers until I came to the fifth-grade report:

"He's a behavioral disturbance in class. He is very aggressive, wanders around the room, does not come to class prepared. He is capable of doing his work, but procrastinates and then is last to finish. He doesn't seem to be able to stay put for long."

I compared the fifth-grade teacher's account with that of the first-grade teacher. It didn't take a graduate degree to see that nothing of consequence had changed in five years of school. Bobby's behavior had been the same in fifth grade as it was in first grade. So much for school learning. I left the office and headed out to the parking lot, determined to put all thoughts of school behind me and finish off the summer holiday with a restful Labor Day weekend. Come Tuesday, I'd be ready for Bobby.

With 11 years of teaching in my pocket, you'd think I'd no longer have any butterflies the night before the beginning of a new school year. Wrong! Visions of children danced in my head, with Bobby dead center, all night long. At 5 A.M., I decided to call it quits and make some coffee. I was already beginning to formulate a game plan for Bobby but would need to gather more observational data of my own before I could safely identify teaching strategies that might work with him. As competent as his previous teachers were to make those behavioral assessments that appeared on his records, I preferred to make my own observations and evaluations.

He shuffled into the room, all 5'8" of him, sweaty and puffing from playing in the schoolyard—kids making the most of those last few moments of totally free time, the very last bits of the summer rapidly passing into history. He looked me right in the eye, and I saw a sweet, shy smile come to his lips. I returned his smile and his eyes brightened. I thought of Joey, in my last year's class, who had written in his journal, "A good teacher must have love for all the children, even the bad ones." The chill in my heart melted. I promised myself that I'd find a way to work with Bobby, to appreciate him, perhaps even to love him. This, after all, was teaching.

Four weeks into the term, I was finding it hard to keep that promise. I kept a close watch as well as careful anecdotal records that I hoped would allow me to develop a thoughtful, informed, working hypothesis of his behavior that would, in turn, lead to informed, effective teaching interventions. What were his special needs? Why had his behavior continued in such an aggressive pattern? Why all the roaming around, and the inability to stay with a task? I knew I could find the answer to these questions in his behavior, if I only knew how to look. I kept watching and keeping notes, while his behavior continued to drive me crazy.

He seemed to be unable to function without close supervision and structuring, unable to stick to a job and finish it on his own, unable to make choices or think things out for himself. I saw, too, his racially prejudiced outbursts and his extreme dogmatism in presenting his opinions as truths. Routine physical tests revealed good physical health, with no evidence of visual, auditory, or motor impairment. Checking back on his cumulative record, I found that in the third grade, he had scored 114 on a group IQ test. Whew!

By the first week of October, I felt I had enough evidence to generate a working hypothesis. I sat on the floor of my study, sipping coffee and sorting out scraps of anecdotal comments that I tried to put together, like pieces of a giant jigsaw puzzle, into a picture of Bobby. If I could see the picture clearly, I would know what to do, how to help him.

The anecdotal data fell into two categories. In one group, the data pointed overwhelmingly to Bobby's inability to think things through, to his need for constant and close supervision and structuring. In the second group, the data revealed consistent and repeated acts of aggression. The pieces began to form a picture. Was Bobby showing signs of dependency behaviors—a child unable to think for himself? Was he operating out of an extreme "thinking deficit"? Was his frustration with his deficits in thinking causing him to act aggressively? Frustration = Aggression? I sat back on the pillow, chewed my thumbnail, and looked at the puzzle pieces again. They seemed to fit. There was no indication of physical causation, so that was out. There was no impaired intelligence, if you could believe the group IQ test score. So that was out, too. If he could be given a program that helped him think for himself, would his need to act out diminish? Would he be able to function more effectively on his own? Would he lose some of that extreme dogmatism that made him always certain, in circumstances where he needed to be thoughtful, reflective, and circumspect? The hypothesis pointed to a teaching plan: Bobby needed to learn to think for himself.

I hit the books that I thought would give me some good ideas and set about devising a program to provide Bobby with activities that would challenge his thinking. I would see to it that his school work included more comparing, classifying, summarizing, hypothesizing, interpreting, observing—the higher-order tasks. I would also ensure that he had many more opportunities to choose, to make purposeful decisions and reflect on them. Smug and satisfied, like a pedagogical Sherlock Holmes who had cracked the case, I smiled and took a long drink from the now-cold coffee.

It was not hard to follow through with the plan. The program I created for Bobby was similar to what I was attempting to do with the rest of the class: a plan for children to learn to think for themselves. But Bobby would get more concentrated doses. He, like the others in class, would make his own decisions about curriculum tasks. Like the others, he would have his own planbook, in which he would reflect on choices for certain subject areas. What choices would he make? How much time would he allow for reading? for writing? for word study? Worksheets and assignments emphasized higher-order operations and avoided activities that called for single, correct answers. How are the Navajos and the Pueblos alike? How are they different? What hypotheses can you come up with that might explain the racial tensions in South Africa? How can these data be classified? Like the others in class, Bobby was caught up in a well-organized, rigorous program of increasingly challenging tasks that demanded his self-sufficient functioning. And each time he came to me to ask "What should I do now, Miss Allen?" or "What am I supposed to do here?" I bit my tongue to keep from telling him what to do, instead turning the question back to him: "What do *you* think, Bobby?" I watched him turn from me, shrug his shoulders, walk back to his table, pick up his pencil, and study the wall. I knew my plan needed time to work, that Bobby would not learn to think for himself in one day or in one week. But in my heart, I wished I could, somehow, speed up the process.

It was getting close to Halloween, and the lovely autumn days were showing the early frost signals of cold weather to come. I came into class that morning, cheeks red and nose cold from the walk to school, feeling invigorated, ready to take on the world. The kids came in from the playground at 8:45, and I reminded them to get out their planbooks and think about how they would spend their language arts time, from 9:00 to 10:30. I reminded them, too, to schedule art for 10:45 to 12:00 that morning, since the art teacher was coming in to work with them on making Halloween masks. For language arts, the children could choose to read, or to write, or to design a project to share a book, or any combination of those or other language-related activities. The choice was theirs to make, but they had to have a thought-out reason for making that choice.

No sooner did the words leave my lips when Bobby rose to his feet, arms waving in the air, shouting: "I can't do this stuff! I need you to tell me what to do! I need you to tell me what book to read and how many pages to read. I need you to tell me what to write. I need you to do that for me. You're the teacher! It's your job to tell me what to do."

Shocked from the verbal assault, I took two steps backward and muttered to myself, "Boyoboyoboyoboy! What do I do now?"

Study Questions

1. What do you consider to be the significant issues in this case? Consider each, then decide which, in your view, is the key issue.
2. In this case, Maggie, the teacher, has gathered data about Bobby that suggest a relationship between his behavior and his inability to think for himself. What is your view of this hypothesis? What data inform your position?
3. Maggie used a student-centered, open-classroom approach to her teaching, in which many choices of consequence are left to students. Where do you stand on such a teaching philosophy? How do you see such strategies as appropriate for Bobby? What data support your ideas?
4. Should Maggie have chosen an approach to instruction that is more traditional than the one she used? What, in your view, is a more traditional plan? What are the benefits of a more traditional plan? What are some weaknesses?
5. How, in your view, does a teacher assess individual students' learning needs? What skills do you suppose a teacher needs to do this?
6. How does a teacher determine which teaching methods and materials are most appropriate for an individual learner? How does the teacher assess the effectiveness of the selected strategies? Why, in your opinion, would this be important?
7. Based on the data in this case, what diagnosis would you make of Bobby Miller's behavior? What kind of teaching plan would you see as appropriate? How does your diagnosis and teaching plan concur with/differ from Maggie's?
8. What, in your view, explains Bobby's outburst? How should Maggie respond? How do your suggestions reflect the data in the case?
†9. To what incident in your own teaching does this case relate? Discuss the incident with members of your group, describing what happened, what actions you took, and your reasons for choosing those actions. Discuss, too, how the incident shaped your view of teaching and learning.

4.2   IS IT WORTH THE EFFORT?

"Mrs. Olson," the principal's voice came through the intercom, "would you come down to the office after class?" I looked up at the speaker, cursing silently, wishing that I had had the courage to go after its connecting wires with my toolbox, silencing once and for all its disruptive and disrespectful intrusions into my teaching day. I glanced up at the clock—2:45 P.M.—and made a mental note not to forget to stop by at the office after school. Given that this first week of school was crammed full of all sorts of after-school demands on my time, it would be easy to let that request slip through the cracks. Not a good idea.

"Sit down, Heather." Mrs. Tindell, the principal of the Caulfield Intermediate School, pointed to a chair. My mind started to compute what this could be about. Obviously, the problem was a major one, otherwise I wouldn't have been invited to sit. This could take some time.

"I've just had a call from Dr. Herbert Jennings, a psychologist from the Denver public school system. Dr. Jennings has been working with a young boy, Bernard Miller, for the last two years. To make a long story short, Heather, the family is moving to Central City, and Bernard will be coming to Caulfield Intermediate. I want to put him in your class for two reasons. First, you've got the lowest enrollment of the three sixth grades. Second, and more important, given your college major in psychology, you are likely to be the one who is better able to deal with Bernard's special needs."

I thrust my anxious fingers through my hair, a nervous mannerism that I had picked up in my long-lost youth, and worried the unruly strands into place. "What's he like then? Is he going to be a real problem?" The question formed a knot in my neck. This was only my third year of teaching. I was hardly a seasoned practitioner. Yet, with each succeeding teaching year, the administration kept upping the ante. Last year, Donna Duthie nearly drove me nuts with her whining behaviors. This year was to bring its own special form of endurance test. How come, I wondered, they never told you in college about these children with special needs? If they had, would I have stuck it out or packed it in? Would I have believed that there were kids who could make a teacher's life hell on earth?

"Before you commit to this plan altogether, Heather, let me also add that I'd like to put Bernard in your class on a trial basis. Based on what Dr. Jennings says, Bernard, who was in a special needs classroom in Denver, may now be ready for the challenge of a regular classroom. Putting him in your class will give us all a chance to see how things work out, and if he is ready to make that move. If you agree, you would have the back-up of the resource room teacher, who will come into your class four hours a week and work individually with Bernard. If you choose not to accept him, I would have to make arrangements to place him in the special needs class for children with behavior disorders."

I ran my fingers through my hair again, pulling it away from my face, where it was bound to fall again seconds later. At this rate, I'd be bald on top by the time I was 30. Elsie Tindell was leaving the choice up to me. Thanks a lot. You'd have to have a heart of steel to send a child with any chance at all to the behavior disorder class, where, as everyone knew, a child's behavior would be more likely to deteriorate with each year he or she spent there. It was no choice at all. I'd have to at least give Bernard Miller a chance.

"Could you tell me a little about him?" I asked, thinking that any information could be helpful in determining what I could expect. Perhaps it was not going to be as bad as I originally thought.

"I can't tell you too much more than this," Elsie Tindell's voice softened with her awareness of what she was asking. "He is still a behavior problem, although he has been undergoing private therapy for two years. However, I should add that Dr. Jennings feels that if he has the chance to be in a class with his agemates, he may become more familiar with more age-appropriate behavior. In his special needs class in Denver, he was virtually isolated from any examples of good behavior. So this is a very important step for Bernard."

I stared out the window and watched the children from the Caulfield Intermediate School board the school bus, some quietly and orderly, others rambunctious and full of vinegar. What produced their differences? How did a boy like Bernard Miller grow up so "haywire"? If we teachers didn't go the extra mile to see what we could do to help, who would help them? Where could they turn?

"Of course I'll take Bernard." The words came tumbling down my lips before my mind had made itself up. "He deserves a chance." My heart softened, even though the beat quickened. I knew the kind of extra effort children like Bernard took, and I knew that the gains could be very small. Was it worth the effort?

Elsie looked at me gratefully, her body relaxing with my acquiescence. I hadn't thought how much she might have cared; I had seen the picture only from my own point of view. "Thanks, Heather. I know this will be a real challenge for you, but I'll support you in anything further you decide later on about Bernard."

As I left the office, I knew that this was going to be a tough weekend. Bernard arrived with his parents on Monday morning.

Elsie Tindell took my class and arranged for me to meet briefly with Mr. and Mrs. Miller and Bernard in the conference room. Both parents seemed visibly anxious, as if their comprehension of what was at stake for Bernard was threaded into their small courtesies. They seemed willing, eager to be of any help. All I had to do was call. I would find them very cooperative.

All the while we were trying to communicate these elementary ideas to one another, Bernard was in motion. It was as if someone had wound his spring, which now lay internally coiled, taut, on the verge of release. In between his parents' words, sentences, pauses, he constantly interjected, and his demands grew more incessant:

"Can I go to the class?"

"Can I go now?"

"I'll just go to the class now."

"Where is it?"

Each time Mrs. Miller looked at him with a reproach, Bernard stopped, but only for a few seconds, until the next interruption. I watched this behavior with a growing fascination of what lay in store for me and for the other children.

Before they left, both parents assured me that what they wanted most for Bernard was that he be a well-behaved student. They had talked at length to Bernard about this, and they had his promise that he would really try. Bernard and I watched as his parents left the school, and he walked with me down to the classroom.

The first week of classes with Bernard was considerably better than I had had any reason to expect. There were times when his behavior was quite acceptable. There were other times when his spontaneous outbursts were unnerving. "I can't do this!" he'd shout to the fluorescent light fixture. Or "Why are you always picking on me?" he'd accuse, turning me into the villain.

His outbursts were most in evidence when other children were talking or when his work needed correcting. He seemed unable to allow that other children might also have something of value to say or that his work efforts were imperfect. His need to be in control, to have attention focused on him, to be perceived as "perfect" was extreme and seemed out of hand.

There were moments, if I remembered to keep some of my humor, when Bernard's outbursts could be funny. Like the time he shouted out during assembly, where the whole school had gathered for a talk about caring for our planet, "Pizza is junk food. Why do they serve it for lunch?" The ironic part of that outburst showed Bernard as particularly knowledgeable and able to communicate his thoughts in an intelligent and quite adult manner. So what if he was yelling and so what if his timing was inappropriate?

There was also the time that the class walked over to the John Muir Park to collect pine cones, and Bernard talked nonstop all the way there and back. I thought my ears would vomit, as he assaulted them with the secret cures that he had invented for many diseases, using revolutionary laser techniques. This was not a boy who was joking or pretending. My alarm about Bernard grew as I saw the dividing line between what he actually knew and his delusions of grandeur evaporate.

It was not difficult to see that, as the weeks progressed, Bernard was isolating himself from his classmates. The hoped-for relationships with children of his own age were not happening.

Gathering background data from Bernard's parents was easy. They were very forthcoming and very cooperative. In a series of conferences, I learned that Bernard was an only child, born when both his parents thought they no longer would be able to have children. Even in Bernard's early months, it seemed that he was a very aggressive and demanding child whose needs took much time and energy from his parents. Bernard seemed to require their full attention, full time.

When Bernard was in the second grade, his parents had felt that his academic progress was too slow, so they decided to tutor him at home. This they did for two hours each day after school, and for three hours on Saturday. Sunday was Bernard' s day off. His mother, a former teacher, assumed the full burden of his tutoring, and worked intensively with him on basics, especially spelling and math. As a consequence, she said that she had been able to "raise his achievement level from second grade to fourth or fifth grade." The family had made many trips back and forth to Denver by car, which further enhanced Bernard's knowledge about geography and history. In spite of this tutoring and enrichment, Bernard was unable to spell even the most commonly used words. Mrs. Miller also informed me that he had not been toilet trained until he was 4—until "she forced him to remain on the toilet until he had learned."

From Dr. Jennings, I learned that Bernard's intelligence "fell into the normal range" but that his achievement was erratic. For example, Bernard was considered "gifted" in science, social studies, and reading but weak in spelling and math. Dr. Jennings also added that Bernard was "extremely egocentric, demanding, and socially inept."

I also learned that Bernard's involvement with his "projects" at home was "obsessive" and that family life was focused on the exhausting task of meeting Bernard's demands. While the Millers insisted that they were firm with Bernard, I wondered if they weren't, somehow, contributing to, even exacerbating, his behavior. It wasn't easy to put a label on Bernard. He might be a royal pain in the place where you sit down, but he was also a complex and challenging boy, with many problems.

Both the resource room teacher and the counselor were assigned to help me help Bernard. He had four hours a week with the special needs teacher, plus two additional hours per week with the counselor. Bernard had no difficulty manipulating both of these "special help" sessions to his advantage, adjusting his attendance so that he would be able to avoid his least favorite classes, which were math and physical education. Bernard was smart enough and manipulative enough to find ways to maneuver himself into the catbird seat, no matter who the teacher or what the class. This created ongoing problems for him wherever he was—in the library, on the playing field, in the hallway, in the lunchroom, and even in the toilet.

After only three months with Bernard, I found myself thinking about him all the time. He was a dysfunctional student, creating a tense situation in my class, and I couldn't get him out of my mind. Even though the teaching load for Bernard was shared, I felt that I was the one who was ultimately responsible for what happened to him. At the end of each school day, I left utterly exhausted and returned to school the next morning feeling as if I would not be able to last through the day. Bernard was siphoning every last ounce of energy I had; I began to think how nice it would be to incubate some dreadful flu, so that I could lie in bed for the next three months and put Bernard completely out of my mind.

What could I do to help him become a functioning member of the class? Was there something I had not done, something I had overlooked? Was there something I should have done differently? I knew I would have to confront the problem of what to do if there was to be any chance of success.

It seemed reasonable to begin with an assessment of what I had done so far. I had to drop my defensiveness, my need to "do battle" with Bernard. As much as I didn't like to admit it, I had been trying to outmanipulate him. Because he was such an accomplished player, we were, of course, always at war. When I won, he became more demanding and obsessive. When he won, I felt defeated. Bernard could not be my enemy if I was going to help him. Neither could he be my puppet whose strings I could pull to get him to do exactly what I wanted. Neither could I allow him to destroy my class.

In examining the intervention strategies open to me, I rejected further use of behavior modification. I did not consider this to be a viable option since I had never felt quite comfortable with interventions that dealt with children as if they were being trained like pigeons. The teachers in Denver who were responsible for Bernard had originally begun with a behavior modification plan, and they had initially tried to teach Bernard strategies like "counting to five before speaking out" and other behavioral cues, but these had not been successful. They did nothing to improve Bernard's self-control.

I had to come up with some strategies that would work for me, for Bernard, and for the other students in the class. I believed that Bernard had become a very manipulative boy and that he used these manipulations to get his needs met. I saw him constantly striving for the upper hand as if his life depended on it, totally involved with his own wants and needs, unable to appreciate or care about the feelings of others. In spite of three months with his agemates, he had not formed friendships or even tenable working relationships with any of the other children. At best, they barely tolerated him. At worst, they disliked him for his intrusiveness, insensitivity, and egomaniacal ways.

Instead of giving all my attention to Bernard, I now turned my energies to the other students. Perhaps I could begin by teaching them coping strategies that would empower them and take the burden of responsibility for Bernard away from them. During one of Bernard's time-out periods, I approached the class about Bernard. I spoke seriously, showing concern for Bernard and for all of them. I tried to ensure that there were no heroes or villains in what I said. I spoke of how much I cared for all of them and how important they all were to me. I spoke of the problem of Bernard's behavior—a problem that was not Bernard's alone. We were all affected. Perhaps I should not have spoken so openly to them? It was a terrible risk I was taking, and I had never done this before nor read in any book about the possibility that involving the class in this way might help.

I then went on to make the following suggestions to the class. If Bernard yelled out at me, and I ignored his outburst, then that was an indication that the children, too, should ignore such behavior. If Bernard yelled to another child "Stop looking at me!" or "Don't touch my book!" when that child was trying to help, and I did not respond to that outburst, then the children should follow suit, even if it didn't seem fair to them. The children were not responsible. I would deal with Bernard's behavior. In putting these strategies to work, I was trying to respond to Bernard without threats or guilt-invoking questions. As I began to use these strategies, I could see that when I could respond to Bernard in these ways, his responses to me were less aggressive. We did not become entangled in a power struggle.

In order to "spread Bernard around," I instituted a plan to change the seating arrangement in class so that the burden of sitting close to Bernard was shared by all. Changing groupings often helped to mitigate some of the stress of daily proximity.

A third strategy was to take Bernard with me whenever I left the room. Because his behavior was so outrageous and upsetting to them, the other children would gang up on him when they were left on their own, if only for a very few minutes. I knew that such confrontations were not healthy for Bernard or for the others, and this was my way of heading off these skirmishes. This violated one of my primary teaching goals: I had hoped that the other students would eventually accept Bernard and he, them. This intervention, while effective and insuring safety, would further prevent any social bonding.

These were, however, only strategies of logistics. The more important strategy I employed was to unload my own needs to control Bernard's behavior and to treat him more respectfully. He could make choices, but choices did not mean unlimited choice. Choices were made from among given alternatives. Each day, I found time to listen to Bernard and to treat what he had to say respectfully. I also had to let go of my needs to be punitive, guilt-invoking, and authoritarian, while also never abandoning my role as the person in charge, the one who was ultimately responsible.

The winter snows had melted and the days were getting longer. We could see the first robins in the bush behind the school, and the trees were showing signs of coming back to life. I sat at my desk in the back of the classroom and observed as the children were working away on their art project, making Haida masks out of *papier-mâché*. The art teacher was working with them, and I had the chance to watch my own class for a few minutes without being responsible for what they were doing. I glanced over to Bernard. He was sitting with a group of three other students, and they were working on their masks without disruption. Bernard seemed calmer, more settled. He was certainly less noticeable. He could read for longer periods now; he also read fiction, instead of his earlier diet of only science books. Bernard more often got his work done, usually on time, but not always to specifications. He had made a friend, who spent time at

Bernard's house, working on a science fair project. Bernard's mother called me to say that he had never had a friend from school visit their home before.

That is the up side of the story. Bernard is still unable to use "freedoms" without close supervision. He is still immoderate and excessive, and his relations with other students are far from amiable.

I ask myself about the cost of all of these gains—gains that may appear, on the surface, to be minuscule. What prices have the children paid in terms of learning time taken away from them and given to Bernard? And what of the cost to the teacher? Here it is barely spring, and I'm counting the days until summer. I glanced again at Bernard, who was putting another strip of paper on his mask, his face and eyes bright, and wonder: Was it worth the cost?

Study Questions

1. What do you see as the central issues in this case? List them, and then identify the one that you see as the key issue.
2. How would you describe Bernard? Write a profile of him that would describe his behavior to his next year's teacher.
3. What hypotheses can you suggest that might explain Bernard's behavior? What other data would you need in order to inform your working hypotheses?
4. How would you describe Heather Olson? What do you see as her positive characteristics? What negative characteristics would you identify?
5. What is your view of Heather's plan for Bernard? What do you see as some of its strengths? What do you see as some of its limitations?
6. What options does a classroom teacher have, given a student whose classroom behavior is dysfunctional?
7. Should students like Bernard be placed in regular classrooms? Where do you stand on this issue? What do you see as some important advantages? What are some disadvantages?
8. What would you have done with a student like Bernard? What readings and research support your ideas?
†9. To what incident in your own experience does this case relate? What were the events in the case? What did you do? Were the gains worth the cost to you?

4.3 "HE'S DRIVING ME CRAZY!"

The screen door in the kitchen banged shut with a resounding thud, and Betty Costa could tell from the sound that there was going to be trouble. Another day full of frustration and anger for her son Walter, and another afternoon and evening of complaints. She touched the control-save keys on the Mac to insure that her afternoon's work on the instructions to the jury would not be lost, and she turned around to face the latest outrage.

He came into her study, his eyes manic, his mouth a well of fury. "That's it, mom. I've had it. I'm never going back to that class again. Fini. Kaput. It's over. Toast." The words, staccato punctuation points, gave emphasis to his feelings, leaving no room for negotiation.

"Come on, sweetie," Betty Costa's voice mollified. "Tell me all about it." This was hardly the first time that her son had come home from school in a purple rage. In fact, fifth grade seemed to be one long and endless battle between Walter and his teacher, with Walter always the loser. How many times was it now that Betty Costa and her husband George had been up to school for meetings with Walter's teacher, Hillary Esterhaus? Five? Seven? She had lost count; the meetings never took them anywhere near resolution of the problem. Hillary Esterhaus was adamant. Walter was a terrible behavior problem, a boy who was "too old for his age" and who insisted on having things his own way. Betty thought that the implication was that the Costas had spoiled Walter, but Hillary Esterhaus had not said so explicitly. The fifth-grade teacher did, however, put the onus on the Costas to see that Walter "behaved"—otherwise, there would be more trouble.

Walter Costa did not sit where his mother had beckoned. He stood his ground and began to plead his case. Betty Costa, a district court judge, had to admire her son's presence, his ability to articulate his ideas, his presentation. He could plead his case persuasively. No doubt, he would make a good lawyer. Like mother, like son, she thought proudly.

Walter had done a report on the recent environmental conference in Brazil. She had seen how hard he had worked on it and how much time he had spent on gathering his information. Both she and her husband had talked with Walter extensively about the conference and the different agendas brought by the different nations about the future of environmental protection. They had both been eager to help Walter understand the issues—to help him see that they were complex, not just a matter of good versus bad and right versus wrong. For a child of 10, Walter did possess a great ability to understand issues on more complex levels. Both his parents had taken great pains to enrich his life and to engage in dialogue with him, on an adult level, from his very early years. Their work with him had paid off. Walter was a sophisticated, gifted, and very articulate boy, well read, well traveled, and very opinionated. He could be a bit much in class, Betty was quick to admit, but surely any teacher would be able to see and appreciate the talents of this exceptional boy.

"Well, what happened when you gave your report?" asked Betty.

"Well, in the first place, she never even called on me. And I had my hand up, too, from the very beginning. She called on Tony Huston, and of course, that bimbo, Sheila Cutler. Their reports were so boooorrrrrring, mom, you would have fallen asleep. Probably copied right out of the encyclopedia. They couldn't even read their own words! Then the bell rang and we had to go to gym. When we got back, she said there was no more time, and we should turn the reports in and she would read them. So I gave mine to her and she gave it right back to me and told me to take it home and do it again 'cause it was too sloppy for her to read." Walter, crushed, held his paper out for his mother to see. It was true, his handwriting was about as legible as alfalfa sprouts, but was penmanship the critical issue here? Walter had never developed the kind of small muscle control that allowed for neat and clear cursive writing. But in this day of word processors, what was the problem?

Betty Costa did not rush in to condemn Walter's teacher. Like the fair-minded jurist that she was, she strove to see both points of view and tried to encourage her son to do likewise.

"But, sweetheart," she began, "perhaps Mrs. Esterhaus had important reasons for choosing Tony and Sheila to give their reports? And perhaps you could have done a bit better about making your writing more legible. You have important ideas and they're no good unless they can be read."

"Well, *I* can read them," shouted Walter, perceiving his mother rising to the defense of his teacher. Whose side was she on, anyway? He picked up his bookbag, tossed it over his shoulder, and powered out of the room, motor running. Betty heard the door to his room close, and wondered if she had done the right thing. She didn't think it was right simply to take Walter's side against his teacher, since that would likely exacerbate an already tense situation. Yet she also believed that Walter's case about the handwriting was legitimate. Shouldn't she have stood by him?

Ever since Walter entered fifth grade, he had had trouble with Hillary Esterhaus. The way Walter described it, Mrs. Esterhaus gave him no slack. She insisted that he do things her way. Walter found the endless worksheets and textbook exercises tedious and unchallenging. His rich experiences at home contrasted radically with the mundane activities of the classroom. Walter was bored, and from what Betty Costa saw of the work he brought home, it was no wonder. If that hadn't been the only fifth-grade class in the school, Betty would have asked for a transfer in the first month of school. Without an option, the only other possibility was to transfer Walter to a private school. Betty and George Costa had considered this but rejected that option on two counts. First, Walter would have been uprooted from his neighborhood and his friends, which did not seem to be a good idea for a boy who had only a few friends to begin with. Second, and perhaps more compelling, was the argument that the private school smacked to the Costas of elitism. Walter was already enough of a snob about his intelligence and did not need any more push in that direction.

Betty wondered every day whether that decision had been wise. Shouldn't the public school be more equipped to deal better with a gifted child? Shouldn't Walter's activities in class reflect his advanced competencies? Why was he being made, again and again, to conform to the grade norms, without the opportunity to have his own horizons extended? Now that it was spring, and the school year nearly over, Walter was just going to have to make the best of it. We all have our crosses to bear. Walter might not be getting any enrichment at school, but that was certainly being made up for at home.

Hillary Esterhaus tossed her long blonde hair back with one flick of her head, thumped her daybook down on the table, and sat down audibly. Her friend and colleague, Jaime Alvarez, took a single glance at her face and immediately zeroed in on the problem.

"Don't tell me. It's Walter Costa, right?"

"Damn straight. Walter today, Walter yesterday, Walter tomorrow. That boy is driving me crazy! Jaime, I just don't know how I'm going to make it through the year with him." Hillary's shoulders folded down, and her body seemed to shrink with fatigue.

Jaime did not say anything. He knew that Hillary needed those few minutes of silence to calm down and get hold of herself. He knew that she knew that he was listening, whenever she was ready to give him the latest chapter and verse about that "demon 10-year-old" who was making her life miserable.

"You know, Jaime," Hillary said, gathering her energies, "I'm beginning to think of this as war. It *feels* like a war between Walter and me. I know that he hates me. I know that he thinks I'm the enemy. But I'm damned if I'm going to let that controlling, obsessive, self-centered 10-year-old run my class. I'm older, *and* smarter, *and* stronger, and I'm going to keep that upper hand, or else!" She looked out the window to the wooded hills across the road, where she could see signs of life returning to the trees. She tossed her silky golden hair again, and looked Jaime Alvarez in the eye.

"You've heard this story before, right?"

He smiled warmly, his eyebrows reaching toward the ceiling. "So what else is new?" he chuckled, trying to lighten the effect.

"So tell me. I must be doing something wrong, right? You've got six years of teaching experience under your belt. This is my first year. So give me the benefit of your wisdom. Am I partly responsible for what's happening between Walter and me? Is he just a swift pain in the keester? Am I doing something that's maybe making the situation worse? Is it wrong for me to try to get him to do what the other students are doing? Where is it written that he should be allowed to make his own decisions about what he's going to study? Is there a fifth-grade curriculum, or isn't there?" Her voice softened, cracked. "You know, Jaime, this is the first time in seven months that I'm beginning to think that it's not just Walter's problem, that maybe it's also mine." She looked down at her hands, folded into her lap.

"Tell you what, Hilly," Jaime said, lifting her hands into his with gentle reassurance. "Not just because I'm the part-time helping teacher for the intermediate grades in this school. Not just because I've got the years on you. But because I think you are a good and decent person who really cares about kids and about being a good teacher. And because this is the very first time that you've looked at the situation from the vantage point of your own role in it, as well as from Walter's. I think maybe I can help. So I'm going to ask you some questions, okay? And you tell me whatever you think you want to."

Hillary nodded, the long hair bobbing in the sunlight.

"Tell me," Jaime pressed gently, "about your impressions of Walter. What kind of boy is he? What's his background? What are his interests? What behavior gives you trouble?"

"Well, I told you," her voice took a sharp edge. "He's a controlling, obsessive, self-centered boy who is used to having his own way about everything."

"Yeah, I already heard that part." The gentleness never left his voice, as he chuckled, trying to cut the tension. "So tell me about the details. And see if you can forget the labels."

For the first time, Hillary softened, smiled. "Hey, Jaime. Give me a break, okay?"

"So?"

She looked across at the trees, as if trying to project a picture from her mind into reality.

"Okay. From the first weeks of school, way back in September, he was already showing me how smart he thought he was. I began to think, all right, already, I can see you are smart; stop trying to impress me. I began to think of him as a nuisance. Smart, yes. But a terrible nuisance. He was always 'on me'— you know, like, in my face. If I had an idea, he had a better one, or a different one." She sighed, the memories painful in the recall.

Jaime took her pause as a sign to interject. "So from the beginning, he was trying to assert himself, to gain some power. And your response was . . ." he left the sentence open for her to finish.

". . . to battle him for control. It was my class, and the control belonged to me. I was going to make the important decisions about curriculum, and I wasn't about to give that control over to him." She spoke in a whisper.

"Tell me more about him, Hilly."

"Well, his mom's a district court judge, very well-to-do parents, very ambitious. He's an only child, gets to go on all their posh holidays. Twice a year to the Caribbean, with Aspen. Honolulu, San Francisco thrown in for good measure. He told me that he's asked his parents to take him to Australia when he finishes sixth grade. That's going to be his graduation present. He's treated very much like an adult at home. You know," she reflected as if coming to a new awareness, "I wonder if he's ever had a chance to be a little boy. He surely is very bright—I mean, conceptually way beyond his years in what he knows and in how he reasons—but he is also very driven and I think also very anxious. I'm not sure I can explain it."

"Would you consider his behavior beyond assertive, Hilly? I mean, is he aggressive? Hostile?"

"Hmmm, funny you should ask that, Jaime. I tended to think of Walter as obnoxious. But now that you raise the question, I do see aggressiveness in how he behaves. And he certainly is hostile to me. I can often hear his voice in my ears, after class. There is a sharpness, a shrillness in the way he talks that seems to be on the edge of shrieking. I tell you, it's very grating on the nerves and very exhausting. His voice is so demanding."

"What about his interests? Does he have any interests in particular?"

"This is funny, Jaime, and I've never thought of this either. But his interests seem to shift from topic to topic. At first, I thought he was just interested in everything. But now I'm thinking, maybe his interests are only superficial. That is, he's really not interested beyond surface levels.

"There's something else that occurs," she continued, almost without pausing. "He doesn't seem to stick with any job, that is, he just dispatches the work, lickety-split, and tosses it in, and moves onto the next job. I think that's what exasperates me. I can see that he has the ability, but the quality of his work is shoddy, like he's not giving his best effort, like it's not worth his time."

Hillary, Jaime sensed, was for the first time gaining some perspective about Walter Costa. She was beginning to look beyond the labels she had assigned to him, and beyond her anger. She was beginning to see the problem with Walter in new ways. Perhaps this would be the first steps on the pathway of dealing with the problem more effectively?

"But what about his interests, Hilly? Is he actually interested in anything?"

"He says he's interested in animals. I'm not sure if it's a real, deep interest. The environment, too, but I'm not sure about that. I don't know if he trots these ideas out because they're supposed to impress me."

"Have you talked with him, you know, just you and Walter? About his interests?"

"Yeah, well, no actually. You trapped me on this, Jaime. I haven't ever really sat down and talked with Walter. I've disliked him too much." She turned her face away, lest he see the guilt she felt at her disclosure.

"So tell me a bit more about his behavior in class. You know, what he does that makes you so mad."

"That's too easy, Jaime. I assign a topic for writing a story, and he wants another topic. I assign a research project on Peru, and he does one on the meeting in Brazil. I give the children a story to read, and he picks a different story.

He always has a reason for the choice, too. This is too silly or too dumb or too boring. He wants it his way. Then he gets furious with me when I don't call on him to read his report. Never mind he's on a different topic altogether. I'm prepared to be liberal, but I'm not prepared to be that liberal. The kids have to know who the teacher is!" Once again, the hair flew back, defiant strands falling over her shoulders.

"There's more, Jaime. With all his insistence on having his own choices, he's also very anxious about his work being less than perfect. If he should get a paper back that's less than an A, you'd think he was going to have apoplexy. He doesn't want to take any advice from me, or any direction about how his work might be improved. As I told you when we began, he's arrogant, spoiled and obsessive. I know he's gifted, but he's driving me crazy!"

Hillary Esterhaus looked across the table into Jaime Alvarez's concerned face. "So tell me, Mr. Helping Teacher. What do I do to survive the rest of this school year?"

Study Questions

1. What kind of boy is Walter Costa? Based on the data in the case, write a two-paragraph profile that would describe him to his sixth-grade teacher.
2. In what ways are Hillary Esterhaus and Betty Costa's views of Walter similar? Different?
3. What do you see as the "problem" with Walter? What aspects of his behavior suggest that he is a "problem"?
4. In what ways do you see Hillary Esterhaus contributing to her difficulties with Walter? What, in your view, does she do that makes a difficult situation worse?
5. How would you describe Hillary Esterhaus as a teacher? Based on the data in this case, write a one-paragraph confidential report that describes her teaching.
6. If you were Jaime Alvarez, what advice would you give to Hillary Esterhaus about what she should do for Walter Costa? What about her suggests that she will be able/unable to act on that advice?
7. What action, if any, should Betty and George Costa take with their son regarding what is happening in school? What educational principles guide your thinking on this question?
8. Should Betty and George Costa have removed Walter from this class and sent him to a private school? On what educational values does your decision rest?
†9. To what experiences of your own does this case relate? What student in your own class "drove you crazy"? What was the nature of the difficulty? In what ways, if any, did you see yourself exacerbating the problem?

4.4 BARRY

"Are you crazy?" my father looked at me as if I had just told him I was planning to become the wife of Tarzan and live in a tree house in the jungle, dressed in leopard-skin underwear. "No one goes to live in the mountains," he continued his assault. "What will you do there? It's so far from the city!"

His words stung me and I stepped back, looking for support from the oak-paneled door. "Dad," I faltered, "I really need your support here. It's not easy for me to take this job so far away, to be away from the family. But there are no jobs close by. And I do want this chance to be a teacher."

He shrugged his shoulders, for once at a loss for words. I knew he would, in the end, understand. But why was he making it so difficult for me to leave? I was a grown-up person. I was entitled to have a chance to live my own life, to make my own decisions. It would have been nicer, easier, if my decisions were not encumbered by such a family opera!

I would have preferred to find a teaching job closer to home. First year of teaching—it's got enough turmoil on the job, without being alone, in a strange place, far away from friends and loved ones. But as jobs went, this was the only one available for a new teacher in this time of budget cuts and teacher cutbacks. I felt lucky to get it. So what if it were in the mountains, in a small town about 300 miles from the coastal city where my parents lived? I might even get to like it.

Twin Pines School, nestled in a grove of conifers, served the township of San Remo, in what was becoming the most rapid-growth area in the state. Drawn by the clean mountain air, the beautiful landscapes, the low-cost housing, residents found the rural life a refreshing change from the smog, high-density and high cost life on the coast. But there was nothing about the school or the beauty of its setting that had prepared me for this first year of teaching. If the scene was serene, life as a teacher at Twin Pines was anything but!

It didn't take many days for me to discover Barry in my group of 26 combined fifth and sixth graders. He was a gentle and courteous boy, as if someone had actually taken the trouble to teach him some manners—a pleasant change from the other hell-raisers who made up the male complement of the class. On the athletic field, he excelled in virtually every sport offered. During lunch hour, or recess, I liked to watch him shoot baskets, his skill and grace an elegant counterpoint to that rumble-tumble world of unorganized play activity that teachers see twice daily, at the designated hours of recess and lunch. Off the sports field, and in the classroom, he was like a walrus out of water. The grace and skill fell from him, as he wrestled clumsily and unsuccessfully with the demands of the sixth-grade curriculum.

Ever the butt of other children's grim and devastating put-downs, Barry struggled with reading, his pace plodding and his ability to concentrate overpowered by his fierce struggle to decode words. But at least he could achieve some marginal success. Where he succeeded in distinguishing himself as an utter failure was in math. While the other children were making headway into the wonderful world of fractions and decimals, Barry was defeated by simple, basic number facts. Computation was a puzzle to him, and even the sums given to first graders were a total mystery. He was able to make some headway with 2 + 2 = 4, but he was in trouble if the amount of either numeral was increased by a single digit. Two plus three was outside his reach. Forget subtraction.

The other kids did not help. *Retard,* was a word frequently tossed in his direction, and even though I made numerous attempts to quell the flood of children's cruelties toward one another, Barry could not help but be further diminished by his classmates' low opinion of his academic performance.

Remembering what I had learned in Education 423: Teaching Strategies in Math, I studied Barry's papers, trying to make sense of the kinds of errors he was making. But the more I studied his errors, the more a pattern eluded me. There seemed to be no pattern to his errors, no consistency to what he knew or did not know. It was as if a different child was turning in the papers each day. If he knew the sum of 2 + 3 on Monday, there was no guarantee that he would do that sum correctly on Tuesday. His responses shifted so radically, I began to think he might just be wildly guessing. On the other hand, maybe the "math chip" in his brain had been rendered dysfunctional. I had heard in my college classes of children who had reading disabilities, but I hadn't heard about children with math disabilities. I tried to remember what I knew about learning-disabled children, but given that he could function, albeit in a marginal way, in reading, I was totally mystified as to what the problem might be.

Mrs. Newhouse, Barry's mother, lost no time in coming to school for a visit. She brought with her the diagnostic assessments made in the educational clinic of the large coastal city, where she had taken Barry for an evaluation last year. Barry had been given a battery of tests, and the clinical results seemed to me ambiguous. He was given an individual IQ test, and scored 80. I interpreted that to mean "low average." This, in itself, would not explain his math difficulty. He could read and comprehend at a fourth-grade level and he did seem to be making at least some gains in this area, although they were slow. The tests revealed that his math functioning was "poor," but there was no indication of where the problem came from. The report from the clinical psychologist suggested that Barry showed no indication of "psychological problems that might interfere with his learning." The speculation seemed to point in the direction of low IQ as the causative factor, but the professionals at the clinic were better at explaining *what* he couldn't do, rather than *why* he couldn't do those things. Since I already knew *what* he couldn't do, and needed to know more about *why*, the diagnostic assessments were not very helpful. I began to intuit that maybe there was some physical dysfunction that was outside the scope of the clinic staff's ability to detect. Could there have been a birth defect? Might there be some genetic malfunction? Were there infant or early childhood experiences that put him at risk? Had his mother taken drugs or alcohol during pregnancy? None of these lines of inquiry had been pursued by the clinic staff. And if the educational clinic in the city struck out for me, the resources at the school district level were even less helpful. Diagnostic services at the school and in the county were few and far between. I could make a referral, but it would be months until any information would be forthcoming. And would the results be any more illuminating than what I already knew? I could try it, but in the meanwhile, Barry was still sitting there in my class, being defeated by the simplest numerical tasks.

Mrs. Newhouse wanted something different from me. She was not concerned with finding out more about Barry's difficulties with his schoolwork. She seemed to have already accepted as a given that he had these academic limitations. What she wanted was some reassurance that this new teacher (me) would be sympathetic to the learning problems of her only son. Would this new teacher work with him, to the best of his ability? Would she see any value in him as a person, outside of his limited academic performance? Would she use his academic failings to further undermine his confidence in himself? Would he, at the end of sixth grade, be more convinced than ever that he was a capital-F Failure, ready for the garbage heap? I looked out of the classroom window to the schoolyard where Barry was waiting for his mother, shooting baskets. Pity, I thought, that basketball could not substitute for math on his report card. Then he would be "gifted" instead of a "retard."

I was touched by Mrs. Newhouse's plight. She cared deeply about her son and was hoping for some magic, something that could happen in sixth grade that would not propel him further down into a sea of hopelessness as a learner. But I didn't want to build up her hopes. I wanted to tell her: "Look here, I'm only a first-year teacher! What do I know about how to help him? Even the professionals at the educational clinic bombed out when it came to pointing to what was wrong! How can I succeed where all his other teachers failed?" I wanted to tell her all of that, but I could only look into her eyes, filling with tears, and assure her that I would do whatever I could. I spent the weekend thinking about Barry. And even though I tried to get him out of my mind, he was never far from my thoughts.

Remembering what I learned in my coursework—that the use of manipulatives in math would increase comprehension as well as skills—I approached the first-grade teacher on Monday morning to ask her for some Cuisenaire rods. This seemed to me to be the right way to begin work with Barry. I sat with him, dumped the rods out on his table, and showed him how he could use the manipulatives as an aid in calculation. He took the rods from me, with a look on his face that told a story, but I could not read it.

I saw him pushing the rods around on his desk as he worked on the math worksheet I had given him, with ten simple addition facts to sum. His paper, however, was no different from those that I had seen before: the pattern of errors that made no sense persisted. I blue penciled "two correct out of ten" with a heavy heart. The next day, when I looked over to Barry's desk, I saw that the rods were nowhere in sight. "Where are your rods, Barry?" I asked when I approached him. Barry looked at me, his eyes blazing with open hostility, as he reached into the inner recesses of his desk and drew them out. Three days, three rod-instruction periods, and three worksheets later, we were still at square one.

The following Monday, I decided I'd give it one more try.

"Hey, Barry. Take out the rods and let's do some math."

Slowly, as though he were swimming through glue, he began to extract the bag of rods from his desk. I pulled a chair over to him and got a good look at that cold, hard face. It didn't take many questions to find out the trouble. Cuisenaire rods were for babies. I had publicly humiliated him with my choice of hands-on materials. Never mind that we had used them in my college course in math methods. Everyone at this school knew they were only used in the primary grades. Why didn't I just put a dunce cap on his head and be done with it! Numb with shame, I took the sack of rods from Barry and retreated to a neutral corner where I could assess my losses.

After dinner, I opened a bottle of wine and had two glasses before I sat down to rethink my next moves with Barry. If rods were for babies, I had to find some other manipulatives that would be more appropriate. They needed not just to help him conceptualize numbers, but to restore his dignity. I decided on money.

I put together a bag of coins, about five dollars' worth in pennies, nickels, dimes, and quarters, and told Barry that this would be his bag of money. "Barry's money," the other kids called it. No one could say that these manipulatives were for babies. He began to use the money as counters. Each day, he and I would put together a group of 10 arithmetic examples requiring him to add and subtract money. At the end of the day, he'd turn his worksheet into my "in basket" for marking.

His score of correct responses was fairly consistent, usually three or four out of ten, with five correct being a major event. If there was a consistency about his low score, there still was no discernible consistency to his pattern of errors. Working with him one-on-one on a daily basis did not increase his ability to compute or to comprehend these basic numerical concepts in any significant way. In the evenings, at the dining room table where I read students' work with my after-dinner coffee, I tried to think of what I might write on Barry's paper that would not demean him further, that would not destroy the remaining vestiges of confidence that he had in himself. I could not be false and write that his paper was good work because it was not good work; that would have been a lie.

If I wrote that, why would he ever trust me again? If I wrote, "You are trying," that, too, could be seen as a reproach. It sounded too much like, "You are trying, but not succeeding." I couldn't think of something to write that would be honest as well as supportive, encouraging and validating.

In a move that no teacher in any education course ever taught me, I picked up my gum eraser and rubbed out a few incorrect digits in Barry's answers. Deviously, I selected a matching pencil, forged his handwriting, and put the correct digits under the examples. Would he know? Would he remember the answers he had put down? Would such a lying, cheating maneuver doom us both? I poured a shot of brandy into my coffee cup, picked up my blue pencil, and wrote, "Hey, Barry. Eight correct today! You are really making some big improvement in your work." I downed the coffee-brandy in a single gulp.

I played out this scenario with Barry for the next few months. Barry, despite extensive one-on-one instruction, practice with his bag of manipulatives, and math worksheets, never learned to master computation with increased accuracy. I continued each evening to erase and change his incorrect answers so that I could return his paper with a response that validated Barry-as-person. I never breathed a word of this to anyone in school.

In the early days of spring, three boys from another class came into the after-school disarray of my classroom to hang out and talk with some of my "hangers-on." I heard them talking from where I was putting together a photo display for the bulletin board.

"Who's the dumbest kid in your class?" one of them asked.

Larry looked up from what he was doing and looked over at Mark, who liked me to call him "Bob," and said, shrugging his shoulders, "I don't know."

It would be nice if Barry's story had a happy ending. But the truth is, I left the Twin Pines School at the end of that school year to take a job in the city, near my family and friends. I lost touch with Barry altogether. Did he ever get through high school with any shred of his self-worth intact, even though he could not do his numbers? Is self-worth a reasonable price to pay for the inability to add and subtract? Maybe a college coach picked him up, got him a basketball scholarship, and gave him a free ride through the academic requirements? Did I do the right thing with Barry, choosing to bolster his feeling of self-worth rather than giving him a correct and earned mark? If I teach for 100 years, I'll never know for sure.

Study Questions

1. What do you see as the key issues in this case? Identify them.
2. What do you make of Barry's performance in math, given the data in the case? What hypotheses can you come up with that might explain his inability to add and subtract simple numbers?

3. What is your opinion of the action taken by the teacher? What risks were involved? What were some potential gains for Barry? For the teacher?

4. What beliefs might this teacher hold that allowed her to take this radical action? What are your thoughts on it?

5. What, in your opinion, is more important: letting a child know that his or her performance is incompetent or protecting a child's sense of self-worth? Where do you stand on this issue?

6. What action would you have taken if you were this boy's teacher? What beliefs do you hold that would dictate those actions? Can you envision a time when you might have to act in ways that are incompatible with those beliefs?

7. Imagine Barry 10 years later. How might this teacher's actions have influenced his life? Imagine Barry 10 years later, if his teacher had continued to grade his papers accurately. How might that have changed his life? What scenarios can you create?

†8. How is a teacher's need to feel success related to students' achievement? How might such needs impact on a teacher's actions? Talk about an incident in your own teaching experience where your own needs to feel successful were tied up with a student's success, and how these needs influenced your behavior.

†9. In your own teaching experience, were there times when your concerns about marking and grading and protecting a child's feelings of self-worth were in direct conflict? Talk about those times and about how you resolved the conflict. Talk about the beliefs you hold that helped you to resolve the conflict. Talk about the consequences of your actions. Talk about what you would have liked to do but, for whatever reason, were unable to.

4.5 BETWEEN TWO CULTURES

"Tunafish sandwich, two chocolate chip cookies, and a Gravenstein apple," she mused to herself as she took the lunch items out of her "Teacher's Pet" baggie and spread them on a paper towel on her desk. It was her husband's turn to make the lunches this week, and he had been thoughtful about giving her her "faves." She hadn't planned on eating in the classroom today but, at the last minute, changed her mind. She needed the time to catch up with the anecdotal reports to parents that were scheduled to go home at the end of the week, and a quiet hour in the room could give her a considerable advantage.

When Betsy Cairns had chosen teaching as her profession, she never dreamed that it was going to be such an all-consuming job. "Does it get easier after your first year?" she wondered. What with preparations for class, reading students' papers and writing helpful comments on them, trying to figure out the best instructional approaches for individual learning needs, parent conferences, staff meetings, and the hundreds of details that made up her teaching life in fifth grade, she often found herself coming to school early, leaving late, and working at home evenings and weekends. What was that smart-aleck crack she had heard from the garage mechanic the other day about the "sweet" job teachers had—home at three o'clock and two months off in the summer? Get real, Charlie! At least her husband, Brian, knew what teaching was like. He had his own exhausting job teaching second grade in a school across town.

Betsy picked up half of her sandwich, took a large bite, and groaned as cucumber, tomato, alfalfa sprouts, and mayonnaise leaked out of the end of the bread. Brian could always become a short-order cook if he ever decided to quit teaching. She didn't know anyone who could make a sandwich taste so good. Idly, she wondered what he had planned for tomorrow's lunch as the first half of the sandwich disappeared and she removed the rubber band from the stack of anecdotal record cards.

She could hear the interruption gaining crescendo as it worked its way down the hallway and approached her classroom door. Pauline, the school aide, stood in the doorframe, with Arnold and Woody in tow. Arnold was crying and Woody's face looked as if he had just run the Boston Marathon, while Pauline's agitated commentary broke into the short-lived silence of the noon hour.

"Well, here's Arnold and Woody," she said, "to sit out the rest of recess. They're not the villains, mind you, but I thought it would be good for both of them to have a bit of a time-out. There was quite a kafuffel, and I had to take Rudi to the nurse with a bloody nose. But he started it, mind you. I was watching, and I saw the whole thing." Pauline nudged the boys into the room, and they both approached her desk. She reached out in a reflex, to put one arm around each of them, while her eyes stayed with Pauline.

"What happened then?" she asked, the smell of tunafish hovering over her desk as she saw another lunch hour go down the tubes. Pauline, a widow who took the job as school aide to give her something to do with her empty days, puffed out with the importance of having a tale worth telling.

"It's always Rudi, mind you. He's always the one to start it. Punching, kicking, spitting, he's like some wild animal let out of a cage. He's walking along, across the playground, and suddenly he goes berserk, striking out at whoever is in his way. Babbling at the top of his voice in Persian; I can't understand a word he's saying. He took a swing at Arnold, then Woody, and the next thing, they're both piling on top of him, the three of them yelling, punching. I tell you, I'm getting too old for this, Betsy."

"Thanks, Pauline. Thanks for stopping the fight and for bringing Woody and Arnold up here. I'll take it from here. Did you say that Rudi was in the nurse's office?"

Pauline nodded. "I'll get down there later," Betsy said, "but first, I want to talk to the boys."

"I'm not blaming these two, mind you," Pauline was having a hard time disconnecting from the heat of the moment. "They were provoked." Her gaze shifted to the boys. "You tell Mrs. Cairns what happened now. She'll deal with it." Now looking at Betsy, "I better get back to the yard. Who knows what's next!" She huffed out, nose sniffing the air two inches above her head.

Arnold was crying softly and Woody's face had faded from bright red to pink, as Betsy said, "Okay, guys. What happened?" Their answers didn't surprise her. Rudi, always Rudi. He'd been in class only four weeks, and each day he'd been in another fight. It was incredible that this small 10-year-old was so full of rage. She couldn't begin to understand it.

It was mid-October when Rudi first appeared in her classroom, no warning, no time to get herself ready, just this small boy with deep, dark eyes that held a thousand secrets, his hand firmly in the grip of Ann Wallace, the principal. "Here's Rudi," Ann announced, a small smile tried to mask the furrow in her brow. "He's got to go on your register, Betsy, I'm sorry. The other fifth-grade teachers are up to their armpits. He doesn't speak any English at all. Only Persian. How's your Persian?" She tried to make light of it.

"Let's see. I think I've got one word, *imam*, from that eggplant recipe, but that's about it. Hardly enough for a scintillating conversation. Maybe Diane Redding can help out. If Rudi is going to spend some time in her ESL class, she may be able to give me some ideas for what to do in my classroom. Otherwise, I may be in deep trouble."

Ann tried to be placating. "I know you'll do the best you can, Betsy. We're not expecting miracles. Rudi has already been in two other schools since September, and as I understand it, he only arrived in this country in mid-August." Ann rolled her eyes skyward as she continued the story of Rudi. "I have to tell you, Betsy, the school records are not very encouraging. There's been a lot of trouble. When Rudi first started school, he was put in a special ESL class placement, where they hoped he would learn to speak and develop some social skills, and they would worry about the academics later. I don't know what happened there, or in his other placement. He certainly hasn't been in this country long enough to see any real gains. But I do know that he's way behind academically, and I know you're going to love this—he's quite a hostile and angry boy."

Ann and Betsy both looked down at Rudi, whose eyes darted anxiously around the room.

"Come on, sweetheart," Betsy's tone was reassuring. "I'll find you a seat." She took his hand, extracted him from the principal's protective custody, and led him to a seat close to her desk. "Where's he from, Ann?" Betsy asked, as Rudi settled into the chair.

"Iran, seems like. His brother brought him in early this morning. I don't know about a father or mother. I imagine we'll find out more as we get more detailed information from the other schools. You let me know if there's anything in particular you need from me and I'll try to get it for you. And Betsy," she paused to meet the teacher's eyes, "thanks."

Betsy Cairns barely heard her. She was already assembling spare pencils, markers, a scribbler for Rudi, which she placed on his desk, touching him lightly on the shoulder. She felt his body stiffen and withdraw, pulling away as if her hand had been hot. She made a mental note of that behavior and filed it away for future reference.

A few minutes later, the rest of her rambunctious fifth graders began to fill the room. Her first day of Rudi was about to start.

Duncan Elementary School was not exactly on the direct flight path of new immigrants seeking asylum in the country. Yet, in a bedroom community that was within spitting distance of a major metropolitan center of the state, it was natural that newly arrived families would eventually find their way here, too. Duncan was trying bravely to keep up with the influx of newcomers, doing its best to find ways to help non-English-speaking children to traverse the bridge between the cultures that spawned them and the high-tech world of this North American suburb, but the task was formidable. Diane Redding, the ESL teacher, was having a tough time of it. Despite her fluency in Spanish, she was out of her league when it came to children whose native languages were Chinese, Russian, Rumanian, Polish, Portuguese, and now Persian. Her ESL class was getting pretty interesting! Betsy did not know if Diane was going to be able to help her, but at least Rudi would have the advantage of specialized instruction for one hour a day, and that was something to be grateful for.

Rudi's first week in fifth grade was unforgettable. It seemed that every effort made by the other children to befriend him was perceived by Rudi as a threatening act, to which he retaliated violently. It did not take the rest of the fifth graders very long to figure out that their best plan was just to keep out of Rudi's way. By the end of the week, Betsy had refereed dozens of verbal and physical fights, and Rudi had become increasingly isolated from the other children. Betsy soon realized the futility of her urging the others to "be especially nice to Rudi and make sure he knows he is welcome in this class." Why would the other children take the chance of extending a hand of friendship, when they were likely to receive a kick in the shins for it?

By the beginning of week two, Betsy knew that she had better get some information from home, and in response to her request for a conference, Rudi's aunt, Mrs. Fatima Sahadi, came up to school with a 2-year-old toddler at her side. Mrs. Sahadi, Rudi's mother's sister, had been in the country for four years. Her English was heavily accented, but understandable. She told the following story:

Rudi's parents were still in Iran, and while they were trying to emigrate, they so far had been unable to obtain the papers they needed to leave the country. Rudi's brother, Yasim, had been sent here two years ago to go to college to study engineering. This summer, the parents had sent Rudi over, on his own, to live with Yasim.

Mrs. Sahadi watched as her little girl investigated each desk in the classroom and said, without apparent emotion, "He's only 19, Yasim. He's not able to look after a boy like Rudi properly. He has his own studies, and I think he's too strict with Rudi. I think he hits him too much. These are the old ways, the old customs. That's all he knows. They live upstairs from us now, and Rudi comes to stay with me when his brother is in school. But I have my own family, my husband and my daughter, to take care of. I can't accept the responsibility for Rudi."

Mrs. Sahadi did not know when Rudi's parents would be coming. She didn't know *if* they were coming. She didn't know what was going to happen to Rudi, and she seemed to have already closed her heart against the forces that were shaping him in his new country. When she picked up her daughter to leave, Betsy had the uneasy feeling that much of the story about Rudi, Yasim and the Sahadi family was still untold.

What was clear about Rudi, and it didn't take any master sleuth to figure it out, was that he was a terribly unhappy child who seemed to be teetering on the brink of violent behavior all the time. Living with Rudi was like waiting for a powder keg to go off. What could his life have been like in Iran, up to the point of his departure? What could it have been like for him to have made the long plane trip from Teheran to Capital City, alone and without the ability to speak or understand English? What did he understand about when he would see his parents again? What was it like for him to have only a strict, disciplinary, and punishing 19-year-old brother as his primary adult? What was it like for him to have an aunt and uncle who seemed more emotionally distant and rejecting than strangers? If Rudi was angry, confused, hurting, the events in his life had conspired to shape this unhappy boy.

After her meeting with Mrs. Sahadi, Betsy began to initiate a plan of action to help Rudi academically. Perhaps, she thought, if he could learn to speak, read, and write English, he might not feel so alienated, so powerless in the group? Perhaps he would need to rely less on aggressive acts if he could communicate verbally with his classmates? Would learning to read help him feel that he belonged here? Or was Rudi too far gone, too alienated, too troubled, too much steeped in violence to be brought back to a pathway of stability and emotional health? Betsy couldn't help wondering, too, whether, given the sad tale of Rudi's life outside of school, anything positive she did would be canceled out by his treatment at home.

She set aside 15 minutes each day for one-on-one work with Rudi. On the first day, she began with some words that she thought might be "key words" for him. *Rudi* was one; *Yasim* was another. For the third, she took a chance and gave him *Yna*, the name of his little 2-year-old cousin. Using strategies that she remembered from her studies in college about organic reading, she printed these words on cards for Rudi, said them aloud to him, and then had him read the words back to her. She then gave him some chalk and demonstrated how he was to copy his words on the blackboard. Rudi was caught up in the experience but was unable to stick with it for long. His attention shifted to where some boys were standing near his desk, and Rudi immediately took off and shoved them both vigorously. Betsy wondered if Rudi's notoriously short attention span was an indication of his fear that someone standing near his desk was, somehow, a personal threat to him? Was he worried that someone might make off with his pitifully few possessions?

Rudi was becoming Betsy's *bête nóire*. She couldn't get him out of her mind, either in school or out. In the third week of classes, Rudi used his black felt pen and scribbled in several library books. Betsy was furious and for the first time, she lost it, found herself yelling at Rudi, the anger and frustration of the last three weeks built up to a pitch and erupting in a terrible stream of ugly words.

Rudi did not need to understand English to understand the tone of the message. He retreated to his seat, his eyes never leaving her face, while the other children fell into a stony silence. That afternoon, she watched from the classroom window as the children walked home in groups of twos and threes, chatting and laughing, while straggling far behind, alone in the solitary confinement of his own world, walked Rudi. Her heart softened, and the anger she felt over the defaced library books was obliterated by her compassion. What was it like, she wondered, to be only 10 and so desperately alone?

Two days later, in response to her note, Rudi's brother Yasim came after school for a conference. Betsy saw a young man with his own agenda and his own needs thwarted by having to accept adult responsibility for a small sibling, full of his own anger about it. Yasim kept Rudi very close to the small attic apartment in which they lived; he did not want his brother "in the malls or at the video arcades" like the other children here. He did not want Rudi to be influenced by the "evil Western ways" that would corrupt him. He was acting *in loco parentis*, and his parents would expect him to be strict and tough.

Rudi had to come right home from school; otherwise he would get a beating. He had to do his lessons at night, practicing writing the English alphabet for two hours. If he did not do the work, or if he dawdled, Yasim would smack him. There was no TV in the attic room, but sometimes Rudi would get to watch if he was downstairs in his aunt's house.

As gently as she could, and trying not to be excessively judgmental, Betsy asked Yasim if, perhaps, he was being too strict with Rudi, too punishing?

His eyes never wavered from her face. "These are our ways, teacher. I treat my brother as he would be treated at home. We do not believe children should have such freedom as they have here. Rudi must learn to obey. He must do as he is told. I am in charge."

There didn't seem to be any point of taking the conference further. Yasim believed that what he was doing was right. He saw Betsy's suggestions to be more lenient as potentially corrupting for Rudi. Betsy didn't see any chance for getting Yasim to change his views. She got up, thanked him for coming, and walked him to the door. When she returned to her desk, a shaft of late afternoon sunlight caught Rudi's desk and dust motes danced in the air above it, an artist's view of the confusion of her thoughts. Was this a case of child abuse, Betsy wondered? Should she report this to the authorities? If she did and Rudi was taken out of his brother's care, would his life be happier or more secure?

Betsy took her cookies from the desk and gave them to Arnold and Woody. She told them that she understood that Rudi had started the fight and that Rudi had provoked them. Still, she felt that they might find better ways to deal with Rudi than fighting back, but she was silent on what those ways could be. She felt herself at a loss as to how to help these boys respond to Rudi.

Settling Woody and Arnold in, she looked at the clock. Damn, 12:50! Lunch hour shot. Anecdotal report cards shot. Rudi still down in the nurse's office. It was tempting to forget about him and leave him there for the rest of the afternoon, give the class a holiday from Rudi. She snatched her apple, bit it, and raced down the corridor toward the nurse's office. Where did you begin to help a boy like Rudi?

Study Questions

1. What do you see as the central issues in this case? Talk about the central issues, and then list them in what you consider to be their order of importance.
2. How would you describe Betsy Cairns? What attributes would you use to describe the kind of teacher she is? Write a one-paragraph profile of this teacher that might describe her professionally.
3. How would you describe Rudi? What attributes would you use to describe the kind of boy he is? Write a one-paragraph profile of Rudi that would describe him to his sixth-grade teacher.
4. From the information given in the case, what do you see as the factors that might explain Rudi's behavior? What data support your ideas?
5. Given what you know about Rudi, what are some options open to Betsy Cairns with respect to how she might help Rudi in class? What are some options for Betsy with respect to how she might help the other children deal more effectively with Rudi? What reasons do you have for thinking that those suggestions are going to be helpful?
6. Given what you know about Rudi, what do you think Betsy should do about Rudi's home situation? What reasons do you have for thinking that those suggestions will improve Rudi's situation?

7. What, in your view, can teachers do to help themselves ease the trials and tribulations of dealing with children like Rudi? What suggestions can you make? What reasons do you have for thinking that those suggestions are going to be helpful?

†8. Talk about a child in your own student teaching/teaching experience who was having considerable difficulty making an adjustment to a new culture. Talk about the child's behavior, and talk about your own responses to this student. Talk about the strategies you used and how successful they were. Talk about what you might have done in retrospect.

4.6 I DON'T WANT HIM SITTING NEXT TO ME!

They were the meanest-spirited children who were ever put together under one classroom roof, this combined fifth and sixth grade that I'd just inherited from a teacher who had gone off on maternity leave. Lucky her! I was grateful to have a job, true. I was grateful to be in this beautiful, suburban school district, in a new school with modern, up-to-date equipment. Things could be a lot worse. But I was not prepared for these children. I had never dreamed that 10- and 11-year-olds could develop such antisocial attitudes.

Their offhand remarks to one another were full of barbs. They didn't share. Cooperation was "stupid," patience and tolerance nonexistent. I didn't know what egg they'd hatched out of, but I did know that their cruelties to one another made me dislike them intensely. My two college courses in human growth and development had not prepared me for these suburban, elitist, affluent, and disagreeable children. Was this what children had become at century's end? If so, maybe I had better reconsider my choice of profession.

Teaching was not my first career choice. I'd danced around the idea of journalism since my days as a cub reporter for our high school newspaper. When I'd been given the assignment to interview Sylvester Stallone in my junior year, even though this opportunity had been arranged for reporters from all the city schools as a publicity stunt to generate interest in his waning career, I was dazzled by the glamour of a reporter's life. Woodward and Bernstein became my heroes and I must have seen the movie *All the President's Men* a dozen times. I'd imagine myself as an investigative reporter getting the goods on some high-up, public official, exposing him and his evil ways, and going on to Pulitzer Prize fame. That was my dream.

When I finished college, I put together a portfolio of my work on both high school and college papers and set off, hat in hand, to the large metropolitan newspaper offices. The best I could get was, "We'll contact you if there's any opening. Please leave your card. Thanks for coming in." Me and a hundred other wannabes every week, all dreaming of the glamorous life of a reporter, left sitting at home, waiting for the phone to ring.

"Not bloody likely," Uncle Harry told me. "Newspapers are in trouble. Nobody reads these days. Everybody gets their news from the TV. Unless you've got a contact in the business, you're as likely to get a job as a Martian is of becoming the next Celebrity Chef. Get a life, Curtis," my uncle told me, "and stop sitting around waiting for a job that's never going to happen."

As much as I resented his tough-minded advice, I knew in my heart that he was right. I couldn't sit at home, sponging off my folks and waiting for my dream job to fall into my lap. I had to find something else to do—something I might enjoy, something to challenge me, something to give me a life. My friend Marilyn suggested teaching, and it sounded like a reasonable alternative.

I enrolled in a Master of Arts in Teaching program at a private university in the city. They were happy to take my tuition dollars in exchange for giving me a one-year course in how to be a teacher. The twelve-month wonder! The one-year program was designed for liberal arts majors like me who wanted to become teachers. Most of us in the small program were adults who had had second thoughts about their first career choices, and we got to know each other pretty well. The work was intense, but not excessively challenging intellectually. I made it through easily, with a GPA of 3.85, and received at the end of it a state certificate to teach. In June I put together a CV and, with accompanying letters, sent copies to 10 suburban school districts that surrounded the city. Having heard too many horror stories about teaching in the city itself, I thought the teaching life would be sweeter, easier, and infinitely more bearable in the suburbs.

To all my letters of inquiry, I received polite but unequivocal replies. Thanks for your application. There are no positions available at this time, but we'll keep your letter on file in the event we have an opening. By September 1, I was still sitting around my parents' house, wondering if I was any better off waiting for a job as a teacher than I had been as an aspiring reporter.

When the call came on September 15 from the Greenwood County School Board office to come for an interview, I was ready to take anything. Greenwood County was considered *the* place to live, a suburb of large, elegant, high-priced homes, high-income residents, well-equipped, modern schools. A teacher who was pregnant had decided suddenly to take early maternity leave. They needed a teacher immediately and were particularly interested in my journalism background. Perhaps there was a chance to get a small school newspaper started. I couldn't have been happier. I could combine teaching with my first love. It wouldn't be *The New York Times*, but it might be fun. By the time the interview was over, I had accepted the position to teach a combined fifth- and sixth-grade class at the Collingwood School.

Chuck Spector, the principal at Collingwood, seemed like a "real" guy. No phoniness, no hiding behind a professional facade—he was direct, straightforward, genuine. I liked him right away. He told me that the children at the school were "advantaged" and that most of them were quite bright. I remember his saying that these kids' idea of a fieldtrip was a long weekend in Paris, that parents would take the children out of school for winter skiing trips to Aspen, and that the school authorities felt it was better to ignore these absences than to make a fuss, because the parents were powerful and would have it their own way, anyway. And who was to say that a child would not benefit from two weeks in Aspen in place of two weeks in school?

Chuck was giving me a clear and unmistakable message about the children and the parents of Collingwood School: wealthy, influential, and used to having things their way. How would this translate to life in the classroom? I couldn't even begin to guess.

At first appearance, they were the most physically attractive children I had ever seen. Designer clothes, designer haircuts, the healthy looks of children who had summered at Martha's Vineyard and eaten the best and most expensive foods, prepared by the world's finest chefs. These kids were the "right stuff"—the children who would doubtless grow up and become the next generation of leaders in business and government.

We spent the first few days getting acquainted, and I could see that whatever I did was met with marginal politeness but, underneath, was marked as terribly uncool. I was becoming increasingly self-conscious about my clothes, my city "accent," my working-class origins. By the end of my first week, I had concluded that my kids were snobs, and I wondered what I would have to do, as part of my curriculum plan, to "humanize" them.

As we got to know one another better, I could see other ugly behavior leaking out. Clean-up, for example, was met with the greatest resistance, including loud carping and bitching and what my mother would call "a lick and a promise" effort:

"I don't see why we have to do this!"
"This is the janitor's job."
"The maid does this at home."
"I'm not a janitor."

To my rejoinder that they must accept responsibility for cleaning up their own space, they'd retort, "Why should we? We don't do it at home!"

The first time I organized the class into groups for work on social studies projects, I was appalled at the overt and cruel interpersonal comments.

"I'm not going to be in Tenniel's group," Elizabeth shouted. "She's disgusting."

"Well, I'm not working with Roger, either," yelled Mark. "He's just too stupid for words. I mean, cosmically stupid." The class laughed.

They hurled insults around and toward one another like volleyballs. Not wanting to force the issue of who was to work with whom, I decided to allow them to sort out their own working groups. This took the better part of two hours and, in retrospect, I would rather have had five teeth drilled. When the groups had finally been set, I thought I should say something wise about how badly they had treated one another.

"Why are you so mean to each other?" I began, figuring that the best way was to put it right out on the table.

"We're not mean," said Mark, defensively.

"Well, what do you call the way you were acting in the last two hours?"

"We're just kidding, Mr. Lester. That's the way we are with each other," answered Abby. "That's the way we kid around."

"Besides," Mark countered, "we were just wasting time anyway. Who cares about groups? As far as I'm concerned, the whole afternoon has been wasted in this useless activity."

Good shot, Mark, I thought. The best defense is a good offense.

I wondered if it would be profitable to take the discussion further, that is, me accusing, and them well-defended and denying, and in the end, making me the culprit. We could be in the "I'm not/You are" mode for the next three days. I shrugged my shoulders and turned to the chalkboard to write some notes for math. Their win.

During PE their competitive and insulting behaviors were raised to levels I hadn't thought possible in 10- and 11-year-olds. I thought of carrying a tape recorder out to the field to capture some of their comments. There could be an important article in it for some local rag—what kids were like these days—but I didn't have the heart for it. I watched from the sidelines as they cut one another to ribbons verbally.

"Hey, Anthony, you blimp. Can't you run any faster?"

"You're out, Greg. You loser!"

"That's not my fault. It's her fault. She runs like a bottle."

"You bimbo, Julie. Your legs are like tree trunks."

By the end of two months with my class, I had spoken to them at least two dozen times about their behavior to one another. I tried anger. I tried persuasion. I tried cajoling. I tried pure, unadulterated reason. It was as if my words were spittle on a hot gridiron. No sooner had the lecture passed from my lips than we were back to where we were in the first place. Exactly.

But not quite. The one major change was what I saw happening to me. I had come into this class in September a cheerful, caring, generous, giving guy. I wanted to like these children, to be nice to them, to share happy times together. Now, in mid-November, I found myself increasingly angry, disgusted with them, and unwilling to "give of myself"—my real self—to such a selfish and merciless bunch. They were winning, and I was losing. I had tried to convince them that it was nicer to live with one another harmoniously, but they didn't believe me. At least, if they did, they didn't show it in any way in their in-class behavior.

I hadn't thought it could get worse. But the following Monday morning, Chuck Spector came trotting down to my room with Roland Michaels, a black boy whose family had just moved into the neighborhood. Roland was the only black student at Collingwood School, and he had just been put on my fifth-grade register. I didn't even think to be aware of how Roland must have felt, looking at that sea of white faces. I only thought about how my students would respond to Roland, and my heart was heavy with anticipation of the worst.

"Roland's dad," Chuck told me, "is a graphic artist whose work has been exhibited in several major shows in New York. His mother, a designer-artist, works for *Vogue* magazine." Chuck told me about a younger daughter, Felicia, who was only 4, and not yet in school. The family had just moved to Greenwood County from a fashionable loft in the city's "artist" community, because they wanted more room and a better environment for their children to grow up in.

I turned to Roland and extended my hand to welcome him. "We're glad to have you, Roland, and I look forward to getting to know you better," I told him. "Let's see," I said looking out over the classroom, "where will we put you?" My mind silently computed the best grouping arrangement. Where would the boys be more accepting, less rude? It was a crapshoot. I sucked in my breath and headed over to where Anthony, Phillip, and Maxwell were sitting. "I'm putting Roland here with you guys," I said, and I saw their faces contort and mouths turn down, as if they had just bitten into lemons. Roland could not have escaped the message, but at least no words had been spoken. Was it because Chuck Spector was still in the room? Did the principal's presence mean that they were reining in their nasty comments?

Somehow, we got through the first day without incident, but the silence was an uneasy one. As I watched out of my third eye, the children seemed to ignore Roland, as if he weren't here at all. The invisible boy. Anthony, Phillip, and Maxwell talked together and did their usual high-jinks. It was as if there was no one else at their table. Nor did Roland make any effort at contact. He kept to himself, not speaking to any of the other children throughout the day.

At three o'clock, when the rest of the class had gone, I noticed Roland still at his desk, collecting his belongings and slowly packing them up into his backpack. He was obviously lingering, I thought, perhaps because he had something to say. I thought I'd give him an opening.

"I hope you had a good day, Roland," I said with sincerity. "If there's anything you need, any help you need, I hope you will let me know."

"Thanks, Mr. Lester," he said, sounding like a small adult. "You know, I think I'm going to like it here, really like it here. I love Greenwood. The city is fun, lots of things to do, but I love being in a house and having a lawn and trees in the backyard. I've got my own room, now, and my sister has her own room, too. I just love it here."

It was as if a finger had been pulled from the dike, unleashing a torrent of emotions in this boy. I was touched that Roland would speak so openly to me about what was in his heart. I was touched that this city boy had found a home that he loved. I suddenly wanted, with all my heart, for his experience in my class to be a good one, a happy one, a positive one.

The next morning, when the children were scrambling around, unpacking their school things and getting ready for the morning's activities, I noticed that Roland's desk had been evicted from the group and had been shunted off by itself, to a space near the window. I noticed, too, that Roland had gone to it, and sat down, without complaint, without bringing the matter to my attention. Should I confront this right away, in front of the whole class, I wondered, or should I do it privately, just with the group of boys who were responsible? I didn't know which course of action would be better, but I knew that I had to do something, take a stand, tell the kids that what they had done was objectionable.

My anger was too great to let it percolate any further. "Hey, you guys," I said, looking directly at Maxwell, Phillip, and Anthony. "What happened to your group? Roland is supposed to be sitting in your group and now I see that he is off by himself. What happened?" I looked at Roland and hoped, a bit late, that I had done the right thing for his sake. He was sitting looking out of the window, as if there was nothing happening in the classroom that had any relationship to him.

"We don't want him with us," Maxwell said indifferently, as if he was talking about a pair of socks that weren't his.

"But how come? You don't even know him, so how do you know you don't want him?" I pushed it a little further.

"We don't sit with blacks," Maxwell said, looking directly into my eyes.

Roland continued to stare out of the window, to a world of trees, green lawns, and suburban serenity, while the tension of the classroom boiled up behind him. I saw his profile, which registered no trace of affect, and looked back at my young offenders, pushing down the torrent of feelings that wanted to burst from my heart.

Study Questions

1. As you see it, what are the significant issues in this case? Talk together and list them in the order that you consider important.
2. Working together, develop a profile of Curtis Lester that describes how you see him as a teacher. What do you consider to be his strong teaching points? What do you see as his weaknesses?
3. Based on the data in the case, talk about your perceptions of this fifth- and sixth-grade class's behavior. What diagnosis would you make of such behavior? Where do you suppose such behavior comes from? What data are you using to support your ideas?

4. How would you describe Curtis Lester's strategies in dealing with the children's offensive behavior? How would you evaluate Lester's strategies? What reasons, in your view, would explain their lack of effectiveness?

5. What, in your view, should a teacher do when children reveal racial, ethnic, or religious prejudice? What assumptions are you making? What makes you believe that the strategies you are advocating would be effective?

6. What might Lester have done differently when Roland came into his class? What assumptions have you made? What leads you to believe that your suggestions would work?

7. How do you explain Roland's behavior? What, in your view, accounts for his "indifference" to class events? What does his behavior tell you about him? What assumptions have you made?

8. What should Lester do now? What assumptions have you made? What leads you to believe that those suggestions would be effective?

†9. Talk about a time when you had to deal with a class that expressed open hostility to a child of another race. Talk about what you did, and what happened. Talk about what you might have done, in retrospect.

4.7 "MR. ANSARI IS COMING ON TO ME"

The advertisement reached out and punched me in the eye:

SCHOOL DISTRICT NO. 33 (BRADFORD)

PHYSICAL EDUCATION TEACHER

A full-time teacher is required immediately for the William S. Hume Secondary School, in Bradford. The position involves junior and senior physical education, plus guidance.
Preference will be given to individuals who possess: a) a valid state teaching certificate; b) a university degree with a major in physical education; c) a previous record of successful teaching experience in a similar position at the secondary level.

I thrust my bowl of oat bran from me and reached for the phone. At this point in late August, I had despaired that anything would turn up in my area, but here was a position made just for me. I had a strong physical education background, plus six months experience as a substitute teacher. I was ready for this job and more than ready to take on the responsibilities of full time teaching.

"Hello, Mr. Blancas," I said when I was finally connected to the assistant superintendent in charge of personnel. "My name is Pam Harris. I saw your ad in this morning's *Free Press* and was wondering if I could come in to interview for the physical education position."

I could tell that Keith Blancas was interested in me from the start. It was a woman physical education teacher that they really wanted, although the discrimination laws forbade them to advertise a gender preference. The interview was a piece of cake. The assistant superintendent was impressed with my file and was doing more to "sell" me on why I should take this job than to actually interview me for the position. The only possible wrinkle lay in the add-on requirement that I teach one guidance class.

I wasn't about to pretend that I knew anything about guidance counseling. But Keith Blancas reassured me that there was not much to know. "It's just a matter of common sense, really," he said. "Some of these girls will have much more experience than you do," he said with a smile and a wink that made me uneasy. "There is, of course, a textbook and a teacher's manual, and if you follow these, the material is rather straightforward.

"Of course, we would expect you to be able to counsel students who got into any personal difficulty—uh, you know what I mean, Pam. And in matters of extreme seriousness, well, uh, you could always call on support from the administration. Really, you know what I mean. Girl-to-girl stuff. Some of the girls just need another, more mature person of the same sex to confide in."

It seemed to me that Keith Blancas was trying to brush this part of the job off, as if it meant little and didn't carry a lot of weight. Perhaps it was because he himself did not value what guidance, done well, could bring to young women wrestling with puberty and other psychosocial dilemmas. He put his emphasis on building the girls' field hockey team and wanted me to know that this was a high priority for the school and for the district: to build a winning team. He convinced me that I could do it, and by the time I left his office, my doubts about taking on the guidance class had all but melted away.

Bill Martin, principal of William S. Hume Secondary, was waiting for me when I arrived at the school. His manner was stiff, and he lacked any of the personal warmth shown me by Keith Blancas. For nearly 40 minutes, he lectured me about the school, spelling out in detail the physical features, as if I were a reporter assigned to deep background. He talked about the design of the building, the number of classrooms and teachers, even the number of books in the library. He told me more about the lunch program than he did about the students. When I finally got a chance to raise a question, I asked him to tell me about what the students were like. He said, "They're just kids, Ms. Harris. Like any other kids. Just normal, everyday kids." Bill Martin did not seem to be a rich resource of human or educational information, and I left his office unimpressed with his leadership. But perhaps there was more to the man than was revealed at this initial conference? Likely I would find that out as the school year evolved.

We were deep into Labor Day weekend when I began to experience the gut-wrenching anxieties that are probably commonplace for all beginning teachers. My friend Judy suggested that we take a picnic lunch and spend the day at the beach, say "goodbye" to the summer. We piled into my old car, and I nosed it in the direction of the lake. It was a soft morning, still warm, but with a hint of fall in the air. Without having planned to dump my anxieties into Judy's lap, I found myself bubbling over, spilling out some of the worries that had made knots in my head, neck, and shoulderblades.

"It's not as if I'm worried about the teaching, Jude, or even coaching the field hockey team. That I can handle. I know it. But I would have liked to know more about the kids. For Pete's sake, you'd think the principal would have been able to tell me something helpful. I feel as if I'm entering a black box."

Judy Fletcher, my best friend of many years, looked at me and smiled. "Whatever they're like, you'll handle it, Pam. You've done enough substituting to have had a wide range of experience with all kinds of kids. You're good with them. They like you and they trust you. Whatever you find in the black box of William S. Hume Secondary, you'll handle it. You'll be fine."

The butterflies in my midsection went on a holiday. Judy was right. I would be able to handle it. Somehow, deep within myself, I knew that to be true.

The Tuesday after Labor Day, I met the staff of William S. Hume School for the first time. Fifty-four teachers assembled in the cafeteria for the first meeting of the school year. Bill Martin introduced me as the new girls' physical education teacher, and the other teachers applauded, making me feel like a celebrity. He also introduced Joe Ansari, the new biology teacher. Joe also got a hand, and I watched his handsome face blush and smile. "Golly," I said to no one in particular, "he doesn't look very much older than the students."

Bill Martin's handling of the staff meeting did little to disabuse me of my first impression of him. He seemed inept, inarticulate, and disorganized. Once again, he did virtually all the talking, rambling on and on in a discourse with himself that most of the staff had long tuned out of. At the end of the meeting, several of the staff raised questions about program, but Martin's responses seemed to be incomprehensible. At one point I caught two male teachers glancing at each other and winking, as if they were sharing some private joke about the principal. He continued his discourse, however, without taking notice. For me, the two-hour meeting was unhelpful and tedious. It didn't do much to inspire my confidence in Bill Martin as an educational leader. If I was going to need help in getting my own program off the ground, I thought I'd be better off to look elsewhere.

It's funny how quickly the "midnight dreadfuls" about beginning to teach diminished with each passing day of the school term. The brain is so packed with the demands of the job, there's little room in it to hold onto anxiety. The more a teacher works the job, the more experience he or she collects. The more experience, the more secure the teacher feels about what he or she is doing. By October, I was no longer feeling like the new kid on the block. I felt very much rooted in the school and very purposeful about my teaching responsibilities. The teachers who cheered me on my first day continued to be warm and friendly, and I never had any reason to have a single regret about being on the staff.

The students were primarily kids from working-class families, some quite talented, some average, and a few real klutzes—the normal array of physical education competence. My physical education program was varied enough to keep me hopping and challenged. I taught a dance class for tenth graders, aerobics classes for eleventh and twelfth graders, and general physical education for ninth graders. Coaching the field hockey team I did as an extracurricular activity, and I enjoyed being out there on the field, in all kinds of weather, with that group of energetic young women who had, I thought, the makings of a winning team. In the guidance class, which I ran for twelfth-grade girls, I felt over my head and I could see myself very much playing it by ear. It was difficult to follow the text and the teacher's manual. The students wanted to talk about personal issues— about sexual experience, about AIDS, about how boys treated girls, about alcoholic parents, about siblings, about their dreams and aspirations, about their lives.

Was it okay to let them talk about their own lives, I wondered? Should I be more authoritarian and try to keep them to what the students considered to be the more boring stuff in the textbook? Was it more important to allow them a chance to talk about the issues that directly affected their lives? And what was my role supposed to be in all of this? If they were going to use the period as a time to "mouth off" how was I supposed to respond? What did teaching "guidance" involve? If I didn't try to make some comments in response to what they were saying, this class would be no better than a pajama party. If I did try to respond, what should I say? I could tell them about the dangers of infection, about protection, about AIDS, and they would listen. I could give them that kind of information when it was needed. But what should I say in response to a student's talking about her father's alcoholism? I didn't have a clue. If I did one thing right, it was, at least, that they were able to talk openly and considered me sympathetic. But how much good was that? And was this, technically, *teaching*?

The months were marked in a series of holiday distractions—Thanksgiving, Christmas, Easter—and when I next looked up, I could see new growth on the elm trees and robins on the lawn. I had so immersed myself in this first year of teaching that I hardly noticed the time. I was going to make it through to June after all, and perhaps even accomplish something. It was prematurely warm that Tuesday, and we opened the windows wide to the smell of spring in the guidance class.

The students were talking about smoking—how tempting it was to smoke and how "cool" some of them felt when they had a cigarette between their fingers. Many of them talked about cigarettes and lung cancer and said it was stupid to smoke. Others told of parents who were unable to quit and about whose health they worried. The class, with a little help from me, carried the discussion about smoking to the end of the period. I did what I usually do when I'm uncertain about what to say. I listened sympathetically and affirmed comments that I knew to be true. I gave information when it was asked for. But I didn't see it as appropriate to lecture them about the evils of smoking. Instead I said, at the end of class, that I knew that once hooked, it was hard to give it up and that there were clearly grave health hazards in persisting with a smoking habit. I tried very hard not to preach or admonish them, figuring that they got enough of that from most adults anyway.

I could see, when the bell rang, that Vicki Frost was tarrying over the small job of gathering up her belongings and I knew, from experience, that such lingering often meant a private word was wanted. I lingered, too, ignoring the growling in my stomach that signaled lunch time, and waited for Vicki to take the initiative.

"Can I speak to you for a moment, Ms. Harris?" she asked.

"Of course, Vicki," I said and moved over to sit down at the desk directly across the aisle from her. She, too, sat and looked me in the eye.

"I think I'm going to fail biology," she said, her face serious, soft. "I have to talk to someone about it and I don't know what to do." She became quiet then, inspecting her fingers as if they had just begun to grow warts.

Vicki Frost was not a great student, but she was certainly better than average. She worked hard, got her work in on time, and what she did was competent. She was not much of a high-profile class participant, but she was not shy, either. When she did speak, she seemed to exhibit a great deal of "street smarts"— the kind of intelligence that made her seem old beyond her years. What distinguished her for me was that she was extraordinarily attractive. There was also something about Vicki that I found hard to like, something hard to define— something, I don't know what, that put me off. However, our relations in class had always been amiable.

"Tell me, Vicki," I asked, "what makes you think you're going to fail biology? Have your marks been down? Has your teacher said anything to you?"

"Well, the truth is, Ms. Harris," she continued, still studying her fingers, "that Mr. Ansari is coming on to me, like, you know? And I haven't encouraged him. I mean, actually, because I ignore him, I know he's going to get back at me by failing me. I just know it."

My mouth went dry, as if I had just swallowed an economy size box of cotton swabs, and my voice seemed to come out of my nose, filling the silence with what could be considered the most stupid question on earth. "How long has this been going on, Vicki?" But I didn't know what else to say, I was so shaken by her disclosure. I flashed back to that first staff meeting, at what seemed now to be years ago, remembering Joe Ansari, his incredibly handsome, youthful, shy face—he and I the two new teachers, being greeted by the applause from the other teachers. Could it be true? Could Joe Ansari be guilty of sexual harassment? Would Joe do this? It was hard to believe. One thing I did know for certain was that I ought not to make any premature or precipitate responses to Vicki. I had to find out more, to be certain, before I took any action. If Vicki's accusations were true, Joe was a menace to his classes and to the profession. If Vicki was imagining things—things that she thought to be true, but were exaggerated— a teacher's career and life could go down the tubes if falsely accused.

"Thank you, Vicki, for confiding in me," I managed to force out of my shriveled vocal cords. "You realize these are serious accusations and I'm going to have to think about what to do next, before I take any decisive action. We'll talk more on Thursday. But in the meanwhile, I'd appreciate it if you didn't mention this to anyone else. May I have your word on that?"

Vicki nodded, her head still down. Then she looked directly at me and said with a cry in her voice, "Oh, Ms. Harris. You're not going to let him fail me in biology, are you?"

I patted her on the arm and walked her to the door. Suddenly, I was not a bit hungry for lunch.

In the staff lunchroom, I saw Alice Carrillo on the sofa, just hanging up the telephone, and I made a beeline for her. "Alice," I blurted, "I've got to talk to you. It can't wait."

Alice was a veteran social studies teacher on the staff, and she had gotten me out of other sticky situations in the past. She was close to retirement, and I often thought of her as my guiding angel, someone I could always turn to for good and sensible advice. Every new teacher should have a colleague like Alice Carrillo.

"You look as if you'd just met Anne Boleyn with her head tucked underneath her arm," she smiled.

"Worse than that, Alice. Much worse." I proceeded to spill out the story of Vicki Frost and Joe Ansari, working my voice back to its natural pitch.

Alice looked thoughtful. "Yes, I know Vicki," she said. "I've had her in two of my classes and I think you have to reserve judgment about what she's telling you. Vicki is not as smart as she'd like to think she is, and science is definitely not her strong subject. She may be pulling your chain here, Pam, using the sexual harassment angle to cover the fact that she is getting exactly what she deserves in biology. You know, this wouldn't be the first time that Vicki has had trouble with a male teacher. If I were you, Pam, I'd talk to her more before you make any decisive moves."

I stared at Alice Carrillo, thunderstruck. It had not occurred to me that Vicki might have been manipulating me to intervene on her behalf with Joe Ansari, to get him to jack up her grade when she did not deserve it. This was beyond me.

"But," I bumbled, "aren't we supposed to report any suspicions of sexual abuse directly to the principal? And isn't this a suspicion? I mean, Alice, we have to think of the other students, too. If Vicki's allegation is truthful, there may be other girls at risk."

"I know, Pam. But one or two days? Is that going to make such a difference? Even if what Vicki has described is true, this can hardly be considered sexual abuse. Besides," she said with a smirk, "are you thinking of taking these suspicions to that enlightened figure of an educational leader, our esteemed principal, Bill Martin?"

My body went limp. Bill was the last person I could count on to respond in an intelligent, informed way. After eight months, I had found my first impression of him to be dead-on. He really was a jerk.

Two days later, Vicki came into the guidance class without so much as a nod in my direction. If she was experiencing any tension around the disclosure she had made on Tuesday, there was no sign of it. When the bell signaled the end of class, I asked if she would stay for a few minutes to talk with me.

"I'm concerned about what you told me on Tuesday," I went right to the point.

"Oh, that," she dismissed it with a wave of her hand, as if she had gotten the wrong change. "Forget it, Ms. Harris. Just forget I ever said anything. Okay?"

"Forget it?" I gasped. "How could I forget it? You've made a very serious accusation about a teacher in this school."

"Look, Ms. Harris," Vicki said, fixing me with her light blue eyes, "I've talked to my mom about it and we've decided that we're not going to do anything. I'm out of here in June, just two months from now. I just want to graduate and go. I'm not going to start making trouble here. It will ruin my last two months and spoil my graduation. Who needs it!"

"But, but," I couldn't find the words, "but if Mr. Ansari has harassed you, it's important to report it. There are other students to consider."

"I won't do it, Ms. Harris. Like, I just want to graduate without any trouble. What I told you the other day, that's history. And besides, I found out that Mr. Ansari is giving me a C in biology. I'll still have the grade-point average I need to get into college, so it's okay. After all, it's not like he actually *did* anything to me. It's just what he said."

Vicki picked up her books and turned on her heel, her long, blond hair bouncing jauntily from shoulder to shoulder. I watched her disappear down the stairs. What actually did happen between Vicki Frost and Joe Ansari? And what was my responsibility now?

Study Questions

1. What do you consider to be the substantive issues in this case? List them in what you see as their order of importance.

2. How would you describe the teacher in this case, Pam Harris? What do you see as her strengths as a teacher? What do you see as her weaknesses?

3. How would you describe the student, Vicki Frost? Talk together, and based on the data in the case, generate a list of characteristics that you think would describe her to another teacher.

4. How would you describe the principal, Bill Martin? How might teachers' views of a principal's competence influence critical decisions teachers have to make?

5. What, in your view, is the purpose of a guidance class? What do you suppose makes for a good guidance class experience for students? Where do your ideas come from?

6. Based on the data in this case, how would you evaluate the way Pam Harris taught her guidance class? What were some good features of what she did? What did you disapprove of? What knowledge base are you using in making these evaluations?

7. Based on the data in the case, what is your response to Vicki Frost's accusations against Joe Ansari? What data are you using to draw your conclusions? What assumptions have you made?

8. What, in your view, is sexual harassment? Where is the line drawn between a teacher's natural giving of affection to students, and sexual harassment? On what data are you basing your determinations?

9. What do you see as some of Pam's options? What do you see as the implications of the options you are suggesting? What do you see as the potential consequences?

10. What should Pam do? Faced with the data in the case, what would you do? On what values does your decision rest? What assumptions have you made?

†11. Talk about an experience you have had that is similar to the one in this case. What were the similarities? What were the significant differences? What action did you take? What might you have done in retrospect?

4.8 "I JUST WANT TO BE NORMAL"

"You'll want to have a look at this, Julie," Carol Ouiderkirk's crooked finger beckoned Julie Gardner through the private door into the principal's office. Julie's eyes immediately took in the fat, blue file folder on the study table as the principal shut the door.

"I thought you should have a read through the file before you make up your mind. Cole Hummel is not just a disturbed 11-year-old. He's probably the most difficult challenge you will face as a teacher. I'm afraid if we don't do something for him, he's going to wind up as a statistic."

Julie picked up the blue folder. Clipped to the inside cover was a copy of a newspaper article, headline screaming: ELEVEN-YEAR-OLD BOY ATTEMPTS SUICIDE. She pulled up the hardwood chair and began to read. It was not her idea of an ideal way to begin the school year.

Julie Gardner had come to Phoenix Park Elementary School directly from her professional training program at a nearby teachers college. When she was being interviewed for the job, Carol Ouiderkirk did not pull any punches in her description of life at the school. "This is not going to be anything like what you've been learning at the college, Julie," the principal said directly, and without a trace of paternalism. "This school has special challenges. I just want you to know what you'll be facing if you join this staff."

Julie's eyes followed the principal's finger as she pointed out the window to the area behind the school. "Over there are 100 units of subsidized city housing, and one-third of our children come from these facilities, living at the poverty level. Many families are dysfunctional, and there is a high incidence of child abuse.

"This immediate area behind the school has become a gathering place for teenage gangs that collect here from all over the city. They come on weekends, at night, to do drugs. The area is secluded, you can't see it from the street, so it makes for a particularly opportune gathering place. Last weekend, the police came and arrested eight kids. On Monday mornings, I have to get the custodian out there to clean up the garbage and the discarded drug paraphernalia—hypodermic needles and cookers used to make freebase. We've asked for more police patrols but haven't been successful in getting that support. You see, the school is right at the rapid transit station, so kids are coming in here from everywhere. At times, it gets so rowdy and out of control that the neighbors have gone out there with baseball bats to drive the kids away. It's been quite a mess." The principal paused, staring out the window as if she were willing the area behind the school to vanish. Julie waited until Carol Ouiderkirk was ready to continue.

"On the other side of the road, across the main street from the school, are all these new high-rise condos. To the parents from the subsidized housing project, these condos represent wealth beyond their dreams. And they are angry, very angry. Social services have been cut back drastically in this community, and these people literally have nothing. How do you suppose they feel to see their neighbors who go out and buy ripped designer jeans, for $85, from Saks Fifth Avenue, because 'ripped' is fashionable? It's a crazy world out there, Julie," Carol said, her voice soft with the enormity of the educational challenge.

"But, on the other hand," Carol's smile was filled with warmth, "you will never find teaching here boring!"

Julie didn't need a lot of time to decide. She knew that her learning and growing as a teacher in Phoenix Park School would be rooted in the fertile soil of urgent need and guided by the informed, wise, and caring hand of this principal. Without hesitation, she told Carol Ouiderkirk, "I want very much to join this staff."

In her first year at the Phoenix Park School, Julie saw that Carol Ouiderkirk had not exaggerated the situation. The incidence of children in trouble was very high. In a school with 330 children, more than 100 of them had been referred, at one time or another, for special services help. That could mean anything from psychiatric evaluation, to therapy, to court-authorized removal from home to foster care, to arrest. Julie, whose own growing-up experiences had been strictly suburban and middle class, had had only the vaguest appreciation of the kind of poverty she saw at Phoenix Park every day. One of the school services initiated by the principal was the Sharing Table—a table set up in the hallway that was the repository of any food left over, or unused, from the school lunch program. Parents from the project houses could come in and help themselves to sandwiches, fruit, milk; and children could also take food home for parents or siblings. Julie remembered the first time she was on lunch duty, when she saw Alvin stuffing half of his lunch in his schoolbag. She hadn't known then that he took food home every day for his mother.

Yet an outsider coming into the school would immediately perceive the calm, orderly, and caring learning environment. If the world outside the school was bizarre, the school was a haven for children—and for many children, the most safe and nurturing environment in their unhappy lives. How did the principal and the staff make this work? Not easily.

Julie's first year at Phoenix Park was full of the kind of experiences that she had never dreamed of during her preparatory years in college. It wasn't that the teaching itself was difficult. That she could handle. At the sixth-grade level, she enjoyed finding inventive ways to make the curriculum more interesting. The children liked working in cooperative learning groups, and they enjoyed reading from self-selected library books. Writing stories from their own experiences gave them opportunities to tell about their lives and to unload, in a climate of safety and respect, some of the personal baggage they carried in deep, dark places. Teaching the curriculum was the most satisfying and enjoyable part of Julie's time at school. It was the other "stuff" that was so hard—the endless telephone calls to deal with crises, the abusive parents, the inadequacy of social service agency help, and the outbursts of rage of individual children, who had endured so much and who, when triggered, released their fury in wild and hair-raising eruptions. But whenever Julie felt that she was unable to endure, there was always the staff, who shared her experiences, who knew and understood, and who would listen and support her through the latest crisis. And there was Carol Ouiderkirk, whose strong and stable leadership could always be counted on to steady the foundering ship.

Nothing in her first year, however, had prepared Julie for what was in Cole Hummel's file. Cole was being transferred to Phoenix Park from another elementary school in the district, where he had been enrolled since kindergarten. Cole had been badly abused physically and sexually by his biological father, who was now in prison for raping two teenage girls. A physically small, red-headed boy, who "looked like an angel," Cole might well be the single greatest challenge of Julie's entire teaching career. Carol was asking if Julie would be willing to accept Cole into her sixth-grade class.

As she turned the pages in the folder—reports from teachers, psychologists, psychiatrists, social workers, mental health workers—Cole Hummel's life played out, like a horror movie, in her troubled mind.

The physical and sexual abuse inflicted by Cole's father during his preschool years was horrifying. It was beyond Julie's credulity that an adult was capable of committing such sadistic and bestial acts on anyone, let alone his own child. After his father's imprisonment, life at home continued to be unstable and chaotic, his mother's behavior fluctuating wildly between bouts of desperate personal concern for Cole and violent, aggressive outbursts in reaction to Cole's own aggressive behavior. In Cole's 11 years of life, he had been removed from his home, at his mother's request, and placed in foster care on four different occasions. While Mrs. Hummel was aggressively vocal in her demands that "the system" help her deal with Cole, she was also negligent about following through on appointments with social service agencies.

The result of these early traumas and of the ongoing upheavals on Cole's current behavior was both horrifying and heartbreaking to Julie. Cole had severe emotional and behavioral problems. It was no surprise to Julie that his ability to learn was seriously compromised, that his motor skills were poor, that he was emotionally very immature, that he was full of anger and self-hate. It was no surprise that Cole was depressed a lot of the time and had a very negative self-concept. Frequent mood swings shifted from extreme depression, during which he would lay his head down on the desk and suck his thumb, to wild rages, when he would lose control, shout obscenities, kick and bite, and otherwise try to inflict bodily harm on others. Once Cole had picked up a skateboard and hurled it through the classroom window.

Adults who had tried to restrain Cole during his violent outbursts quickly found that restraint enraged him further, putting the adult in physical jeopardy. The urge to hurt, even to kill, surfaced repeatedly in Cole's behavior and in what he said to others. In one psychologist's report, it was noted that Cole's response was, "I wonder what it would be like to kill my mother and father."

It was understandable that Cole was disliked and rejected by his peers, some of whom had troubles of their own and some who were openly afraid of his outbursts. This was a boy who was intensely preoccupied with his victimization and confused about his sexuality; who masked his apprehensiveness about schoolwork behind an attitude of defiance; who needed one-to-one, highly personalized attention on any learning task.

By the time Julie got to the end of the file, her hands and feet had turned ice cold. Carol Ouiderkirk sat quietly and waited until Julie finished before she asked, "Well, Julie, what do you think? You realize that there's no hidden agenda here. You are completely free to decide for yourself whether you'll accept Cole. If you do, we'll all give you all the help we can. If you don't, I'll have to find another alternative."

Julie's face composed itself into a gray mask. In making her decision, she reflected on two pieces of information in the file. One was the item about Cole's having drawn a face of a boy weeping on the top of a spelling test paper. The other was the newspaper article that reported Cole's suicide attempt. In an interview with the psychiatrist at Children's Hospital following Cole's attempted suicide, Cole had told the therapist, "I just want to be normal." Both of these expressions of feeling touched Julie profoundly, eroding much of her resistance.

"I'll take him, Carol," she said, with a stone of doubt in her heart.

"Are you sure, Julie? I want you to be really sure. Because if you decide to take Cole, it would not be very good for him to have you change your mind later on. I want to avoid his being rejected again, at all costs. I'm sure you understand the implications of that."

Julie Gardner sucked on the bottom of her lip, a habit she'd had since she was a child that made her seem very much younger than her 22 years. "I'm sure, Carol. That is, I'm sure I want to give it a chance. I'm not sure that I'm up to the challenge, but then, who is? What makes me sure is that I know I can count on your help and support."

"Totally, Julie. Totally." The principal's voice closed the discussion, and the two women embraced. Julie left the inner room through the main office and passed the secretary's desk without seeing her. It was going to be a long weekend.

Was there a better way to prepare herself for her new sixth-grade student? Suit of armor, perhaps? Five years of clinical training at the psychiatric unit of Children's Hospital? She didn't know.

Cole Hummel was small for his age, a little red-headed boy who truly had the face of an angel. It was only a half an hour into the first day of school when his attention-seeking behavior came into full play. As Julie called the children's names and tried to get to know who they were, Cole took off his shirt and put it on over his face. During recess, he was taken to the office for throwing eggs, which he had brought from home, at the school building.

To Julie's repeated requests for class participation, Cole responded defiantly. "I'm not going to do this stuff. This stuff is boring. It's doo-doo."

Julie tried hard to keep her cool. She felt that the best response to Cole's defiance was to ignore him, not to make a big deal over these initial testing behaviors. The school day seemed 48 hours long with Cole in the room. His rude, flippant remarks played a constant counterpoint to all classroom activity.

When reproached, he would respond, "I don't care." At the end of the first day of school, Julie was ready for the Christmas holidays.

By Friday, nothing had changed. Cole continued to be defiant when he was asked to do schoolwork. He continued to be apathetic or indifferent to potential consequences. His response, "I don't care," seemed to Julie a rebuff to her efforts to establish any rapport. In the staff room on Friday afternoon after school, Julie talked to a veteran teacher, Mollie Askwith, who told her nothing that she did not already know.

"Look, Julie. This is a deeply troubled boy who is full of rage and self-hatred. You're not going to make major inroads with him in a week. He has every reason to be mistrustful of adults, so why on earth should he trust you? Why should he allow you to get anywhere near him emotionally? His defenses are way up. He's protecting himself, and maybe that's the best he can do at this moment in his life. I know that kind of clinical analysis doesn't help you a lot with his day-to-day behavior. But there are no miracle cures for anything, and certainly no magic wand to fix what is broken in Cole Hummel's life."

"That's not exactly what I needed to hear right now, Mollie," Julie pouted.

"Okay, then, how 'bout let's go down to the pub with the rest of the staff and we'll raise a glass to the end of the first week of school?"

Julie smiled. "Yeah, sure. Maybe the best thing to do is to put the week behind me. But how do I gear up for week number two? Is there a book I can read that will help?"

Mollie chuckled. "How about Peter Blatty's *The Exorcist*? At least you'll know you're not the only one with problems."

Monday began with new problems. Cole had brought several pornographic magazines to school and was showing them to a group of boys in the back of the room. When Julie came over to see what was going on, she overheard Cole telling the boys in the group that he could get younger children to do what he wanted sexually and that he had "humped" a neighbor's 5-year-old daughter in the garage. She also heard him tell Foster, another boy in the class, that he would "suck his dick" after school if Foster would give him two candy bars.

Julie felt as if she had been struck dumb. She stood there, listening and watching this angel-faced boy unloose the vilest sexual obscenities she had ever heard. Her first reaction was to charge into the group and begin yelling reprimands, but she held herself back from that hysterical response. Instead, she stood there, paralyzed with indecision, wondering what to do next.

Study Questions

1. What do you see as the important issues in this case? Talk together and list the issues in what you consider to be their order of importance.
2. Given the description of the school in this case, what kind of teacher is

needed to do a good job here? What do you consider a "good job?" Write a profile describing the ideal teacher for this school.

3. What toll does a child like Cole Hummel take on a teacher? How does a teacher manage to keep his or her positive attitude toward teaching when faced with the day-to-day behavior of a Cole Hummel?

4. What do you see as the necessary conditions for a principal and a teaching staff to make a school like Phoenix Park a safe and nurturing learning environment for the children described in this case?

5. Using the data in the case, develop a 50-word working hypothesis about Cole that contains information about his *behavior*, the *causative factors* contributing to that behavior, and recommendations for *classroom treatment.*

6. How do you suppose Julie Gardner might have prepared herself for Cole Hummel? What ideas do you have on this? What, if anything, should she have done differently in response to Cole's behavior on the first day of school?

7. What, in your view, is behind Cole's statement, "I don't care"? What data, from the literature on child development, support your position?

8. What do you suppose is a reasonable projection about the time involved before Cole's dysfunctional behaviors can be expected to diminish, given high-quality, effective classroom treatment? What assumptions are being made?

9. What teaching plan (including curriculum, teaching strategies, and psycho-social interventions) do you see as appropriate for Cole Hummel? How is your teaching plan congruent with the working hypothesis you developed in Question 5?

10. How would you advise Julie to act in response to the last scene in the case? What assumptions are being made? What do you see as some potential consequences of the actions you are recommending?

†11. Talk about a student from your own teaching experience whose behavior was dysfunctional. Talk about the child's behavior, how it affected you, the other children, the learning climate in the classroom. Talk about how you responded and what, in retrospect, you might have done differently.

4.9 I THINK HE'S STONED

The windows of the seminar room looked out on the park-like lawn of the campus, giving an illusion of pastoral serenity to this urban state college campus located on the southwest edge of a bustling city. Carl Hackman dropped his books on the table, hung his jacket on the back of the chair, and went over to the windows. The warm spring afternoon was not exactly conducive to a meeting with his student teaching seminar group. But he'd certainly rather be here, on this Friday afternoon, than back in his classroom. Maybe he'd have a chance to talk about some of the things that were happening in his class that were giving him sleepless nights. Wasn't that what the student teaching seminar was supposed to be about—to share classroom experiences and get some practical help? Up to now, these Friday afternoon meetings had been long on theory and very short on real, practical help. How was he going to face his own class if he couldn't even begin to resolve the problems of his student teaching practicum?

Carl Hackman was delighted when he received his student teaching assignment. He had heard all the "war" stories about being placed in an inner-city school and had already made up his mind to protest such an assignment if it came to that. But a lucky star landed him in Hawthorne Middle School, right in the heart of Forest Hill, the most affluent neighborhood in the city. Carl was sure he had it made. Bright, advantaged kids, seventh grade, all the equipment and supplies he could wish for—it was a student teacher's dream come true. But even lucky stars have a dark underside. Kate Miramonte, his mentor teacher, had suddenly become ill and had to take extended sick leave after the first two weeks of Carl's term. The long-term substitute brought in to replace Kate didn't seem to know much more about teaching than Carl did. Harold Tribe was glad to leave most of the important classroom decisions to Carl, as they both waited for the return of Kate Miramonte. Having Harold there as another body didn't do much to alleviate Carl's stress. Since Kate's sudden and untimely illness, Carl felt as if he had been thrown into the sea without a life preserver. Harold had a funny habit of manipulating situations so that Carl would bear the full brunt of classroom activities, and Carl found himself thrust into the role of "teacher" long before he had acquired the experience to feel comfortable in the job. His college supervisor, Greg Poirier, told Carl that the student teaching experience he was getting was invaluable. But Carl didn't see it that way. It was now six weeks since Kate took leave, and it seemed unlikely that she would be able to return before Carl's student teaching semester was finished. Was he learning to teach, Carl wondered? Could what he was doing in class be called teaching? It seemed to Carl that he was going from crisis to crisis, putting out one brush fire after another. Yeah, sure, he was getting experience all right. But what kind of experience? He was desperate for some practical help, for some good advice, for some how-to's. Having been thrust too soon into a situation in which he had to make the important teaching decisions in this seventh-grade class, he felt he was drowning in a sea of uncertainty.

Carl's ideas about the "advantaged kids" at Hawthorne Middle School quickly went down the tubes. While many of the students did, in fact, come from some of the most affluent homes in the city, and while many of them had expensive clothes, fat allowances, and all the toys in the F.A.O. Schwartz' catalogue, many of them also came from broken families or had parents whose successful and lucrative careers often kept them busy and emotionally withdrawn from their offspring. While Carl originally thought that "behavior problems" in the classroom would not be something he would have to be worried about at Hawthorne Middle School, he was surprised and chagrined to learn that classroom behavior was his most pressing concern. Of course, not all the students in his seventh-grade class were difficult. Some were quite nice. But he did have a group of five boys, who had been together since fourth grade, who were disrespectful, acted out, and were real trouble makers. The parents of these five boys were away most of the time and did not, overall, seem to show much interest in their children. The boys seemed to get a sense of power from belonging to the group, and the group seemed to give each of them license to do things that he might not otherwise do on his own.

Sean Crosby was one of the more troubled boys in the group. Sean's parents were divorced, and he was now living with his mother and stepfather. Sean's father, a successful attorney, had left Sean's mother to live with a young woman whom Sean called "my father's bimbo." He referred to his mother's husband as "that f——wad." Sean's school records revealed that neither of his parents had wanted custody of Sean when their marriage broke up, but that Mrs. Crosby finally agreed that Sean could live with her when she remarried.

To Carl, Sean's behavior was incomprehensible. Sean was constantly off-task; when reprimanded, he was rude and indifferent. Without provocation, Sean would suddenly leap out of his seat and assume the behavior that he had seen in the movie *Awakenings*—spastic, random movements of legs, arms, head; incoherent speech. The school counselor told Carl that there was nothing wrong with Sean and that these outbursts were merely attention-seeking behaviors. But Carl was still at a loss as to how to deal with them. The counselor suggested that Carl try using "positive reinforcement" with Sean, but in spite of Carl's efforts to remember to reward Sean's good behavior positively, Sean would respond to Carl's attempts with further acting-out antics. Positive reinforcement certainly was failing with Sean.

Carl found himself more and more perplexed about what to do, and his feelings of uncertainty began to pervade every classroom decision. He was just never sure about what to do; about what was right. The more Carl revealed his uncertainty to the students, the more Sean and his friends' in-class behaviors seemed to escalate. Carl made a calendar at home and began to mark off the number of days left in his student teaching practicum. He couldn't imagine that an inner-city school assignment could be any worse than what he had been dealt at the Hawthorne Middle School.

On Monday of the week of his student teaching seminar, Carl noticed that the boys in the "Group of Five" had all came back from lunch chewing gum and wearing the same overpowering cologne. Carl couldn't help noticing that their eyes had a glazed look, and even more unusual was the fact that they all seemed particularly quiet. Carl's suspicions were alerted, but he felt that he did not have enough information to act.

On Tuesday, Carl paid particular attention to the boys' discussion just before lunch, and he overheard that they were all going to Sean's house again during the lunch break. After lunch, once again, the "Group of Five" came in chewing gum and smelling like a downtown brothel. Sean put his head down on his desk, but Carl could see that his eyes were glazed over and that he was "out of it." Carl consulted with Harold, who told him to just forget it.

"I don't want to get involved with this," Harold protested. "And what do you expect *me* to do? If you confront Sean, or any of the other boys, do you expect any of them to admit they're doing drugs? And where is your proof? You're just guessing."

By Wednesday afternoon, when the events of the last two days had once again been repeated, Carl decided that it was time to talk to the principal. Over Harold's objections, Carl approached the principal about the behavior of the group of boys in his class. Loretta Hagan was concerned. She told Carl that she would come into his classroom on Thursday, just after lunch, and make some observations for herself, and that Carl and Harold should come to her office Thursday after school to decide on further action.

Based on what she saw, Loretta Hagan telephoned Sean's mother at her office, asking her to come to school that afternoon to meet with both teachers and the principal. Sean's mother, instead of being concerned, was aggressively defensive. First she complained bitterly about having to leave her "highly responsible" job duties to come to school to talk about Sean. Then, when she was told about the classroom incidents, she refused to believe that Sean might be smoking pot. "My son," she shrieked, "would never do anything like that. How could you even suspect him of such a thing!" She turned to Carl and Harold and accused them of making up a story about Sean "just because they dislike him" and because they were not able to help him learn. "You teachers are all alike," she fumed. "When you have a boy who needs help with his schoolwork, and you are too lazy to give him the extra help he needs, you try to put the blame on the child." Harold Tribe looked down at the creases in his trousers. Carl felt that he had been caught up in a hurricane. He had no idea of what he should say in response to Mrs. Crosby's tirade, and so he sat back in his chair and let the principal carry the ball.

In spite of Loretta Hagan's attempts to calm Mrs. Crosby down, Sean's mother's voice kept getting more shrill. She finally got up and stormed out of the office, saying, "I've got to get back to work. I don't want to have this conversation any more." Loretta Hagan looked over at Carl and Harold and shrugged her shoulders. "Well," she said, "obviously Mrs. Crosby is not going to cooperate with us in this. I think we need to monitor Sean's behavior very closely and see if we can get any direct evidence that he's taking drugs. If the situation persists, we may have to override Mrs. Crosby and go directly to the authorities."

On Friday morning, Carl was totally unprepared for Sean's vicious attack. The boy came storming into class and confronted the student teacher directly. "You f——wad," the boy screamed. "How come you told my mother that I was taking drugs. I never did. Now, I'm going to be grounded, and my allowance is cut and it's all your fault, you f——wad. She's going to tell my dad, and he won't take me skiing this Easter." Carl stood there while the boy, his fury spent, let his arms hang down to his side, went to his seat, put his head down, and began to sob. Harold busied himself with counting out social studies textbooks while Carl considered picking up his jacket and leaving that classroom forever. For once, he was actually looking forward to the student teaching seminar that afternoon.

Greg Poirier called his 16 student teachers to attention while he first addressed the "business" agenda of the student teaching seminar. There were matters of teaching credentials to be discussed and other end-of-semester details that needed cleaning up. "What about an end-of-term party?" Greg asked. Thirty minutes into the business agenda and already Carl's eyes were drooping. It had been a tough week.

"This afternoon," Greg announced, "I'd like you to team up in groups of four. All the people in a group will have a chance to talk with one another, with respect to what each of you considers to be a classroom problem that has given you some concern." Carl smirked when he heard Greg's word, *concern*. How about *nightmare*, he mused. "I'd like," Greg continued, "for each of you to tell the others in your group what seems to be giving you difficulty in your student teaching assignment. Now, this may be a problem with curriculum or it may be a problem with a student's behavior. It may be some difficulty that you are having with an individual child. It can be anything. Once the person in the group has presented his or her problem, then the others in the group try to advise the person with the problem about what to do next. Now, are the instructions clear?" The students nodded, and at Greg's signal, they began to arrange themselves into groups of four.

Carl found himself in a group with Brent, Cheryl, and Ivor, and as they arranged their chairs around in a small circle, Carl picked up the ball. "Listen, you guys," he asserted. "I've got a problem that is making me crazy. I need help and I need help now. I'm just about at my wits end, and if I don't get some resolution, I'm thinking about quitting student teaching." Carl looked down and saw that his hands were trembling as he unloaded the story of Sean, his suspicions about the students' using drugs, and the response of Sean's mother. He also told the group about what Sean had said to him only this morning. As they looked at him in disbelief, he remembered to tell them about Kate Miramonte and the long-term substitute, Harold Tribe. When he was finished with his stories, he sat back in his chair, his face flushed, his hands ice cold. "Well, you guys? What do I do next?"

Study Questions

1. What do you see as the critical issues of this case? Discuss these with your group and then, talking together, decide what you consider to be *the* critical issue.
2. Based on the data in this case, what do you consider to be Carl Hackman's strengths as a student teacher? What do you consider to be some weaknesses?
3. How do you explain Carl's uncertainty with respect to classroom decisions? What hypotheses can you suggest that would account for it? How, in your view, do the classroom events in this case contribute to Carl's uncertainty? How are Carl and Harold Tribe alike? How are they different?
4. How does uncertainty provoke the need for specific, concrete answers to complex situations? How do you explain the way this works?
5. How would you describe Sean Crosby? What is your professional view of his behavior?
6. Based upon the data in the case, what conclusion do you draw about the "Group of Five" and the possibility they have been using drugs? What data have you used in drawing your conclusion?
7. What, in your view, should Carl have done about his suspicions? What, in your view, should Carl have said (if anything) to Sean and the other boys? What might he have said to Sean's mother during the after-school conference? What do you see as the potential consequences of the actions you are advising?
8. When a teacher (or a student teacher) has suspicions that a student is using drugs, what actions need to be taken? Why do you believe such actions are appropriate?
9. If you were a member of Carl's seminar group, how would you respond to his urgent request for help? What "answers" would you give him that would be appropriate for his situation?
†10. To what student teaching (teaching) situation of your own does this case relate? Talk about your own situation and describe how you dealt with it. In retrospect, what do you consider to be appropriate actions? What might you have done differently?

RELATED READINGS

Ashton-Warner, Sylvia. 1972. *Spearpoint.* New York: Knopf.

Baroody, Arthur. 1987. *Children's Mathematical Thinking.* New York: Teachers College Press.

Boehm, Ann E., and Weinberg, Richard A. 1987. *The Classroom Observer.* New York: Teachers College Press.

Cohen, Dorothy, and Stern, Virginia, with Balaban, Nancy. 1983. *Observing and Recording the Behavior of Children.* New York: Teachers College Press.

Deutch, Charles. 1982. *Broken Bottles, Broken Dreams.* New York: Teachers College Press.

Dorris, Michael. 1989. *The Broken Cord.* New York: HarperCollins.

Elkind, David. 1978. *A Sympathetic Understanding of the Child from Birth to Sixteen.* Boston: Allyn & Bacon.

Farrell, Edwin. 1990. *Hanging In and Dropping Out.* New York: Teachers College Press.

Johnston, Bernard. 1971. *The Literature of Learning.* New York: Holt, Rinehart & Winston.

Kendall, Frances E. 1983. *Diversity in the Classroom.* New York: Teachers College Press.

Landau, Elliott D.; Epstein, Sherrie Landau; and Stone, Ann Plaat. 1972. *Child Development Through Literature.* Englewood Cliffs, NJ: Prentice-Hall.

Meyers Briggs, Elizabeth. 1980. *Gifts Differing.* Palo Alto, CA: Consulting Psychologists Press.

Mongon, Denis, and Hart, Susan. 1989. *Improving Classroom Behavior.* New York: Teachers College Press.

Paley, Vivian. 1988. *Bad Guys Don't Have Birthdays.* Chicago: University of Chicago Press.

Paley, Vivian. 1990. *The Boy Who Would Be a Helicopter.* Chicago: University of Chicago Press.

Paley, Vivian. 1992. *You Can't Say You Can't Play.* Chicago: University of Chicago Press.

Postman, Neil. 1982. *The Disappearance of Childhood.* New York: Delacorte.

Purkey, William W. 1970. *Self-Concept and School Achievement.* Englewood Cliffs, NJ: Prentice-Hall.

Ramsey, Patricia G. 1991. *Making Friends in School.* New York: Teachers College Press.

Raths, Louis E. 1972. *Meeting Children's Emotional Needs.* Columbus, OH: Merrill.

Raths, Louis E.; Simon, Sidney; and Harmin, Merrill. 1978. *Values and Teaching.* Columbus, OH: Merrill.

Raths, Louis E.; Wassermann, Selma; Jonas, Arthur; and Rothstein, Arnold. 1986. *Teaching for Thinking: Theory, Strategies and Activities for the Classroom.* New York: Teachers College Press.

Stevens, Linda J., and Price, Marianne. (Ed.). 1992. "Special Section on Children at Risk." *Phi Delta Kappan,* 74(1), 15–40, 57–71.

Webber, Marlene. 1991. *Street Kids.* Toronto: University of Toronto Press.

5 | CASES: The Teacher and the Curriculum

In the cases in Chapters 3 and 4, teachers wrestle with decisions that emerge from the evolving self-as-professional and the teacher's relationship with individual and groups of students, respectively. In this chapter, the decision-making dilemmas enter that professional domain called "the classroom." It is in this context that teacher-as-person and teachers and students combine, forming a triangular relationship with the myriad events that make up classroom life. What curriculum concepts should be emphasized? How should instruction be organized to meet individual needs and articulated learning objectives? Who should play significant roles in shaping curriculum? What evaluation practices are both fair and congruent with students' learning needs? How do teachers take the risks of innovation? Trying to decide what to do in these cases is further confounded by the increased number of both players and variables. Shifting conditions add further to uncertainty. The classroom is not a place for sissies.

Using the best data on hand, choosing appropriate actions, and making good decisions are what life in classrooms is all about. The experience of choosing and practice in reflecting on choice make for more thoughtful, intelligent decision making. Wrestling with the challenge of making choices, and getting practice in reflecting on choice, should arm you with tools to serve you well in your own quest for "what to do."

Each case is followed by a list of questions, with additional questions for those with classroom teaching experience denoted by a dagger.

5.1 WE ONLY DO THE TRIED AND PROVEN THINGS

The morning in August that she was interviewed for the job was beastly hot and humid—summer's last gasp. Her linen dress was limp with heat exhaustion, and she was afraid that circles of sweat were framing her armpits. Heat and nerves were a deadly combination. How could she hope to make a good impression when she felt so damp and smelly, like an overused dishcloth?

The school secretary didn't seem to notice. She smiled warmly, and as their eyes met, Naomi was reassured. "Mrs. Milton is expecting you. I'll tell her you're here. Would you like a coffee while you're waiting?"

"No, thanks very much," Naomi shook her head. "I'll just sit here and try to cool off a bit. The drive over was pretty grueling."

"I know what you mean. The traffic can be awful at this time of morning. And if you don't have air conditioning in your car, by the time you get here, you are ready to be hung out to dry. I'll be glad when this summer is over." The secretary smiled again, and Naomi thought that if this was the tone of the school office, the interview with the principal couldn't be all bad.

Ursula Milton came out of her office to greet her in person. "Mrs. Kline?" She offered her cool, soft hand and took Naomi's sweaty one. "I'm very pleased to meet you. Mrs. Van Pelt called me from the board office and spoke to me about her interview with you yesterday. She thinks that you're just right for this job."

Naomi felt her shoulders release some of the tension she hadn't even known she was carrying. She had thought that the interview with the superintendent, Mrs. Van Pelt, had gone well, but she had not expected that her recommendation to Ursula Milton would be so strong. Naomi felt some of her confidence return as she sat in the chair across the desk from the principal of the Wisdom Valley School.

Ursula Milton got right down to business. Her manner, her language, her appearance were all of a whole—formal, reserved, distant, but never unkind. Naomi wondered how she could manage to look so cool on such a sweltering day. Even though the office was not air conditioned, Ursula Milton looked as if she just stepped out of a page of *Women's Wear Daily*—the right attire for the professional, fiftysomething woman. Naomi knew, even from this brief interview, that once Ursula Milton made up her mind about something, it would not be easy to persuade her otherwise.

"Tell me something about yourself, Mrs. Kline," Mrs. Milton asked, the smile never leaving her face.

"Well, as you know from my file, I've had six months experience as a long-term substitute downstate. I just moved here with my husband, and I was hoping to find a teaching position close to home. When I called Mrs. Van Pelt at the board office, she told me that a position at the primary level had opened in your school."

"I see from your application that you took your teacher training at State College," Milton formed the statement as a question.

"Yes, that is correct," Naomi replied, not sure where this line of questioning was leading.

"I happen to know that program quite well," Milton smiled. "You get a very good grounding in the important courses—history of education, educational psychology, and, of course, the whole methods sequence. I know that is a very good preparation for teaching. You will have the kind of background I believe is very important for a beginning teacher."

Naomi looked past the principal to the window behind her. She was afraid that if she looked into her eyes, Milton would somehow see the truth there, as she lied and said, "Oh, yes. The program was very good." In truth, she knew that the courses she had taken were only as good as the teachers who gave them. Those good teachers made whatever courses she took with them exciting and meaningful. In those classes where the teachers were less than good, the courses left her unchallenged and unfulfilled. It was not the program itself that made the difference, it was the good teachers who made certain parts of the program good. On this issue, she and the principal seemed of different minds, but she knew well enough not to open this debate with the principal at this time, certainly not if she wanted this job.

If Ursula Milton suspected Naomi's true feelings, she did not let on. Instead, she began to talk about the teaching position at Wisdom Valley School as if it were already Naomi's.

"As you know, Mrs. Kline, this school is one of the first built in this community, and we pride ourselves on its record. The parents in this district expect quality education for their children, and we believe it's our job to give them quality education. I think you will enjoy these children, and I know that you will enjoy being on our staff." At this point, Ursula Milton stood up, extended her hand across the desk, and said, "Let me be the first to welcome you to the staff of Wisdom Valley School." Keeping a tight grip on her hand, the principal ushered Naomi to the door.

As Ann Sweet, the school secretary, offered her welcome to Naomi as well, Naomi couldn't help observing the difference in style between the women in the outer and inner offices. Ann was warm, friendly, relaxed, while Ursula Milton was distant, cool, and very formal. "Well," thought Naomi, "if Ann can get along with her, why can't I?"

"I'll bet you'd like to have a look at your classroom," Ann offered, and Naomi was overcome with gratitude. "I also have a class list for you. Even though you won't know any of the children, you'll at least know their names. Now what else can I help you with?"

Naomi surveyed the classroom: standard school issue—a four-sided box with one window wall that looked out onto Wisdom Valley Road. The room was like an oven, but it was clear that it had been shined and polished to make it ready for the first day of school. Barren walls, scrubbed chalkboards, the desks arranged precisely one behind the other, in five military-looking rows, with the chairs neatly placed on each. As Naomi looked around, she could already see what it would look like with a little color, a few pictures and plants, a reading corner, and lots of children's work on the walls.

"Ann, I'll want to spend some time fixing up the classroom before school starts, maybe early next week. Would that be okay with you? And, of course, I'll need some supplies. You know, posterboard, newsprint, paper, primary pencils, felt pens—all that stuff."

Naomi thought she detected a sign of something, she didn't know what, on Ann's face. "Oh, supplies," she said. "Of course. Those you'll have to get directly from Mrs. Milton. She's the only one who has the key to the supply closet. She'll be in all of next week, so when you come in to work on your room, you can get the supplies then. But I think it's probably a good idea if you come to her with a list of what you need. She would much prefer to work with your list."

Naomi shrugged. In her other school, the supply room had always been open and teachers were trusted to get what they needed when they needed it. This business of having to ask the principal each time you needed a piece of chalk or some masking tape seemed to her to be a colossal waste of time. A worst-case scenario suggested the principal's excessive control needs in full play. "Uh, oh," Naomi thought. "What have we got here?"

It didn't take long for Naomi to be caught up fully in her teaching at the Wisdom Valley School. She found her first graders delightful, the parents concerned and supportive, the school staff friendly and welcoming. Even the custodian, Ellwood North, was a helpful and cheerful ally, although he frankly would have preferred that she let go of her "progressive" ideas of room arrangement. "It was infinitely easier to sweep up when the tables were in rows," he had told her during that first week of school. "These desks in groups of four are a damn nuisance." This had become an ongoing repartee between them, but always a good natured one. On the surface, teaching at Wisdom Valley School seemed ideal.

Naomi began her first-grade program with activities that allowed her to get to know her children better. There was lots of classroom discussion, showing-and-telling, and talking about things that mattered to them. Through the ideas that children shared, she was able to find out more about what interested them and what their lives were like outside school. Naomi built into her program a rich array of creative activities—painting, drawing, coloring, clay, fingerpaint, music, drama; never mind that her supplies excluded easels, blocks, and a sandtable, since these were all considered "kindergarten equipment" and inappropriate for first grade. Couched under the rubric of "reading readiness," Naomi's creative activities were never questioned, and on the few occasions when Ursula Milton came into her classroom, she seemed genuinely pleased with the way the room looked and how the children were behaving. In the third week of September, Ellwood North delivered 25 copies of the reading readiness workbooks to her classroom. Naomi looked them over, decided she could do as well or better by instructing her children more informally on those reading readiness skills, and packed the workbooks into a rear cupboard. She did not see the need for formal instruction in skills like left-to-right progression, rhyming words, and letter names, since these skills were already being taught in a more integrated way, through her more experiential approach. She figured that if any child came up "wanting" when her periodic overall class assessments were made, she could always revert to the workbook for that child in need.

By the end of September, she had settled comfortably into her teaching life at Wisdom Valley School and was enjoying herself immensely. As she mentioned to her husband, Carl, one evening, "This is as close to perfect as it can get."

He looked at her over the rims of his glasses and said, "Don't jinx it, babe!"

It was at the staff meeting the following Monday that a different picture began to emerge. Ursula Milton liked to have the staff meeting separated into "primary" and "intermediate" cohorts, with the primary teachers meeting on Monday, and the intermediate teachers on Tuesday. Because much of the agenda was grade-specific, Milton felt it was more efficient to address these groups separately. Naomi wondered whether double the number of meetings was worth it for the principal, and whether this separation of teachers was a good thing for the overall unity of the staff. Perhaps it didn't matter? Perhaps an ambience of two separate schools contained in one building was also an effective way to run a school? What did she know? After all, this was only her first permanent teaching assignment.

In the staff room, Ursula Milton sat at the head of two long tables linked together at their short ends, as the primary teachers filled all the spaces around the long, narrow rectangle. Ursula smiled, chatted pleasantly with the two women who sat nearest her, both veteran teachers who had been there since the school opened. Naomi thought that this was the most friendly behavior she had yet seen in her principal. Yet beneath the pleasant chatter, Milton managed to keep her distance from the group. How did she do it? How did she manage, through her behavior, to signal that she was not a part, but apart?

"I'd like to get down to business, please," Ursula tapped the table with her pencil, and the teachers became quiet. "There are several bulletins from Mrs. Van Pelt. I'll pass these copies along to you so each of you can have your own copy."

"Now, the first item says, 'The school nurse will have hours only on Mondays and Thursdays of each week. If an emergency occurs on other days, we are to telephone the central office.' Is that clear?"

Naomi watched in grim fascination as the principal proceeded to read aloud every word on the bulletins, in spite of the fact that each teacher had a copy of the bulletin on the table directly in front of her. This oral reading of the bulletins took approximately 90 minutes of meeting time. After a few additional school-based announcements, the principal thanked the staff and left. No sooner was she out of earshot, when Priscilla D'Antonio threw her arms up in disgust.

"Here she goes again!" scoffed Priscilla. "She still thinks we can't read and that she has to read these notices to us."

"Boring. Boring. Boring," said Lorraine. "What a waste of time."

"I wonder if she reads aloud to the intermediate teachers," queried Stella. "Would they put up with it?"

Naomi listened to the complaints. The teachers felt infantilized, yet no one would voice her complaints to the offender. So life in the paradise of Wisdom Valley School was not as idyllic as it had appeared.

On the Friday of that week, the district's Professional Development Day allowed for teachers to select, from a large array of activities, those one or two that were appropriate to each individual teacher's professional needs. Naomi chose an all-day workshop on Organic Teaching: The Key Vocabulary Road to Reading. She had heard of Sylvia Ashton-Warner's work with Maori children in New Zealand, and she found the approach fascinating. It made sense to her that children would learn to read by choosing their own words, and that reading would be a very personal, highly individualized journey. The all-day workshop excited her and she was eager to try this approach in her own classroom. On the weekend, she purchased and read Ashton-Warner's book *Teacher*. By Sunday evening, she was convinced not only that the key vocabulary approach to beginning reading would be effective in promoting literacy, but also that it would be a more joyful way to teach reading and writing. Surely there *were* better ways to teach reading than with the Dick and Jane readers! Goodbye, "Run, Dick, run." Goodbye to "See Spot jump." Hello "ghost" and "kiss" and "Mummy" and "dark" and "sandcastle."

In retrospect, she thought she should have known better. Given Ursula Milton's obvious control needs, she should have just gone her own way, kept her classroom door closed, and begun the program as she had planned. But no. She had to be too enthusiastic. She had to tell of her plans. She thought she was doing the right thing.

On Monday afternoon, directly after the children left school, Naomi went down to the general office and asked Ann Sweet if she could see the principal.

"She's not busy," said Ann. "Go right in."

Naomi went into the inner sanctum and sat on the edge of the chair across from the principal's desk. In her excitement, the words came spilling out, tumbling from her lips and into the air space that separated teacher from administrator.

The smile never left Ursula Milton's lips, but her eyes were cold. "Oh, Mrs. Kline. What you are proposing are hardly traditional methods. They are experimental, purely experimental. We do not do any experimenting at Wisdom Valley School, my dear. When you have more experience, you will know that. In this school, we use only the tried and proven ways of teaching." The principal got up, a signal that the conference was over.

Study Questions

1. What do you see as the key issues in this case? Talk together and make a list of what you consider to be the key issues.
2. How would you describe the new teacher, Naomi Kline? Make a list of what you consider to be her chief attributes. Working together, construct a short, one-paragraph profile that would describe her.
3. How would you describe the principal, Ursula Milton? Make a list of what you consider to be her identifiable attributes. Working together, construct a short, one-paragraph profile that would describe her.
4. What can you tell about Naomi Kline's first-grade program from the data in this case? What is your opinion of this type of primary program? What educational beliefs does a teacher have to have in order to operate such a program?
5. What do you know about the kind of program (the key vocabulary approach to beginning reading and writing) that Naomi Kline is proposing to the principal? Based on the data in the case, what do you see as some merits of such an approach? What do you see as some potential disadvantages?
6. What is your opinion of the position taken by the principal—that teachers should not try any new programs; that they should stick to what is tried and proven? What assumptions are implicit in this statement? What educational data support your opinion?
7. Should Naomi Kline have taken her proposal to the principal? What do you think? Should she have closed her classroom door and done what she had planned? What are the pros and cons of both of those actions?
8. What should Naomi Kline do now? What assumptions are implicit in the suggestions you are making? What are some consequences of the actions you are proposing?
†9. To what personal experience does this case relate? Talk about it in your group and tell how you resolved the dilemma for yourself. Talk about the consequences of your actions and what you might have done in retrospect.

5.2   CHILDREN WORKING AS SELF-MOTIVATED LEARNERS?
IT DOESN'T WORK!

There were 36 of them the year I was assigned to teach a sixth-grade class in a suburban school about 35 miles from a large metropolitan area. The size of the class was a challenge in itself. It was also the year that I was determined to put all of my ideas about a student-centered classroom into operation—ideas that I had learned during my sabbatical year, enrolled in courses at the university. My class would have teaching for thinking, student self-evaluation, cooperative learning—the whole banana. I was full of energy and very idealistic about what my classroom could become, and I was convinced that this was going to be my best teaching year.

The students were a mixed lot, much like any teacher finds in a hetero-geneously grouped class. About 12 of them were quite bright, alive, vigorous—the "stars." About 6 of these 12 were smug and self-satisfied with their intellectual skills. They considered themselves to be the intellectual elite, with license to mock and villify all the other children who didn't qualify for inclusion in their group. On the other end of the behavioral spectrum was a group of 12 children whose behaviors revealed other types of problems: extreme aggressiveness, consider-able deficits in their ability to think for themselves, passivity and indifference to learning, lack of self-confidence and diminished self-esteem; poor academic per-formance. In the middle was another group of 12—pleasant, friendly, nice kids, who made no trouble and made no headlines. In other words, a "normal" het-erogeneous class.

The first two or three weeks of the school year, the "honeymoon" period, passed uneventfully. We got to know one another better. We decorated the class-room after considerable debate about who would do what and where. So what if the classroom resembled the horse that was designed by a committee? We estab-lished some routines. I told them about my plans for the school year: emphasis on thinking, working in groups, project work in social studies and science, self-pacing and choice with respect to certain areas of the curriculum, math and reading work keyed to individual learning needs, self-evaluation of growth. Heavy-duty John Dewey. They listened to me politely. It must have sounded like *Alice in Wonderland*, so far removed were these ideas from their previous classroom experiences. If an experience must be lived to take on real meaning, it is no wonder that my words rang no bells and no eyes lit up with understanding.

There was, of course, one small additional problem. Experienced teacher that I was, I had never tried operating a full, student-centered program in my classroom before. I had, in other classes, children working together in groups making puppets, making butter, baking muffins, working with various art projects, but these were always carefully designed exercises, with a beginning and end, carefully controlled and monitored by the teacher. In such projects, the children's choices are carefully circumscribed. Decision making was restricted to the lower realms of choice of design, or color, or shape; it never included the higher realms of the *how* of procedure, or the *what* of inquiry, or the generation and application of new knowledge. Those higher-realm decisions I had always hoarded to myself.

While I had operated individualized reading and writing process programs quite successfully with previous classes, these were only the smallest steps toward what I had planned for this class. My goal was to help these children move toward greater control over their own learning and fuller responsibility over themselves—

and to do this in a full, not partial, way. To give up teacher control, to invite students to play a major role in the significant decisions of classroom life and learning, to empower children as thinkers, as learners, as decision makers—well, I had never even considered such possibilities, let alone tried to put them into practice. I began with my ideals, my enthusiasms, and my strong beliefs about what I felt was important. What was missing was professional competence in those teaching strategies needed to carry out these goals. Never mind. The children and I would be learners together.

Treading cautiously, I began with the subject areas that I knew best: individualized reading and writing process. It was a cinch to gather about 250 trade books, set up a reading corner, and organize instruction around individual conferences and skill groups. It was easy, too, to ask children to produce some writing each day that would be reflective of some personal experience. Although at first not all the children were enthusiastic readers or writers, handling those few who were not did not present major problems. Eventually, through better selection of books and topics to write about, through emphasis on reading for personal meaning and writing to express personally held views and feelings, and through the use of facilitative evaluative feedback rather than marks and grades, the problem of noninvolvement in these subjects disappeared. If I could get individualized language arts to work, how about math?

In shaping a student-centered math program, there were certain principles that I wished to maintain as fundamental to the program's operation. First, emphasis should be on pupils' understanding of mathematical concepts, rather than on rote application of mechanical skills. Second, students ought to work at their level of competence, and if there were a range of competencies, that must be reflected in the day-to-day work. Third, there must be opportunity for students to pace themselves in concept and skill development. Those who needed much more time to work out concepts should have that time available. Those who were able to progress more quickly should not be kept from moving ahead. Fourth, manipulatives of all kinds should be available in the math center, so that children could be actively involved in hands-on manipulation in learning mathematical concepts and skills. Fifth, students ought to be learning how to make valid assessments of their own skill needs. As part of learning math, they ought to become self-diagnosticians, learning to observe where their skills were strong and where they needed additional help. Being able to make thoughtful and nondefensive analyses of their skill needs seemed to me to be a critical component of their studies in math. Finally, children should be helping one another to work productively, using one another as resources and support systems. Working out the details of classroom application of these principles proved a great challenge, and as I moved cautiously toward a more extensive mathematics program, I learned that my most important resources were my own wits, my own educational experience, my own ability to observe diagnostically how these ideas were working out in classroom practice. It took several weeks for me to work out the kinks, and the children did not live comfortably with instructional practices that had to be modified from week to week, as I learned my way through each stage of field trials. The children responded to my initial confusion by showing me theirs. There were more behavior problems, and the noise level and aimless activity level seemed to escalate. The honeymoon was definitely over.

If I had little experience in the implementation of a full student-centered program, neither had the children any experience in those skills absolutely critical for carrying out their parts in such a program: self-discipline, self-control, cooperative behaviors. It was my naive expectation that when I announced to the children that they would have to learn to take more responsibility for their learning, they should, in fact, learn to do this simply by following my orders. Naturally, I was astonished by their inability to perform according to these expectations. Because I believed that my program would allow pupils more freedom, more responsibility, more control, I expected them to "buy into" these ideas enthusiastically and show their appreciation and gratitude. Hah! I still had much to learn about children, and even more to learn about teaching and learning. My biggest disappointment was not that I didn't see the children grow in their abilities to function in these sophisticated, mature, and self-disciplined ways. That was bitter, but not unendurable. The killing blow was that children wanted, asked, begged for a return to "the way we did it in fifth grade." That meant, "the teacher tells us what to do, and we do it." In those nightmarish moments, I found I could hate teaching.

Not only would I have to help the children develop those skills required to function as thoughtful, responsible, independent, cooperative learners, I would also have to work on developing new attitudes about what was important in their learning and what school was for. In such moments of truth, there is the overwhelming feeling that the task is too great, that the effort is beyond human capability, that there isn't enough energy in the body to pull it off, that discretion is the better part of valor, and that the whole plan should be packed in. Children working as self-motivated learners? It doesn't work!

Study Questions

1. What, in your opinion, are the key issues in this case? Working as a group, identify them and list them in what you consider to be their order of importance.
2. What do you see as the benefits of student-centered learning? What are some prices to be paid for this kind of teaching? What are your thoughts on it?
3. What do you see as the benefits of teacher-directed teaching? What are some prices to be paid for this kind of teaching? What are your thoughts on it?
4. How does a teacher learn to "hang in" during what seems to be an eternity

as children are learning to work responsibly on their own? What support systems are available for the teacher who is "hanging in" while the children are growing toward more responsible behavior?

5. What does a teacher who believes in student-centered classrooms do, when even the children are asking for a return to a more teacher-directed classroom? What are your ideas?

6. What is your assessment of this teacher? Is she a good teacher? What data in the case support your judgments?

7. What is your assessment of this teacher's plan to help her students grow toward greater autonomy? What modifications would you suggest she make?

8. How do you explain the students' response—their asking for a return to more teacher-directed programs? What hypotheses can you suggest?

9. What should this teacher do now? How would you advise her?

10. If you were in this teacher's shoes, how would you have done things differently? What assumptions have you made?

†11. To what personal experience does this case relate? Talk about it and describe the actions you took. What were some consequences of those actions? What were some important learnings for you?

5.3 "I'LL COME BACK WHEN YOU'RE TEACHING"

"Come in, come in," Rose Saunders welcomed the parents who had been milling in the corridor, waiting for her Parents' Night program to begin. They filed in nervously, the ghosts of classrooms past still haunting their psyches, and sat themselves gingerly in the fourth-grade-size chairs. Rose smiled warmly at them. "I know that these chairs are a bit small for adults, but try to make the best of it, please. The program won't be too long, and then we'll have a break for coffee."

Rose had spent the last two weeks thinking about and planning this half-hour program, her first Parents' Night in her brand new teaching career. She had much to tell the parents, and she wanted this to be good. For Rose, there was a lot at stake.

Mr. and Mrs. Olson sat across from the Dooleys at the table grouped for four. The Olsons and the Dooleys had been coming to Parents' Nights together for the last three years. Bette Olson and Jimmy Dooley were neighbors and classmates; they had gone to school together and been in the same classes since kindergarten. And this year the children had a new teacher who was fresh from the university and full of new ideas about teaching. After three weeks of school, the children were excited and eager about what was happening in fourth grade. The Olsons and Dooleys had come to find out more about Mrs. Saunders's program.

If the children liked school so much, could anything good be happening? Wasn't school supposed to be tough, challenging, and strict, in order to have any educational value? Would Mrs. Saunders, with all her new ways, prepare the children for the hard work of fifth grade?

Rose had anticipated these kinds of questions in her preparation for Parents' Night. She had also expected that some parents would be doubtful about her new methods. She knew from her studies in college, and from her keen intuitive sense, that people tended to resist change, that innovation in schools was suspect, that people were more comfortable when things stayed the same. It did not matter that parents' memories of their own school experiences were largely negative. They still wanted more of that for their own children. What was it that John Dewey had written? "We grow to love our chains"?

Rose began the presentation with a short video that she had made, showing her own class in action. She had chosen to focus on science, a subject she loved, and even after only three weeks of school, the children had captured her enthusiasm and developed a love for science that thrilled her. The video, while focusing on science, would also serve as an example of her particular pedagogy, which included active learning, children's cooperative group work, teacher–student interactions that called for higher-order thinking, and emphasis on learning to understand rather than learning to memorize facts. Demonstrating with the video how this worked in science, she would then show how this pedagogy translated to other areas of the curriculum. She would also explain to parents that this pedagogy would not only generate a lot of interest in school and schoolwork but also result in higher-order thinking, better comprehension of important curriculum concepts, more thoughtful pupil behaviors, and, overall, increased knowledge and skill. She had seen how these methods worked during her student teaching practicum and she was convinced that with these methods, she could have the best of all worlds in her teaching. Her job this evening was not simple: to convince the parents that it would work to their children's advantage. She knew that having the parents on her side, rather than as adversaries, would be an important "asset."

After her introductory remarks, she switched on the videotape. The children were shown carrying on investigations with "falling things." They were working in pairs and trios, conducting experiments to see how things fall. Did heavier objects fall faster than lighter objects? Did the shape or size of an object have any relationship to how fast it fell? The videotape panned the classroom and showed 28 children deeply involved in conducting scientific investigations. No child was off-task. While the room was noisy, it was the noise of productive, investigative play.

The camera zeroed in on the group where Bette Olson and Jimmy Dooley were examining the difference in falling speed between a piece of paper and an alphabet block. Dropping both, they remarked that the block fell much faster. "Wait," said Bette. "What would happen if we crumpled the paper up into a tight ball?" She did this and Jimmy said, "I know. The block will still be faster."

Bette climbed up on a chair and dropped both as Jimmy squatted on the floor, observing the paper and block touch the floor at approximately the same time. "Hey," he said. "Hey. Look at that. Do it again, Bette. I don't understand this."

Rose looked around the room at the watching parents, satisfied to see how many of them were smiling in response to Bette and Jimmy's puzzlement. Maybe the videotape could do the job better than if she had talked to them for 30 minutes?

The Olsons and the Dooleys watched their offspring thus engaged, and they seemed to enjoy what they were seeing. They were not sure what the children were learning, but they were certainly interested and very involved.

After five minutes that focused on children's scientific investigations with falling objects, the camera cut to a large-group discussion. The experiments done for the day, the teacher now conducted a class discussion in which children examined their experimental observations and generated hypotheses that attempted to explain the scientific phenomena. In the group discussion, the parents could see how respectfully Rose Saunders treated every child's idea, and how, with great care, she made it safe for each child to tell his or her theory. When Bette Olson volunteered her hypothesis, "I think it's gravity that pulls those things down," both the Olsons and the Dooleys smiled.

When the videotape presentation concluded, Rose explained that what had been seen here in science was very much in operation in the other curriculum areas as well. She tried to make her points as strongly and as convincingly as she could. "I'm not just interested in children's accumulating bits of information. I want them to become good problem solvers, to be able to use information to understand important concepts, to work together cooperatively, and, more important, to love school and to want to learn. I want them to experience themselves as can-do children, ready to take on the challenges of the twenty-first century."

The Olsons and the Dooleys liked what they heard and liked what they saw, but they were not entirely convinced that Rose Saunders, so new, so young, and so inexperienced, would be able to deliver on her promise. But they, at least, were willing to give her the benefit of the doubt. As the school year unfolded, they would learn more. In the meanwhile, Bette and Jimmy were loving school. It couldn't be all bad.

Arthur Kootnekoff, Nathan's father, was of another opinion. His questions challenged Rose sharply. "These new methods seem to lack structure. I can't see how children will learn anything when they're talking. They should be listening to you and you should be talking, Mrs. Saunders. That's the way we did it when

I went to school and that's how I learned. How will they learn to spell and to do the multiplication tables unless they're sitting down and working? I don't need for Nathan to be a scientist. I just want him to learn to read and write and spell and do his numbers good."

Rose was prepared for this, even though she inwardly winced at the thought of children sitting at desks, practicing multiplication tables until they turned green. In these days of pocket calculators that sold for $5.99, who, she wanted to ask Mr. Kootnekoff, did multiplication without a calculator? Not any adult that she knew.

"I appreciate your concerns, Mr. Kootnekoff," she said without defensiveness. "I, too, want Nathan to learn to spell and to read and to write. I want him to learn to understand mathematics, too. I know the methods I'm using are different from those used when all of us went to school. But I have seen these new methods work much better than the old ones. I'm just asking, Mr. Kootnekoff, if you will give me a chance to show that they will."

Rose did not know if Arthur Kootnekoff had been appeased. But at least he raised no further questions.

"Well, how about having some coffee?" Rose gently eased into the closing. "I'll be available to answer any of your questions individually, and I sincerely hope that you'll take up my invitation to visit the class. My door is always open to you, and I have some very exciting things planned for this school year."

The next morning Rose got to school early and went immediately to the staff room to make tea. She was surprised to find her principal, Chuck Allen, at the coffee urn.

"How did the Parents' Night go, Rose? I had hoped to make an appearance at each classroom, but I got waylaid by Billy Schuey's mother and couldn't get away. That woman can sure talk your ear off!"

"Well, I think it was okay. It seemed to me that most of the parents were willing to give me a chance to show that these methods actually do work."

"What exactly did you tell them, Rose? You're not going to stir up a hornet's nest here, are you? I don't need a bunch of unhappy parents badgering me this term. I've got enough to do with the district's new policies for mainstreaming. Don't make me any more problems, Rosie."

What was it about people in administrative positions, Rose wondered, that put her so quickly on the defensive? In the face of Chuck's verbal challenge, she immediately felt the need to defend herself and what she was doing in the classroom. She grabbed her warm teacup with both hands for moral support and looked her principal directly in the eye.

"You remember, Chuck, when you hired me last summer, that I told you about how I planned to organize my class: active learning, children working in cooperative learning groups, authentic evaluation, higher-order thinking? I told you about it then and you seemed interested in these new teaching strategies.

You wanted me here, Chuck, and I'm assuming that you wanted me to teach in these ways."

"Modern ways are okay with me, Rose. That is why I hired you. You're young, enthusiastic, full of beans. I think we need to move to new methods. But gradually, Rosie. Gradually. You take some of these parents too quickly into the future, and all hell will break loose. I don't want any problems with parents, Rose. I don't want kids falling behind academically because of your new methods, either."

Rose felt under attack and she was glad that there were no other teachers in the staff room to see it. She was not about to back down, either. Chuck Allen had hired her knowing full well what her educational beliefs were and what she intended to do in her classroom. She was not going to let him intimidate her now, in spite of whatever problems he imagined her program would create.

"I'll tell you what, Chuck," Rose said softly in her gentlest, least prickly tone. "I'll make a bargain with you. I'll run my program and make you a promise that my children will do at least as well, or better, on the standardized achievement test in April, compared to the other fourth grades in the school."

Chuck Allen looked at Rose—this 22-year-old, feisty young woman who had so convinced him of her ability as a teacher that he had hired her on the spot. There was something about her strength, her courage, her intelligence, and her conviction that was persuasive. He wanted for his school what he thought she could give; yet he, too, was fearful of change that was too much, too soon. Maybe, Chuck reflected, he wanted omelets without breaking eggs? Change without its concomitant upheavals? The questions disturbed him. Did he have the administrator's disease of wanting it both ways?

"Okay, Rosie, okay. I'll tell you, though, that I'm uneasy. You may be traveling down the road of innovation too fast for this old man and for this community. But you've got to show me that what you're doing is educationally sound. And if these kids don't do well on that April achievement test, you'll be in big trouble, kiddo. I'm going to spend some time observing in your classroom. I need to be convinced. So convince me, okay?"

Rose lifted the teacup in the air as a toast and nodded. "Chuck, come in anytime. I know what I'm doing is right and that the kids are learning. I have nothing to worry about." She watched him leave the staff room, and only then did she feel her knees weaken. Had she promised too much? Had she given away the store? Did she have more faith in herself as a teacher than she had any right to have? As a new teacher, should she have more doubts?

Two days later, Chuck Allen opened the door to her classroom, nodded briefly to her, and found the way to a small, fourth-grade-size chair in the rear of the room. "What luck," Rose thought. "He couldn't have come at a better time." The children were engaged in investigations involving bouncing balls as part of a math unit on measurement. Working in teams of two, the children were observing and recording information about a group of balls. In their records, they were calculating the kind of ball, the weight of the ball, the height of the bounce, the length of the toss. They then compared variables, for example: To what extent did the weight of the ball relate to how high it could bounce? To what extent was there a relationship between the type of ball and how far it could be tossed? Each pair of children was similarly conducting experiments and recording results, in metric measurement, on large sheets of graph paper. These records would later be compared and examined in the large-group debriefing on this measurement task. Naturally the classroom was noisy, alive with the sounds of children as serious players and learners.

During the investigations, Rose observed the children carefully. Which groups argued more? What was the nature of the dilemmas? Which children seemed more open to conflicting data? Which seemed more intransigent? Which children seemed to have difficulty recording? Who seemed to be more deeply involved? Which children needed to be directed by others in the group? Who seemed to be the leaders? While she was making careful mental notes of children during this process, Rose did not intervene in the children's investigations. Unless she was specifically asked, she kept a distance from them and allowed them to conduct their experiments on their own. She did this because she had learned that to intervene during this investigative time would create tension for the children between what they were doing and what they might believe she wanted them to do. Teachers' interventions during investigative play seemed to inhibit, rather than facilitate, children's explorations into the unknown. That Chuck Allen was now sitting and observing did not cause Rose Saunders to alter her methods. She knew what she believed, and she believed in what she did. She was not going to "play to the gallery." Chuck Allen would see her teach exactly as she taught when he was not there.

"Mrs. Saunders, Mrs. Saunders," called Bette Olson. "Look at this, Mrs. Saunders. When you throw the small ball, it goes this far. But the big ball goes less far. Isn't that funny? We did that experiment three times, Mrs. Saunders, and each time it's the same."

Rose smiled. "You're surprised. The small ball seems to be able to travel farther than the large ball. That puzzles you and you haven't been able to figure it out yet. Let me know when you're ready to give me some of your hypotheses." She smiled again, and walked away. It was not easy for Rose to refrain from telling Bette's group the answer, to allow them, instead, to find the ways to explain it for themselves. But she had trained herself to do just this, under the tutorship of her sponsoring teachers during her practicum, and she was proud that she did not "tell" and allowed her students to think things out for themselves.

Chuck Allen seemed restless. His eyes went from the children's activities to the array of posters and children's work on the bulletin boards. He looked at his fingernails and then at his shoes. Finally, he looked at his watch. Less than 15 minutes after he arrived, he was on his feet heading toward the door. Glancing back at Rose, he told her, "I'll come back when you're teaching."

Study Questions

1. What do you see as the pivotal issues in this case? Discuss them in your group and then list them according to what you consider to be their order of importance.
2. What kind of teacher, in your view, is Rose Saunders? Make a list of the adjectives that you would use to describe her. If you had a choice, would you choose to student teach in her class? What reasons support your position?
3. Based on the data in the case, how would you evaluate the program Rose Saunders prepared for Parents' Night? What do you see as some of its positive features? What do you think she might have done better? What, in your view, is the importance of "teaching" parents about your innovative methods?
4. What, in your opinion, is behind some parents' resistance to new classroom methods? What strategies can teachers use to make parents allies, rather than adversaries, especially when teachers are trying to be innovative?
5. To what extent should parents have a say in how a teacher chooses to teach? What are your views on this?
6. What is your opinion of Rose's bargain with Chuck Allen? What chance do you think she has of making good on her promise? What data support your position?
7. To what extent should a teacher try to use innovative methods in his or her first year of teaching? What do you see as some implications of the position you have taken for you as a teacher? for the students? for schools?
8. In your view of what was happening during Chuck's visit, was Rose teaching? What is teaching?
9. What response should Rose make to Chuck after class today? What do you see as some potential consequences of such action?
†10. Talk together about an event in your own experience in which you and your principal were in conflict over teaching methods. How did you choose to resolve the conflict? What were the costs/benefits to you? What might you have done in retrospect?

5.4 "IT'S UP TO YOU, MRS. BUSCEMI"

It was barely 8:00 A.M. when the phone rang. Violet Buscemi was sure it was bad news—someone in the family had died, God forbid. Her heart was pounding in her ears and she could barely make out what the voice was saying. "Mrs. Buscemi?" It was a voice she did not know.

"Yes," she faltered.

"I hope this is not too early to call." Was he trying to sell her something at this hour?

"No. What is it?" An edge of suspicion crept into her tone.

"My name is Frank Carter. I'm the new principal of Mill Basin High School. I've just learned that you've been appointed to our staff to teach math."

She didn't know whether to laugh or cry. Her first teaching assignment. She hadn't expected it so soon. But the wheels of that massive bureaucratic structure called the board of education ground exceedingly strange, and if there was some rational explanation for the way decisions were made in the administrative offices, none of those in the front lines of educational practice could make any sense of it. Violet had taken and passed her city certification exam in the spring, graduated from college in June, and was prepared to wait, who knows how long, until she received word of her appointment. Now here it was, three days before school was to open. Her excitement overcame her nervousness. She was going to be a teacher!

"I want to welcome you to the staff of Mill Basin High," Frank Carter announced, as if he was ringing clarion bells. "I'll expect you in my office on Monday morning, at 7:30 A.M., and I'll give you your teaching assignment. I realize that this is short notice, but the first days of school are primarily for student registration, scheduling, program changes—you know, just getting the kids settled in. Serious instruction won't start until Thursday, so you'll have a little time to get yourself sorted out."

It was just 8:00 A.M. when she hung up the phone. She was a teacher.

Mill Basin High School was in the heartland of the city's residential borough. Like most of the city's other older schools, it was a huge, run-down building, five stories tall, that took up the most of an entire city block. Under normal circumstances, the physical plant might have accommodated about 3,000 students, but double scheduling made it possible to increase the number of students enrolled to 4,400. With a teaching and administrative staff of 125, the school was like a small city. The ethnic diversity—including working-class residents of the neighborhood, a large contingent of newly arrived immigrant groups, and students from the massive city housing project that butted against the expressway—made Mill Basin seem like market day at an international bazaar. At last count, 77 languages, including Urdu, were recorded as "language spoken in the home" for Mill Basin students.

Unlike some of the other city schools, the incidence of violence in the school was minimal. Drugs were not sold openly on the streets around the school. Children of the longer-term residents of the neighborhood seemed to put a great value on school as a route to college and eventual entrepreneurial and professional success. Children of the newly arrived immigrant families seemed eager to learn and to make a secure place for themselves in their new country. Although not one of the city's elite and prestigious high schools that creamed off the most academically talented of the city's students for special programs, Mill Basin was certainly a giant step above some of the other urban schools, where teaching felt more like going to war.

Violet Buscemi's first teaching assignment included several sections of general math and one section of geometry, a piece of cake. Her student teaching assignments had prepared her to teach both of these subjects, and she received her schedule with the confidence of one born to teach. Her one handicap, she knew, was that she was small and slight and that eleventh and twelfth graders, especially the boys, towered over her. But what she lacked in physical stature, she made up in energy, drive, and commitment. In the classroom, she was a dynamo. She had the knack that all teachers yearn for—the ability to make a tough subject interesting and relevant to her students, as well as the skill to earn their trust and respect. It did not take her long to win the respect and admiration of her students, and to make her presence on the staff valued.

Each evening, after dinner, as Violet set herself to the task of grading papers and preparing lessons for the next day's classes, she would entertain her husband with stories of her students. Telling the stories, she realized, was more than just an outlet to discharge some of the angst that accumulated, like encrusted barnacles, in the life of a teacher. The telling helped her to view the students through different lenses, to broaden her perspective and point to fresh ways of reaching them.

Adam Wright was one of Violet's stories. As she marked his general math paper, she sighed, knowing that his total score would, once again, be less than 40%. She had tried everything with Adam, but she could not see how he was going to pass the course. Her husband, Walter, listened as Violet poured out her heart.

"You know," Violet told Walter, "I've given Adam every chance. I've worked with him individually in class and asked him to come for special help after school. But he never shows up. His math skills are desperately poor, and his assignments and test scores show it. He's a senior, and he's going to fail math. That means he won't be able to graduate."

Walter Buscemi's eyes searched Violet's face and saw the anguish there. Violet cared for this boy, wanted to help him pass, but she was not getting any help from Adam. "What's the problem, then, hon? His skills are poor, and he's not putting himself out to get the help you're offering him. So he gets what he deserves. A failing grade. You did your best, Vi. It's not your fault he's failing."

Violet winced as she added up Adam's score and put a 40% in red on the top of his paper. The next day, when she returned the papers to the students, she asked Adam again if he would meet her after class for help with his general math skills.

The tall, handsome boy from the city project housing looked at her earnestly. "Gee, Mrs. Buscemi. I just can't come today. I'm taking extra courses so I'll be able to go to college, and I've got other classes after school."

"Adam, I'm really worried about your grades. Your marks are very low."

"I know, Mrs. B.," he sighed. "I'm really trying, too."

There was no place to go with it. Adam was not shirking. There were simply not enough hours in the day for school, extra classes, and the work that he did in the evenings at a supermarket to supplement his pocket money. Violet Buscemi could not get water out of a stone. Without getting the extra help he needed to understand and improve his skills, this handsome, outgoing, and very nice young man was heading for a failure.

The semester flew into June, and Violet, like the other teachers at Mill Basin High, was immersed in marking final exams, writing end-of-year reports, and doing that loneliest of all professional tasks—recording final grades. How many years of teaching does it take before giving final grades gets any easier, Violet wondered glumly. For each student in each class, she tallied up all the marks for the major tests, added one mark that represented the student's work on daily assignments, and another that represented the student's class participation. The final grade would be an average of all of these grades, a fair and equitable procedure. There was no room in math for subjective judgments. The numbers told the whole story, and they took her off the hook with respect to who got what.

When she came to Adam Wright's name, she added slowly, carefully, mournfully and divided the total by seven. Five major tests: 50%, 37%, 42%, 48%, 40%. Assignments: 40%. Class participation: 40%. Total: 297 ÷ 7 = 42.43%. She could be generous and raise the final mark to 45%, but it was still not an easy mark to give.

Two days later, Violet Buscemi was summoned to the principal's office. Frank Carter had asked to review all the students with failing grades, and he wanted to talk to her about Adam Wright.

Violet immediately felt defensive. Had she done enough to help Adam pass? Could she have done more? Was it her fault? She didn't want to have to fail Adam. But how could she justify passing him, given his record in general math this term? If he were to be passed with 65%, what would that mean to the other students who had *earned* a final grade of 65%?

"Violet, sit down. This is a really tough case and I'd like you to reconsider Adam Wright's mark. Adam came to see me yesterday, Violet. Did you know that he had been accepted into a local community college, conditional on his passing all his courses? He would be the first in his family ever to go to college, Violet. Do you know what this means to a black family from the projects? It wasn't that Adam was being lazy, or shirking. He was enrolled in extra courses, off campus, to make up the requirements he needed for college. He was also working part time. That's a heavy load for a grown man, let alone a boy of 18. Can't you see your way clear to giving this boy a boost up by passing him?"

Violet bit her lip, feeling the anger, fighting back the tears. "Look, Mr. Carter. I know that Adam is not an uninterested student. I know that he's deserving. I know what graduating means to him. But I also know what's fair. Adam's class average is 42%. If I give him a passing final grade of 65%, what does this say to the other students who earned grades of 65%? What does this say about any of the other grades I've given, where in-class averages are fair representations of a student's work during the course? How can I be fair to all my students, while being more generous to Adam Wright?"

"Violet, there's more to the picture than just Adam's grade, you know. We don't want to have this school's graduating record marred by too many failing students. It gives the school a bad name, and it puts all the teachers in a bad light. The reputation of this entire school could suffer. Is it going to make such a difference to let Adam Wright pass general math? It's up to you, Mrs. Buscemi."

Study Questions

1. What do you see as the key issues in this case? Talk together, and identify them.
2. What is your assessment of Violet Buscemi as a teacher? What data in the case have you used in making this determination? What assumptions have you made?
3. As you see it, what role did Violet play in trying to help Adam Wright? How would you judge her effectiveness?
4. How would you describe Adam Wright? Given the data in the case, how would you assess his performance in math class?
5. How would you describe the procedures that Violet used in making an evaluative judgment of Adam's work? Is this a good way to evaluate a student's performance in math? What are your views on it? What alternate procedures might have been effective?
6. How, in your view, would you describe Frank Carter? What do you see as his agenda in trying to promote a change of grade for Adam?
7. Where do you stand on affirmative action that would give students like Adam Wright an advantage that might help him to a better future?
8. Based on your own school experiences, what do you see as some inequities in evaluation practices? How does a teacher try to deal with those inequities? What strategies do you suggest?
9. Given the data in the case, what do you think Violet Buscemi should do? What do you see as some payoffs for those actions? What do you see as some negative consequences?
†10. Talk about an incident from your own teaching experience that bears on the question of fairness in evaluation practices. What was the nature of the dilemma? What action did you take? What insight did you gain about class-

room evaluation as a result of this experience? How did that experience change your thinking about evaluations?

5.5 WHOSE CURRICULUM SHOULD WE TEACH?

"Don't forget to write," Jeff Lorber heard his friend Larry call out after him as he raced down the tarmac toward the waiting plane. Jeff's 6' 2" frame had to bend almost in half to make it through the small doorway of the Dash-7, the jet prop plane that would take him from his urban home in St. Paul to remote Setsco Lake. As he heard the engines rev in preparation for takeoff, and watched the tall city buildings retreat into the distance, he wondered what lay ahead for him in his new teaching job. A brand new teacher, scrabbling around for a position with about a thousand other contenders, he couldn't afford to be too choosy. But Setsco Lake? Had he been too hasty in choosing this small, rural community tucked into the northeastern quadrant of the state, about 200 miles from the nearest "large" town? Would he be able to cope with the geographic isolation? Could the spectacular, untamed beauty of the area be sufficient compensation for what city life had to offer?

Jeff settled back in his seat and drank coffee out of a paper cup. Even the plane ride was a trip back to yesterday. He hadn't known that propeller planes were still used in commercial transportation. Later on, he would learn that propeller planes made more sense economically than large jets when small town airports were involved. But more important, given the size of the landing field at the Rutland Airport, surrounded on all sides by the Columbian Mountains, the Dash-7 had a much better chance of getting in and out, especially when the weather was bad, which was often.

When the plane landed at Rutland Airport, Jeff stepped out into what looked like a moonscape, except for the lush evergreen forests that swept up the mountainsides and the fresh smell of pine wood in the air. If Rutland felt like Nowheresville, what would it be like at Setsco Lake, 200 miles farther into the wilderness?

Kelli Shaw was waiting for him in a four-wheel-drive Jeep. "Thanks for coming to meet me," Jeff told his principal. "I couldn't bring my own car. It's really trashed, and I don't think it would've made the trip. I'll have to think about getting a new one when I've collected some salary. But meanwhile, I'll be a bit dependent on the goodwill of my neighbors as well as on my trusty hiking boots," Jeff smiled.

"No problem," Kelli said. "I needed to come down to Rutland anyway to pick up some things at the hardware store. We've got you booked into Tigh-Na-Mara Lodge, a room and a kitchenette that oughta do you until you find your own place. It's not the Hyatt Regency, but it's clean and comfortable and warm."

In the high season, the Lodge is full of sportsmen, come up for the game and fishing. But in the winter, you'll have the place pretty much to yourself. Whatever you need to get yourself set up, give us a shout. People are very friendly and very helpful. You've got to be when you live so far from civilization."

Jeff hunched farther into his down jacket, grateful that he hadn't packed it, deciding at the last minute to wear it for the trip. Even though it was barely September, the air had a chill edge and the Jeep's canvas top let the draft through. "Is there anything more I should know before school starts, Kelli?"

Jeff had heard all the good things about Setsco Lake when Kelli Shaw had been in the city, interviewing him for the position. Perhaps now that he had signed the two-year contract and had actually arrived, he might learn more about the "itches and outches."

"I'm not exactly a historian, but I can give you some background about the area. Maybe you should know a bit about how this place grew and who are the key players," Kelli offered. "Keep in mind, though, that this is only my second year here."

Jeff nodded, beginning to feel the cold.

"Well, of course, the first people to settle and develop communities in the area were Native groups. Metis and nonaffiliated people of First Nations ancestry. In the 1950s began a slow influx of white settlers who chose to live away from urban centers in order to preserve a certain lifestyle. To tell the truth, Jeff, that's probably the source of the greatest tension in the community and the school. Two very different cultures, different lifestyles, different values, different expectations for their children—well, sometimes things get a bit tense."

Jeff sucked on his lip, wondering what this was going to mean for the day-to-day life in his primary classroom. His thoughts about what lay ahead of him played racquet ball in his head and dimmed his awareness for the beauty of the landscape.

"Bear," Kelli said, pointing to the hillock on the right. A large brown bear lay stretched out, eyes fixed on the road, not moving. An omen of things to come?

It was close to Thanksgiving when Jeff finally found a few spare minutes to sit down and write to his friend Larry. The first snows had come, covering the trees with white lace antimacassars and shrouding the area in an eerie silence. In less than three months, Jeff had begun to love Setsco Lake, had embraced its magical beauty, serenity, and isolation. He could easily understand what had attracted early settlers to the region and thought of the possibility of settling here permanently, raising a family, putting down roots. He was even making peace with the tensions at Setsco Lake School. That was, perhaps, why he was so unprepared for what had happened last Friday. How had he been so naive that he hadn't anticipated its coming? Had he been insensitive to the real situation? How was it going to be possible to reconcile these two different cultural pulls? Who was "right"? And how was this problem going to be resolved?

The questions made knots under his shoulderblades as he picked up his pen and began his letter to Larry.

"Hi, old buddy," he wrote and then sat there, warming his stockinged feet at the fire as the events of the past three months played out in his mind.

"Sorry I haven't written to you sooner, but you know how it is, busy, busy, busy. I imagine your own life as a new teacher has been just as hectic, but hey, what can you have down there that in any way compares with teaching at Setsco Lake?

"A few words about the school should tell all: two rooms in what looks like a portable, each with an adjoining cloakroom and washroom. A tiny office, big enough for Thumbelina. I've got the primary group, first through third grades, and my principal, Kelli Shaw, has the intermediate group. She's what they call a 'teaching principal,' with full administrative responsibilities as well as a full-time teaching job. I think she has secretly found a way to add an extra day onto her workweek. I don't know how she does it all. But Kelli and I have made a team, and on some days, we really feel that it's just us against the world. (No, she's not married, and forget that!) Our resources and supplies are in serious short supply. I think we must be on the end of the delivery route for the school district. By the time they get here, they've nothing left! We're like the forgotten school. That pretty much sums it up. A nurse appears about once a month, checking the kids' heads for lice, and that sort of stuff. We've got no special teachers or enrichment materials of any kind. If you want to do a special art project, or even run a well-developed physical education program, the pickings of materials available are *very* lean. One thing I have learned in all of this, old buddy, is resourcefulness. I've become the most bloody resourceful teacher in the state! If we don't have materials on hand, I've learned to find substitutes or create alternatives. There is a great, big, wonderful world out there, and I'm learning to use what's available in the natural environment to build my program. Sometimes I feel like a bloody pioneer. You know, if there's not enough red paint, we go out into the woods together and find the natural materials that allow us to make red dyes. So not only do we get the color, but we get science and environmental studies as a bonus.

"I've grown to love this place, Larry. Would you believe it? Me, the kid from the sidewalks of the city? I've never felt so good and so whole in my life. I love these kids, and I love what I'm doing. And talk about being stretched as a teacher! I'm being challenged every day and growing all the time."

Jeff put his pen down and tugged absent-mindedly at his beard. Should he write the rest of the story to Larry? Should he give him the underside of his teaching life at Setsco Lake? Jeff looked into the fire and tried to remember when it had begun. He had been warned in advance by Kelli Shaw that there was tension in the community between the longtime Native settlers and the relative "newcomers" who represented Caucasian culture. Different lifestyles, different sociocultural values, different expectations for kids collided in different demands on curriculum content and classroom practices. Caught in the war between the cultures were the children. Many of the Native children came to school with little ability to speak or understand English. Where competition was grist for life in a Caucasian value system, it was anathema to most Native cultures. Primary reading materials, issued from the school district office 350 miles away, reflected values and situations that were totally out of synch with the lives of both Native and Caucasian children at Setsco Lake. This boiling brew had bubbled up and over the sides of the pot only last Friday.

Jeff and Kelli had worked hard together, teaming up to develop new curriculum materials that were more developmentally and multiculturally appropriate for the children at the school. Their out-of-school time was largely taken up with the planning and writing of reading materials, social studies and science units that would draw more on children's interests and strengths and reflect more of their community life. These materials were designed to supplement the deficits in the state-issued supplies. Working productively together took a lot of their time, it was true. But what else was there to do evenings at Setsco Lake? Jeff was glad for the chance to work with Kelli and to stretch himself in these creative ways.

Rumblings of discontent were heard in the first parent meeting of the school year, in mid-October. Kelli, as teaching principal, took the full brunt of it, while Jeff, the new teacher, was spared, but only temporarily. A small group of Caucasian parents, vocal and aggressive, did not want to see the social studies curriculum deviate from what the state department of education advocated. That Setsco Lake was isolated from the power center of the state was no reason for the school to adopt an inferior set of curriculum materials. These parents wanted for their children what the children were getting in St. Paul: a social studies curriculum that taught how this great country was settled by the white people, who were instrumental in bringing about a new world.

On the other end of the spectrum, a group of Native leaders was pressuring for curriculum changes that reflected Native cultures more closely. For example, Native children should be instructed in their own language. Textbooks should be written in the Native language, especially at the primary level. The stories in the readers should come from the rich resource of Native folk tales. First Nations children should be taught to have pride in their own heritage, not to learn the ways of the white culture. A school curriculum that taught Native children "white ways" was destroying Native life and was a force of evil.

Between the demands of the small, vocal group of Caucasians and the few Native leaders was the larger group of bewildered Native and Caucasian parents and children, who were having a great deal of difficulty trying to figure out what education at Setsco Lake School should be all about.

Last Friday morning had turned up sunny and cold, and Jeff was settling the children in after the first real snow, always an exciting event that signaled the beginning of snow sports and holidays to come. The children wanted to know if there would be time to play outside, and Jeff was pondering the question when Kelli came to the door.

"I've just had a phone call. We're having a visitor this afternoon." Her face looked tense.

"Anybody important?" Jeff tried to break the tension. "Should I shave off my beard?"

"Not funny, kiddo. This is real. Assistant State Superintendent John Buckley, if you please. I have a gut feeling that he's not on his way here to deliver the toilet paper that we've been begging for these past three weeks."

"Well, should we do anything to prepare ourselves, do you think? Is this going to be heavy, I mean, really, seriously heavy?"

"Dunno, Jeff. I think we're just going to have to wait and see what's on his mind. But I don't like it. This is, after all, the big brass. So something's coming down."

By the time John Buckley arrived at the school, Jeff had long forgotten that he was coming, so caught up was he with the demands and challenges of his teaching day. Jeff had been bending down, helping Naomi with the laces on her running shoes, when he looked up to find a suit and tie watching him from the open doorway. When was the last time Jeff had seen a suit and tie? Was it at the airport last August?

"I'm John Buckley," the assistant state superintendent said as he walked in and extended his hand.

"Jeff Lorber, primary teacher, shoe fastener, and general handyman. Pleased to meet you," Jeff countered.

"Yeah," Buckley smiled, taking in the scene. "I know what you mean."

Jeff wondered if he did know. Could anyone who lived in the comfortable world of St. Paul—where steam heat, air-conditioning, modern facilities, libraries, movie theaters, and markets were simply taken for granted—know about life in Setsco Lake?

"I'd like to meet with you and Kelli right after school. Is there some place where we could sit down and talk?"

"Well, there's only this cubby hole that Kelli uses as her office. It's as big as a shoebox, but the coffee's in there, and it will be warm."

"That's good. I've got to do this fast, because I need to drive right back to Rutland afterwards. I'm scheduled to go out on the first plane tomorrow morning. Got an important meeting at noon in the State House."

"You mean, if the weather be good," Jeff smirked, knowing how often flights were canceled due to weather.

"Don't even think about it," John Buckley grimaced. "If I'm not at that meeting, then I'm toast. Imperative that I be there."

"Uggh," grunted Jeff. He was not in charge of weather.

"I'll wait in the office until you're finished here. But could you get there pronto, please?"

"Yeah, sure, Mr. Buckley. Just as soon as the kids leave."

The two teachers and the assistant superintendent sat facing one another in the cramped quarters of Kelli's makeshift office, sipping freshly brewed coffee.

"Kelli and Jeff, this is a bit complicated, as I'm sure you'll understand. I've had a call from Washington, from Steve Paulos, your local representative to the House. It seems that Steve has a direct pipeline to one of the Native leaders of the community up here, who is really hot for your heads.

"Of course, far be it from me to be telling you how to run your school. I know how hard you both work and what it means to teach in an isolated area. But I think you should both know that you're getting a bad press down in St. Paul and that's not what we need. And especially we don't need this at a time when First Nations people are beginning to get some recognition, some sense of power. We cannot afford, even in Setsco Lake, to be seen as being prejudiced against Indians."

"Tell me, Mr. Buckley," Kelli asked, "what has been identified as the 'problem' here at Setsco Lake School?"

"Well, it seems that the Native leaders are up in arms about what you're doing in social studies. Too much emphasis on white culture. Too much Columbus and the other early explorers. They feel that First Nations people are being shortchanged and inadequately represented in the materials and in the methods you're using."

Kelli glanced at Jeff, who was watching new snow falling down from what had been, a few hours earlier, clear blue sky. Both teachers sat silently, listening to John Buckley's accusations. Neither of them even raised questions, as they both knew that what Buckley knew was already third-hand and would likely be neither accurate nor helpful.

"Look, both of you. Can't you find a way to get together on these issues with the Native community? After all, the Indians do have the right to their heritage and in a school with a large percentage of First Nations children, you should be offering a cross-cultural curriculum, especially in the social studies. Now, of course, this doesn't mean that you should neglect the curriculum from the state department of education! But surely you can find a way to reconcile these interests. We can't have any more calls from Washington. And I'm afraid if this situation isn't resolved, the Native leaders will want your jobs."

John Buckley looked at them both like a stern father who had been greatly inconvenienced by their inconsiderate indiscretions. Neither Kelli nor Jeff offered to tell him what they had been trying to do, that is, to be sympathetic to and give recognition to both Caucasian and Native cultures. Both instinctively knew that this was not a matter of what they were, in fact, doing, but a matter of perceptions. How do you defend yourself against perceptions? And what did John Buckley really know about it anyway? He was just being the hatchet man. And he wasn't even going to stay around long enough to get the information with any accuracy.

"Now, I've got to go, before that snow traps me here. I'm counting on you to bring this problem to a fair resolution." John Buckley got up, picked up his briefcase, nodded to the two bewildered teachers, and hustled out the door to his rental car. Kelli wished fiercely that he'd get stuck in a snow drift on the way back to Rutland. She was angry beyond reason.

"What does this mean, Kelli," Jeff asked. "Does it mean that the curriculum materials we've been cranking out, trying scrupulously to give fair representation to both cultures, are inappropriate? And if so, how are they inappropriate? Does it mean that we shouldn't be talking about Halloween, or Thanksgiving, or Christmas? When Buckley says we've got to give more time and space to First Nations culture, but that we must not neglect the state curriculum either, what the heck is he talking about? Where do you draw the line? Isn't anyone in charge going to help us out with the specifics?"

Kelli, lips pinched together, looked out at the beauty of the white landscape and said, "I don't know, Jeff. I really don't know. It seems that whatever way we proceed, there will be some people who perceive what we do as inappropriate for their cultural heritage. Both groups want different things for this school and we're caught in the middle, trying to dance the thin line between two different dancing masters. And you know what, Jeff?" she said, her eyes blazing. "I'm sick to death of having parents call the shots about this school's curriculum. How can one school, any school, shape curriculum to please every ethnic group that has a legitimate demand for curriculum content? It's making me crazy!"

Jeff looked over at Kelli, his co-teacher and principal, whom he'd come to respect and care for, and saw in her face a defeat that scared him. "Come on," he said. "Let's go down to the Cafe at Tigh-Na-Mara, and I'll buy you a real cup of coffee. Then, if you behave, I might even buy you dinner. Maybe by then, if we put our heads together, we'll figure out what we need to do."

Study Questions

1. What do you see as the substantive issues in this case? Talk together about your perceptions of what the issues are, and then list them in order of what you consider to be their importance.

2. Based on the data in the case, what kind of "case" does the Native community have in trying to influence the curriculum of this school? List some arguments that you believe support their case. List some contrary arguments. Reexamine your list of arguments and consider which of them are based on educationally sound practices. Which are based on political motivations?

3. Based on the data in the case, what kind of "case" does the Caucasian community have in trying to influence the curriculum of this school? List some arguments that you believe support their case. List some contrary arguments.

4. What groups do you see as having a legitimate right to shape the curriculum of a school? The state department of education? The local school district? The principal? The classroom teacher? The parents who represent different ethnic groups? The pupils? All of the above? What data support your position on this?

5. How, in your view, does the isolation of the school in this case make a difference to the way the events in the case are being played out? What differences might you expect if this were a school in an urban center?

6. What response, in your view, would have been effective with John Buckley? What assumptions are being made?

7. What should a classroom teacher do when pressured by parent groups about curriculum? What suggestions do you have for Kelli and Jeff? What are some potential consequences of what you are proposing?

†8. To what personal experience in your own teaching life does this case relate? What were the key issues in that experience? How did you respond? In retrospect, how might you have acted differently? What do you suppose kept you from acting in that way?

5.6   WE'RE WORRIED ABOUT STANDARDS

Charlotte Cormier had hardly settled into her first cup of coffee when the telephone rang in the math office. It was still early, at least a half hour until classes began, when the math teachers congregated around the coffee urn, exchanging war stories about yesterday's crises as a way of priming themselves for the day. Tom Brennan, who, like Charlotte, taught eleventh- and twelfth-grade math, picked up the phone and his eyes turned to Charlotte. "I think you're in trouble, babe," he jested. "Mrs. Rees wants to see you in her office before you go to class." Charlotte smirked at Tom. After two years in Marine View High School, she knew about Tom's sense of humor and was not going to be easily intimidated.

"It's probably about that Gzowski kid who got mugged on the way to school," said Charlotte as she picked up her briefcase and armload of books. "See you guys later," she called, as she sped out the door, glancing up at the clock to see how much time she had before her first class.

The large general office was already swarming with incoming teachers, students and assorted other personnel who populated this elegant school in the affluent suburbs of a large West Coast city. To Charlotte, the scene looked like business as usual, but to an outsider, unfamiliar with contemporary high schools, this might have looked like a mob scene from a movie set. There must have been at least two dozen students on hand, some waiting, some talking to office staff or to teachers, each with his or her tale of woe.

As Charlotte approached the secretary's desk, she got the nod to go right into the principal's office. While Charlotte had thought that this must be about Mick Gzowski, on second thought she wondered what she might have to add of relevance to the situation. True, Mick was in her eleventh-grade math block, and true, these school muggings were becoming more frequent, but what could she contribute that would be of value?

Katherine Rees sat at her desk, facing a man and a woman whom Charlotte did not know. As Charlotte walked into the room, the principal stood up and introduced Mr. and Mrs. Evans, and Charlotte immediately clued in. These must be Robert's parents. But why on earth were they here, at the crack of dawn, on a school day? Had something happened to Robert? She felt a chill spread down her neck and turn her fingers to ice.

When the conference with the Evanses was over, Charlotte left the principal's office feeling a sickness that made her stomach and head ache. She was certain that everyone in the outer office could see the flush on her face and would be able to read the fury in her eyes. She could not even begin to gather her emotions, to pull herself together to face her first class. She had not been naive enough to believe that teaching in the suburbs would be entirely free of racial prejudice. She had known that one day she might have to face this beast and deal with it in some ethical and intelligent way. But she had never dreamed it would take this shape.

Charlotte Cormier was one of fourteen math teachers at Marine View High. When she had accepted the position to teach math two years ago, she wondered what it would be like to teach in the suburbs. It would be very different, she thought, from her student teaching experience, when she taught in the inner city. She remembered her first look at this school nestled on a bluff overlooking the Pacific Ocean, with its award winning architectural design. She thought she had won first prize. If the school was this beautiful, could the students be otherwise?

Charlotte remembered that at first she did not understand why the teachers referred to the students at Marine View as "poor little rich kids." They came from elegant homes. Many homes had servants. Parents were in high-income brackets and were business executives or professionals. It did not take long for Charlotte to understand, to tune into the human climate at Marine View High, which she found considerably less beautiful than its architecture. She saw that the students were intensely competitive with one another, and she saw that competitive spirit show itself in a variety of ugly behaviors in classrooms, in the hallway, in the lunchroom, and on the playing field. She saw students call one another disparaging names; she heard them make sarcastic comments about one anothers' physical characteristics, about clothes, about their work in class. Rudeness, sarcasm, and other acts of verbal cruelty were prevalent in the unsupervised areas of Marine View High. In the supervised areas, a civility prevailed, but, Charlotte saw, it was only surface thin. Charlotte also saw that these affluent pupils were overly concerned with the acquisition of material possessions, the amount and extent of a student's possessions being directly related to that student's status within student groups. Even more distressing to Charlotte was the widespread incidence of both alcohol and drug abuse. The students seemed to have unlimited amounts of money to spend; and if she read the data correctly, the students seemed to be left at home, unsupervised, a considerable amount of the time.

While the students in her advanced algebra class wore the most fashionable designer jeans and shirts to class, sported $100 haircuts, and even drove their own Mercedeses and Porsches to school, they seemed to Charlotte to be unsure of themselves, their self-confidence hardly commensurate with their material wealth. As Charlotte got to know her students better, she learned, to her dismay, that parental expectations were excessive and that the pressure on students to compete and to excel was killing. Killing, she grimaced, was the word for it. Student deaths, from suicide, car accidents, and drug overdoses, were the highest in the state.

Charlotte knew that, underneath the elegant appearances, her students were troubled, and she was quick to recognize that their feelings of insecurity were at the root of their cruel aggressiveness to each other. It was as if there was room for only a very few at the top, and you needed to do whatever you had to do to make sure you were one of those few. If that meant kicking someone off the pinnacle, this you did with both arrogance and contempt for the loser. This students' world had no sympathy for losers.

There was too much at stake. Parents modeled that to be on top was everything, that second place was second-rate. Good grades earned perks—not just ordinary, run-of-the-mill perks, like $5 bonuses, but capital-P Perks, like a trip to Paris, a skiing weekend in Vail, a new Jeep. No wonder the students felt pressure to excel. No wonder they battled constant doubts about their feelings of adequacy. None of them, in their innermost, secret places, could ever feel adequate to meet the challenge of their parents' expectations.

When Fred Kim was enrolled in Charlotte's class, she felt that she had a real opportunity to broaden her students' horizons beyond the teaching of math. Here was a boy recently arrived from Korea, the only one of color in her class. Fred's English was marginal, but she had been assured that his math skills were excellent. Helping him to learn English, and helping him to make a place for himself in the school community, was a job Charlotte thought she could do. Maybe, just maybe, Fred would help her to humanize this cruelly competitive bunch. And her advanced algebra class was just the place for what she had in mind. She was immediately attracted to Fred Kim. She loved his sweet shyness and his hunger to make a place for himself in his new homeland. She loved his enthusiasm, which more than made up for his difficulty with the language. She was glad she taught math. Math, that great equalizer, gave everyone the same breaks.

Charlotte began thinking about trying something new in her class. She had heard about cooperative learning, and had even attended a staff development workshop in which the advantages of cooperative group work had been discussed for students at the secondary level. Charlotte wondered if arranging the class into cooperative learning groups on advanced algebra problems would diminish individual competitiveness, bolster student interest in the subject, create more enthusiasm for learning math, and give students a chance to work with Fred— and Fred a chance to work with them. In that way, perhaps the bridge between the two cultures could be crossed naturally, and Fred would have an easier time becoming accepted. Charlotte dared to hope that maybe, just maybe, she could help her students find their humanity.

Charlotte began by introducing the idea of working in groups to the students. She told them that they would be given a list of math problems, but that instead of working alone, they would team up in groups of four, and that each group, working together, would undertake to solve the problems. When all the groups were finished, the entire class would participate in a whole-class discussion, in which the answers from each group would be examined and evaluated. Grades for this assignment would be issued not individually, but collectively, as a representation of the overall quality of the entire group's performance. Charlotte perceived some uneasiness after this initial announcement, but she attributed this to the new way of working. Students, as well as teachers, she knew, tended to resist the new; they much preferred working in the old, established ways that were familiar. She thought she would be able to deal with that uneasiness, but she was totally unprepared for what happened when the groups began to be formed.

She had not thought she needed to determine in advance which students were to go to what groups; she had thought she would allow the students to choose their own groups. That, she believed, was the more democratic way. As she watched the groups form, she saw that students naturally gravitated toward one another on the basis of their out-of-class friendships. When all the groups had been assembled, Fred Kim stuck out like a sore thumb. Not only had he not been invited to join any of the groups, he had been explicitly rejected when he had taken the initiative by approaching one of the groups.

Seeing this, Charlotte reproached the class for their lack of courtesy and for their rejecting behaviors. "How could you behave this way?" she reprimanded them, flushed with her embarrassment for Fred. But her class surprised her.

Instead of acquiescing and owning up to their cruelty, they countered her reproach with their own brand of insolence. Talking in loud voices, and as if Fred did not exist, they told her: "Nobody wants him in their group! He would pull the group's grade down. His English is bad. Nobody can understand him. Besides, nobody likes him, and he smells bad."

Charlotte felt crushed by their assault. However, she hung in there and tried to persuade them that they were wrong. If they would only get to know Fred, they would find that he had an important contribution to make to the group work in math. She, too, began talking about Fred as if he weren't there, while he listened quietly and took everything in. But what was her choice? Should she have sent him out of the room so they could talk about him behind his back? Should she have waited to talk about this incident another day? Should she have ignored the whole business?

The heck with that, her students told her angrily. They were not going to work with Fred. No way.

"Well," said Charlotte, feeling that she was losing it, "we'll see about that, won't we?" She was not willing to back down, but when she heard the bell, she felt relief. The class spilled their hostility out into the hallway, and she met Fred's eyes with feelings of helplessness as he lingered to gather his books and make sure that the other students were well gone before he went out the classroom door.

Now, two days later, things came to a head. Robert Evans had told his parents that he was being forced to work with an immigrant boy who couldn't speak English and that if his teacher insisted on this grouping arrangement, he wanted his class changed. In the principal's office, Mr. and Mrs. Evans were polite, but their coldness came through like a chilly wind of winter.

Robert Evans, Sr., looked directly at Charlotte, as if he were a judge lecturing a wayward juvenile. "I can see, Ms. Cormier, that you are trying to promote some concern for these minority kids, but I'm damned if you are going to do that at my son's expense. This is, after all, a very competitive world, Ms. Cormier, and Robert is not going to lose marks for the sake of any foreign kid who can't even speak English."

He then turned to the principal, as if he were entering into some private agreement with her—just the two of them, excluding Charlotte entirely. "You know, Mrs. Rees," he said, his voice accentuating the sibilant, "don't get me wrong. I'm not prejudiced, but ever since these foreign students have been coming into our school, the academic standards here have been getting lower and lower. I don't want my son in a class where he will lose his competitive edge. Either Ms. Cormier changes her teaching practice and abandons her socialist notions of cooperative learning, or I want my son taken out of that class."

The 8:30 bell punctuated Robert Evans's last sentence, and Charlotte, doing her best to keep her voice from breaking, and said, "Excuse me, please. I can't be late for my first class."

"Please see me this afternoon, Charlotte, and we'll see if we can't resolve this to everyone's satisfaction," Katherine Rees, ever the political principal, smiled, as if she already had a plan to sweep this problem under the school rug.

Charlotte nodded and gulped. As she walked down the corridor toward her first class, she had never felt so alone.

Study Questions

1. Begin your discussion with an identification of what you consider to be the key issues of this case. List them, and then decide which of these is the most important issue.
2. How would you describe the students in Charlotte Cormier's class? Put together a list of adjectives that would be appropriate descriptors of these young people. Check over your list, and determine what data in the case point to the accuracy of the descriptors.
3. What is your view of Charlotte's decision to use cooperative learning groups in math? How do you see this strategy as appropriate to her goals?
4. What do you see as the factors that contributed to the conflict in Charlotte Cormier's classroom? What do you consider to be the surface factors? What do you consider to be the underlying factors?
5. What, in retrospect, might Charlotte have done differently? What leads you to believe that your recommendations would have made a difference to what occurred?
6. How might a good administrator respond to the Evans? What educational values does that response reflect? How do you believe Katherine Rees is going to respond? What makes you think so?
7. Based on your own values and beliefs about the goals of education, what advice would you give to Charlotte Cormier for when she returns to her advanced algebra class? How should Charlotte respond to Fred? How should she respond to Robert Evans?
8. What do you think Charlotte's next steps should be with her twelfth-grade math block? How do you see those steps as consonant with your own educational values?
†9. What experience of your own, in dealing with racial prejudice, relates to this case? Talk about the events in your group, and compare your experiences with Charlotte Cormier's.

5.7   WHO HAS THE RIGHT TO DECIDE WHAT HAPPENS IN MY CLASS?

The pathway around Lost Lagoon was empty, except for a gaggle of Canada geese that waddled up to them brazenly, bills yawning, desperately seeking the next handout. One goose tugged at the sleeve of her jacket and she had to turn and smile, in spite of the anger that had nearly consumed her that day. She was right to take her troubles into this beautiful, healing park. She knew the water birds from the bird sanctuary would cheer her and that the overhead canopy of Douglas firs and cedars would protect her and give her solace. Already, she could feel the anger slipping away, leaving a dull ache that lingered like the smell of yesterday's cigarettes. Amy turned to Robin, speaking her first words since she had telephoned him and asked him to meet her here. With Robin, she always felt safe, able to speak her heart. He would listen and he would understand.

"It's hard, even now, to talk about it. I was so angry, Robin, so hurt, so humiliated. I came so close to calling him some dreadful names. I wanted to shout terrible curses, all those ugly, rude accusations that people yell at each other when they're driving." Suddenly she snickered and her mouth turned up in a crooked grin.

He looked at her and said, "What?"

"I just thought of the headline in tomorrow's supermarket tabloid: New young teacher cusses out vice principal. Read all about it. The scandal of Templewood School." Amy Baker let the grin spread across her face and light up her eyes.

"What?" he said again.

"I just thought up some new curses." They both laughed as they walked toward the bench, two geese stalking them, reluctant to give up on their quarry.

"Well, are you going to tell me about it?" he asked.

Amy sat down and picked up her brother's hand. They had been close since they were children. Maybe it was because they were only 18 months apart. Perhaps their father's premature death when they were both so young heightened their bond. Robin and Amy against the world. They had been there for each other in sickness and in health, in sorrow and in joy. Amy knew that Robin was there for her now. She turned to him, with a sigh that came from the marrow of her bones, and said, "I don't even know where to begin."

Amy Baker was appointed to teach science at Templewood Junior High School in January of that year. Although Templewood was situated in the suburban school district of South Hillsborough, the enormity of the district and the socioeconomic problems of the community made it seem more like teaching in the inner city. Amy was not complaining. She was glad to have a job and felt particularly lucky to have gotten an appointment in midyear. Many of her friends from university were still out there looking. Times were hard, jobs scarce, and schools, like businesses in the private sector, were cutting back on staff. English teachers were a glut on the market. But with a major in science or math, a new teacher had a better chance. Amy had student taught in South Hillsborough and had had some experience with the hard edge of many of the adolescents enrolled in Templewood. Petty crime, drugs, car theft, gangs, violence, even guns—all were steadily making inroads into the school. What scared Amy more than the rise of violence in and around the school was the insistence by school officials that none of these problems was "anything to worry about" in South Hillsborough. Did they think the trouble would disappear if everyone pretended it wasn't happening? How large did the problem have to become before it would be given serious attention? Amy wondered, as she watched her students get more and more sucked up into the antisocial values of the peer culture.

In spite of her concerns about the problems at Templewood, Amy found that she was able to make a good connection with the majority of her ninth-grade students in general science. Amy's manner with them was respectful, and she was able to communicate to them that she cared about how they were doing and was ready to help them pass the course. She was able to be authoritative, without being authoritarian; kind, without being soft; and concerned, without being soppy. She also knew her subject well and found inventive and challenging ways to stimulate student interest in the material. All of these attributes, however, were not enough to ensure her rapport with every student. There were a few in each class who seemed to be quite beyond her ability to reach; kids who, she felt, in the ninth grade were already lost. Nevertheless, she still kept trying, hoping that some day, in some way, she would break through and find a way to connect with those "turned-off" and disaffected young people. But in the meantime, they sure knew how to give her a hard time.

It was in one of those small groups of "boys in trouble" that Amy's trouble began. On Monday of that week, she had given a test on the material in Chapter 14 of the science text. During the test period, she had looked up from her desk and noted that Tom Fillmore and Randy Holborn were exchanging meaningful glances. It was impossible to approach them without singling them out and this she did, although reluctantly. "Tom and Randy," she announced, "keep your eyes on your own papers." After that, she kept a closer watch, and it seemed to her that the boys were tapping out the answers to the multiple-choice questions. In a hasty response, she told Tom to change his seat for the remainder of the period.

That evening, when she was marking the test papers, she saw that Tom's and Randy's answers to questions 1 through 15 were identical. Even so, she could not be absolutely certain they had been cheating, and it was difficult for her to decide what to do. She could ignore it and assume that no cheating had actually occurred. Perhaps they hadn't been cheating? Maybe she was seeing things after all?

Two cups of strong coffee later, she decided to give the boys a choice. They could take a grade of zero for this test, or they could retake the test later in the week. What they got on the makeup test would become their official mark. The next day, when she presented Tom and Randy with this choice, they both argued vehemently that they had not cheated and that she was picking on them. After lengthy argument, both boys agreed to take the test again on Thursday. On Friday, Amy returned Tom's paper with a grade of 53%, and Randy's with a grade of 48%. To Amy, this confirmed her suspicion that the boys had, in fact, been cheating on the first exam.

At the end of the period, both boys came up to Amy, shouting at her unfairness. As their voices rose, Amy felt her cheeks flush and her temper rise. Her "cool" was evaporating. The boys shouted accusations at her: She was singling them out; they had already taken the test and passed; she was being unreasonable, unfair; she was picking on them for no good reason. In the face of their charges, Amy lost her cool.

"I've had enough. Now get out of here, both of you," she stormed at them.

"I'll get out, you stupid bitch," yelled Tom. "This isn't over yet." The two boys powered out of the room, the air still charged with the tension of the encounter.

Amy spent the weekend at the shore, easing away the tensions of the school week. When she returned to school on Monday, refreshed and ready to take on the new week's adventures, she found a letter from Tom in her box.

"Dear Miss Baker," it began. "I am sorry I got mad and yelled at you. But what you did was un-fair. We did not cheat in the first place and its not right that we should have to fail this test. My idea is that you should let me take the test again. But this time, give me some help and give me some time to stoudy. And I no I could do good. Im sorry I called you a bitch but I was very mad." Amy noted that the spelling left a lot to be desired.

On the bottom of her mailbox, below the junk mail and the pile of school board notices, was a pink memo, the distinctive color of "from the desk of Keith McConachie, VP" asking her to see him as soon as possible. Not once did she think that these two communications had any connection. If someone had told her that they had, she would have laughed it off.

The staff room at 7:30 A.M. was the usual hubub of teachers trying to gather energy to face their first Monday morning classes from the unspeakable brown liquid that was called coffee. The label, however, was its only relationship to the real thing. Amy pulled her "Smile" mug from the cupboard and let the thick, brown liquid pour from the spigot. At least it was hot. Terry Bowman, cup in hand, moved to her side.

"I heard you had a dustup with Tom Fillmore on Friday," she said, without a trace of a smile. Amy wondered if this was going to be a serious conversation. Terry was the school counselor who ran a special program for kids in trouble at Templewood. Tom Fillmore had been in Terry's program last year and Tom continued to see Terry, who had become something of his advocate. Whenever Tom found himself in trouble, it was Terry who took his part with the school authorities. Whatever Tom had done, Terry seemed to have a way of explaining it and setting wheels in motion for Tom to "do better next time." What Amy and other teachers could not fail to notice was that Tom did not "do better next time," and that the incidents of his getting into trouble, rather than diminishing, seemed to be on the increase. Had Tom learned how to manipulate Terry to his advantage? These thoughts slipped across the threshold of Amy's consciousness as Terry continued to speak.

"Tom came to me Friday at lunch, and he was very upset, Amy."

"*He* was upset?" Amy choked on her coffee, spattering it on her clean white jacket. "What do you mean *he* was upset? What about *me* was upset?"

Terry's voice was now cajoling. "He's only a kid, Amy. He's trying, you know. And he needs our help."

"I'm not sure if he's trying, Terry. That's the thing of it. I think he's just manipulating us, you, me, all of us. I think this kid's in serious trouble." Amy tried to stay calm, thinking that calmness and logic were better allies than shouting and emotionality.

"Well, I'm sure you'll agree," Terry was now placating, "that he deserves another chance. Don't you think he should have that chance?"

Amy puckered her mouth, thinking aloud. "He did send me this gosh-awful note this morning, you know, asking for another chance. He even apologized. But you know, Terry, I have this terrible, awful, gut-wrenching feeling that this kid's a real con artist."

"I know he sent you the note, Amy. I told him to do it, that I thought it would be a good idea."

Amy's eyes went to Terry's face, tried to read it, and failed. "So it wasn't even on his own initiative that he sent that apology and the suggestion? You *told* him to do it?" She couldn't keep the edge out of her voice, betraying disappointment in both her colleague and her student.

"Yes, I did. I thought he should appeal to you. I also made a copy of his note and sent it to Keith McConachie. I thought he should be briefed on this situation."

"You did what?" Amy spluttered as the 8:00 bell sounded the beginning of her first class.

As Amy raced down the hall, books and papers clutched to her chest, she could feel her anger mounting and was sure that her face would be beet red by the time she got to room 102. "That insufferable twit," she muttered to herself. "Just who does she think she is!" Amy shoved open the door to room 102 as if it were her worst enemy and stood in the front of her classroom, facing 27 pairs of eyes.

"All right," she managed a small smile, "what did you make of that chapter on the internal combustion engine? Anybody?"

Three classes later, she made her way down to the general office, where Keith McConachie was waiting. She was furious that Terry had taken her problem with Tom Fillmore to the vice principal. This was something between Amy and Tom. Why was it necessary to involve the administration?

Keith McConachie told Amy to sit down and asked her what she was going to do about Tom. Amy, who had not had a chance to consider Tom's request rationally since she had received it this morning, said she hadn't quite thought it out yet.

"Surely, this isn't a matter that requires too much thinking about, Amy?" McConachie smirked at her in a way that she found both patronizing and offensive. "You have some options here. It's not very complicated."

Was it her imagination, Amy wondered, or was his tone of voice paternal, slightly mocking, as if she were a wayward child? Was she reading too much into it, or was it there?

"What are your options, Amy?" he pressed, like a persistent teacher determined to get the right answer.

"As I see it, Mr. McConachie, I have two options. The first is to concede to Tom's demands. The second is to allow the mark on the second test to stand, and to put this event behind me. And now I'd like to tell you, Mr. McConachie," Amy's voice inflection traced his name in bold letters, "what I've decided to do. Tom Fillmore is not going to get the chance to take this test for the third time. His mark of 53% is going to stand."

Keith McConachie got to his feet and his 6'3" frame hunched over Amy, still in the chair. His face stern, and his voice a wagging finger, he proceeded to instruct her in the error of her ways.

"You beginning teachers," he scowled, his eyebrows like large gray worms, inching toward his nose, "you think you know it all. You come out of college so set in your ways, you think that there's nothing in the schools for you to learn. You know, Amy, inflexibility is the hallmark of the least effective teacher." His voice suddenly softened, the good-cop/bad-cop routine. "You've got to learn to bend, Amy, to bend with the demands of the job. Be flexible. Bend to what is required in the situation. Now this is what you are going to do."

She sat there, feeling small and insulted, listening to Keith McConachie talking to her as if he was her father and she was the 5-year-old who had just taken an apple from the neighbor's tree.

"I think it would be a good idea if you wrote Tom a letter and thanked him for his letter, telling him that he has your permission to retake the test and that you will be happy to see him, how many times? three? four? to give him extra help. I think, too, Amy, that you should apologize to Tom. You know, set a good example."

Amy was unable to speak. She felt crushed and humiliated. McConachie had pushed all the buttons, elevating her doubts about herself and the decision she had made as a teacher. She thought seriously at that moment about walking out of his office and walking away from teaching forever.

"You know, Amy," McConachie went on, "Tom is a troubled boy who is trying hard to turn himself around. Our job is to give him every chance. Not to be punitive or inflexible, but to encourage. That's the way we help boys in trouble, Amy. Surely you know that." McConachie took her arm and ushered her out of the chair, and out the door, closing it behind him.

Amy stood there, not knowing what to do. Why hadn't she fought back? Taken a stand? Told McConachie that it was *her* class, *her* students, *her* choice? He had no right to tell her what to do in her class . . . or did he?

Study Questions

1. As you see it, what are the central issues in this case? Talk together about these issues and then list them in order of what you consider to be their significance.
2. What adjectives would you use to describe Amy Baker? Write a profile of Amy, based on the data in the case, that would describe her to the personnel officer of the school where she was applying for a position. Do the same for Keith McConachie, the vice principal.
3. What adjectives would you use to describe Tom Fillmore? Write a profile of Tom, based on the data in the case, that would describe him to the guidance counselor of the secondary school where he is to be enrolled next term.
4. What is your response to the way Amy handled the "suspicion of cheating" incident in her classroom? What action did she take that was, in your view, appropriate? What action was, in your view, inappropriate? What do you believe she might have done differently?
5. What should a teacher do when students are suspected of cheating? What are your views on this?
6. How do you see the role of Terry Bowman having an impact on the events in this case? How should Amy have responded to Terry? What are your views on it? How do you see those actions as appropriate?
7. What is your response to the vice principal's behavior? What hypotheses can you suggest that would explain his behavior to Amy?
8. What should Amy do now? What do you see as some of her options? What do you see as some potential consequences of those actions, both on her self-concept and on the educational climate of her class? What would you do if you were in her shoes?
†9. Talk about an event from your own experience where you suspected students of cheating. How did you respond? In retrospect, what might you have done differently?
†10. Talk about an experience you had with an administrator that was similar to Amy's. What feelings did this provoke in you? How did you respond? In retrospect, what might you have done differently?

5.8 THIS STUFF IS BORING!

Nikolaus leaped up onto the bed and began licking her face. His raspy tongue felt like she was being caressed by a saguaro cactus, and she forced the dream from her mind and edged it into semiconsciousness.

"Nickel," she murmured, voice still thick with zzzz's. "It's not time to get up yet. Give me a break."

The silky-haired sealpoint feline put his full weight on her chest and, kneading the covers with alternate claws, looked her right in the eye. He was serious. Audrey Lee Jackson knew better than to try to ignore this cat who ran her life. She tossed the covers aside, looked at the clock, which had at least seven minutes to go before the radio alarm would have wakened her, and headed for the shower. The cat trailed her into the bathroom, purring along in the key of A-flat.

Seven minutes ahead of schedule gave her time for a second cup of coffee. She sipped the strong, black brew slowly, watching Nikolaus devouring the last morsels of his liver and kidney, kitty blue-plate special, and suddenly realized that for the first time since the term began in September, she was actually excited about going to school. She smiled to herself, thinking, "Yeah, I could really get to like this job."

It wasn't that Audrey Lee Jackson disliked teaching. As a beginning teacher, with a tough seventh-grade assignment in an inner-city school, she had been trying to keep on top of things since the first day of classes. But most of the time, until now, it felt more like she kept missing the train. When she had been a student teacher, she could see how easy it seemed for her mentor teacher, Julia Brown, to keep the class together, interested, on-task, and in control. But whatever magic Julia used eluded Audrey Lee. Audrey's first six weeks with her seventh-grade class were full of tensions. She had yet to be able to orchestrate all the classroom elements that turned teaching into one harmonious tune. How was it possible to meet individual needs, plan curriculum, keep on schedule, maintain discipline, grade papers, and teach lessons—all together—to produce a smoothly running classroom in which children were actually learning something of value?

She had to admit that even though many of her seventh-grade students came from dysfunctional family situations, they were not "bad" kids. Many of them were bright beyond their years. A teacher should not judge kids by their appearance, she knew. Their funny haircuts—the boys' imitations of sprouted wheat on a closely mowed lawn, the girls' dreadlocks—torn jeans, and disheveled T-shirts were not good indicators of their ability to learn. In the first six weeks of school, she had seen that the range of their abilities was as far apart as their heights—from the shortest at 4' 10" to the tallest at 5' 9".

Many of her students actually liked school, and she thought they liked her, too. When they acted out, which they did from time to time, it was usually in response to something she had tried that had not worked—something that fell flat on its face, like the time she thought it might be a good idea for the kids to make election posters to support one of two candidates who were running for president of the school council. In retrospect, she knew she should have allowed them to make a poster for the candidate of their own choice. Instead, she had divided the class in half, down the middle, and assigned each half the candidate of *her* choice. She could see now why many of the children were angry, acted out, used some purple language, and protested the activity. She found herself in battle with them, finally insisting that they do the posters as she had assigned them—or else! It was not a happy day for Audrey Lee or for the class. They had responded in sullen silence and, in an act of tacit group protest, turned out some of the meanest, ugliest, stupidest posters that were ever drawn. At three o'clock, she had dumped the lot into the trash-for-recycling bin.

When she talked with her best friend, Allie Cooper, who had also begun to teach in September at another school across the city, Allie told Audrey Lee that maybe it would be a good idea if she allowed her students to have some more choices in what she was giving them to do. Did Audrey Lee have to be in control of everything? "I mean," Allie asked, "what was so important about your choosing which candidate they should do the poster for? Why couldn't they make that choice for themselves?"

Audrey Lee felt herself getting defensive. "Well, suppose everyone chose the same candidate? Then what? Shouldn't I try to insure that both candidates were equally represented by posters?"

"Listen, Audrey Lee. I have news for you. It's called democracy. We get to vote for the candidates of our choice. Why require a child to do a poster for someone whom he or she is not going to vote for?"

What Allie was saying made sense, even though Audrey Lee was not willing to admit it just then. But she knew she would have to think through this idea of why she needed to exercise control over the students' choices. Where should she draw the line between allowing students more choices and still maintaining control over the class? She did not know.

By mid-October, Audrey Lee was ready to act on Allie's advice. She'd gotten to know the students in her class better and had grown to be less fearful of losing control. She wanted to try some group project work, and as she thumbed through the math textbook one evening, she hit on the idea of teaching bar graphs with a strategy she had learned about in college—cooperative learning groups—but had, until now, been afraid to try.

On Tuesday, at math time, she introduced the concept of bar graphs to the class. First she told the class about bar graphs and how the graphs "represent data, by making a picture of that data, using bars." She then put a chart she had prepared on the chalkboard, showing how information was graphed using bars. (See Figure 5.1).

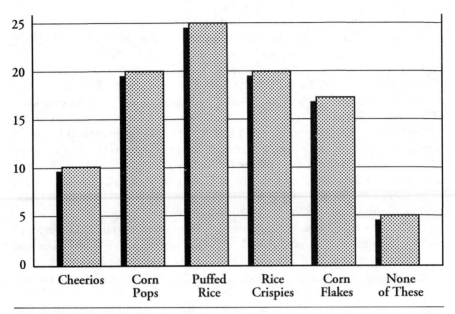

Figure 5.1. What Cereal Do You Eat?

Using her arm as a pointer, she told the class that the numbers on the left side of the graph showed "how many people" in the group ate that cereal, while the brands across the bottom of the graph spelled out the kind of cereal they ate. She then showed, by pointing to the top of the bar for Cheerios, that it was in line with the number ten, indicating that ten people ate Cheerios. Next, she called for hands to tell how many children ate Corn Pops, Puffed Rice, and so forth.

"Okay, now who can tell me how many children eat Corn Pops? William?"

"Twenty. I see 20," William replied.

"Good, William. How about Corn Flakes? How many eat Corn Flakes? Marshall?"

"I don't know, Miss Jackson," Marshall said, his brow furrowed.

"Okay, Marshall. What about Sven? Can you tell how many people eat Corn Flakes, Sven?"

"Twenty?" Sven replied, making his answer into a question.

"No, Sven. That's Corn Pops, not Corn Flakes. Look here, at the Corn Flakes bar." Audrey Lee used her arm to point to the Corn Flakes bar, and demonstrated, by moving her arm across the middle of the space, between fifteen and twenty, where the top of the Corn Flakes bar rested. "How far does this bar reach, Sven? You can see it here." She moved her arm to the left side of the graph that showed the numbers.

"Oh, I see. Between 15 and 20."

Audrey Lee laughed. "Okay, Sven. That's good enough. Between 15 and 20. Would you go for 17? How many would go for 17?" Several children raised their hands. "Okay. Good. I can see that you are figuring it out."

From the students' responses, Audrey Lee concluded that they could understand the concept of bar graphs sufficiently for her to go on to the next step. Her next move was to divide the class into groups of four. To each group of four she gave a question. Tomorrow, the entire math period would be devoted to gathering data on this question that would allow the students to construct their bar graphs. With 32 students in class, she was able to create eight groups. Each group was presented with one of the following questions:

1. How many hours a week do you watch TV?
2. What do you watch most on TV?
3. Do you believe what you see and hear on commercials?
4. Do you think that commercials show stereotypes?
5. Do commercials really make you want the product that is being advertised?
6. When do you listen to the radio?
7. What siblings do you have problems with most often?
8. When do you get along best with your siblings?

The students seemed interested and attentive, and at the end of the math period Audrey Lee was satisfied that she had set the curriculum plan in motion for the next day's group work.

Even though Nickel the cat had awakened her early on Wednesday morning, Audrey Lee only managed to get to school just before the bell. She was scrambling to get her teaching materials ready as the students pounded into the room. One of these days, she reprimanded herself silently, she would get to class in enough good time to put the assignments on the board and get the materials ready before the students were in their seats. As long as she could remember, Audrey Lee had never been an early bird. Was it too late to change? Were her "just on time" patterns too deeply entrenched? She sighed as she picked up the chalk and hastily wrote the assignments on the board, while the class chattered noisily in the background, bringing one another up on the latest gossip.

At eleven o'clock, Audrey launched into the bar graph lesson. "You remember that yesterday, I taught you about bar graphs? How many remember what a bar graph is?"

Lazily, several hands reached for the fluorescent fixtures attached to the ceiling.

"Okay, Rubin. What's a bar graph?"

A long, slow smile spread across the boy's face, as Audrey Lee waited for

Rubin to respond. After a few seconds, she gave up on Rubin, who continued to smile, without speaking, and asked, "Anybody? What's a bar graph? Arabella?"

"It's how you tell how many kids ate Cheerios and stuff like that," Arabella offered, unsure.

"Right, Arabella. That's very good." Audrey Lee filled in the missing ingredients as she reexplained the meaning and uses of bar graphs.

"Now, remember yesterday I assigned each of you to groups? Well, I want you now to change your seats and sit together with your groups. Then we'll gather the information we need to make our own bar graphs."

There was a noisy scrambling around as the students shouted to one another, scraped chairs across the floor, and arranged themselves into groups. It took 10 minutes for them to settle down, and Audrey Lee wondered if there might have been a better way to have gone about this.

"Okay," she said when she again had their attention. "We'll start with group 1, Devi's group. What was your question, Devi? What are you going to get information about?"

Devi rummaged in her book bag, found her notebook, and riffled through the pages. "Just a second, Ms. Jackson. I have it. I know it's here." Audrey Lee's eyes turned to the ceiling as she wondered if classroom teaching was full of scenes of 31 students waiting on a single child. How much time was consumed by waiting?

"Here it is, Ms. Jackson," Devi's voice pitched with relief. "It says, 'How many hours a week do you watch TV?'"

"Okay. Good, Devi. Now, Devi's group, are you listening and watching? You will have to take notes while the class votes on this. Okay. Now the rest of you, raise your hands for how many hours a week you watch TV. How many watch for no hours a week?" The students laughed and chattered to one another. Danny Patel said he watched no hours when he was grounded with no privileges, but that didn't count. Audrey Lee instructed Devi's group to record in their books that zero children watched TV no hours a week.

"Who watches 5 hours a week?" Bradley was the only one to raise his hand, as Audrey Lee instructed Devi's group to record the information that one student watched for five hours a week.

"Okay. Now who watches 10 hours?" Five students raised their hands, and Audrey Lee told Devi's group to note that five students watched for 10 hours.

"Fifteen hours? How many for 15 hours?" Audrey Lee moved, through intervals of five, up to 30 hours, until all the children's TV watching time had been recorded. "Okay, Devi's group. You've got your information. Hold onto it until we're all finished. Okay?" As they nodded, she began the same procedures with the next group.

"Okay, Vanessa's group. What was your question? 'Do you believe what you see and hear on commercials?' Okay, let's take the class vote on that.

Vanessa's group, now you will record this vote, okay, so your group can make the bar graph when we're finished voting on all the questions. Okay?

"Now, how many of you believe what you see and hear on commercials? Raise hands. Okay, let's count."

Ben Dayton yelled over to Charlie Berwicke, whose hand was one of the few raised. "Hey, Charlie, you dweeb. Of course you'd believe anything!" The class roared.

"Okay, Ben. That's enough. Four. I count four. Vanessa, make sure you record four. How many do not believe what you see or hear in commercials?"

Audrey Lee Jackson followed this procedure until all the students had declared their positions on all of the questions she had given to all the groups. Even though this activity took all of the math and the social studies periods as well, Audrey felt it was worth it to finish the data-gathering task in one day.

"Okay, now keep this information handy, because tomorrow your groups will be making their bar graphs." The lunch bell rang, eclipsing her last words, as the students made a scrimmage through the classroom door.

She watched the last of them leave and hoped that the data that they had spent nearly two hours gathering today would not be lost for tomorrow's graphing activity. As an afterthought, she wondered if maybe she should also have kept a record of the votes, just in case.

On Thursday, she planned to allow a full two hours for math, so that the groups would have ample time to complete their bar graphs. By way of introduction, she told the class that she would put her bar graph on the board as a sample that they could use if they needed a reference to guide them. She also distributed a large sheet of newsprint paper to each of the groups. To her surprise and chagrin, she found that most of the groups needed her help in figuring out what they were supposed to do. She had to go from group to group instructing them in how the graph was to be plotted, how the number intervals were to be spaced, and how the data would be represented. Fatigued with their demands for her help, she found herself telling each group just how to do the task, showing them exactly what needed to be done. She would have preferred to work slowly with each group, getting them to try to figure out the procedures for themselves, but the pressure of other groups who needed her help prevented her from using those teaching strategies. She had to sacrifice getting them to figure it out for themselves, in favor of efficiency in providing help to all the groups that needed it.

Even though she had allowed two hours for the task, several groups had not completed their bar graphs by lunchtime on Thursday, and that meant that Audrey Lee had to carry over this part of the task until Friday. The students who were finished were given free time on Friday, while the remaining groups finished drawing their bar graphs.

On Monday each group showed their bar graphs to the rest of the class, and Audrey Lee posted the bar graph charts up around the room. She noted that some groups had used felt pens to make their graphs more colorful, and she was generally pleased with the results of the students' efforts. Just before lunch, in the final 15 minutes of the morning, Audrey Lee sat on top of her desk, her legs dangling over the side, and asked the class how they felt about the activity on bar graphs.

"I liked it, Ms. Jackson. It gave me a chance to work with my friends. That was fun." Audrey Lee smiled at Pam. This was the kind of answer she was hoping for. But she wanted more.

Several other students concurred. There was agreement that group work was appreciated, fun, interesting.

"Anyone have any criticisms? Things we could do better? Come on now, I'd like to hear them, if you do." She was sorry even before she finished the sentence that she had asked.

"If you ask me, it was boring. I mean, there was no real challenge to it. What did we do? We took votes and then all we did was to make these graphs showing how the votes went. There's nothing to that stuff, and the questions were so stupid. I mean, it was fun to work with my friends and I really liked that part. But as a math activity, I found it a total waste of time." Paul, her brightest and most challenging student, sat down with a huff as the other students grew silent. She looked out at the class as they waited for her response, and when the lunch bell rang, she knew that her reprieve was momentary.

Study Questions

1. What, in your opinion, are the critical issues in this case? Talk together and decide on what you perceive as the key issues. Then list them in what you consider to be their order of importance.
2. What kind of a teacher is Audrey Lee Jackson? What data from the case are you using in your description?
3. What are the students like in this class? What data from the case are you using to back up your ideas? Based on your views of these learners, what teaching strategies would you consider more appropriate for teaching them mathematical concepts?
4. In the incident with the election posters, Audrey Lee examines her needs for control. How do her control needs impact on the math lesson? On what data is your opinion based?
5. What, in your viewpoint, are control needs? Where do you suppose they come from? Where do you draw the line between a teacher's control needs and allowing students choices? What are the implications of control and choice for student learning?

6. From the point of view of mathematics teaching, how would you evaluate Audrey Lee's math lesson on bar graphs? What were some good elements of this lesson? What do you consider to be some serious flaws?
7. Make a list of what you consider to be seriously wrong with the math lesson. Talk together about why you consider these aspects of the lesson to be flaws. Talk about how, if you were doing this lesson, you would alter the procedures.
8. What, in your view, did the students learn about math in this lesson? What data are you using to back up that opinion?
9. What should Audrey Lee's response be to Paul? To the class? What would you advise her to say? What would you say and do if you were in her place?
†10. Audrey Lee chose expediency, in providing help to her groups, over giving the kind of instruction that would allow students to figure things out for themselves. What is your point of view on that choice? What do you see as some consequences on pupil learning of her choice of expediency? Under what circumstances were you faced with a similar choice? What do you see as the impact on student learning of either choice?
†11. If you wanted to teach students about bar graphs (or any other math ematical concept) and you wanted to use cooperative learning groups, how would you go about doing it?

RELATED READINGS

Adam, Maureen, et al. 1991. *Evaluation Materials for the Graduation Program*. Victoria, British Columbia: Ministry of Education.

Aikin, Wilford. 1942. *The Story of the Eight Year Study*. New York: Harper & Row.

Ashton-Warner, Sylvia. 1963. *Teacher*. New York: Simon & Schuster.

Bickerton, Laura, et al. 1991. *Cases for Teaching in the Secondary School*. Coquitlam, British Columbia: Caseworks.

Brown, Mary, and Precious, Norman. 1968. *The Integrated Day in the Primary School*. London: Ward Lock.

Christensen, C. Roland, and Hansen, Abby. 1987. *Teaching and the Case Method*. Boston: Harvard School of Business.

Costa, Arthur. (Ed.). 1985. *Developing Minds*. Washington, DC: Association for Supervision and Curriculum Development.

Eisner, Elliott. 1979. *The Educational Imagination*. New York: Macmillan.

Gardner, Howard. 1991. *The Unschooled Mind*. New York: Basic Books.

Glasser, William. 1985. *Control Theory in the Classroom*. New York: HarperCollins.

Goodlad, John. 1986. *A Place Called School*. New York: McGraw-Hill.

Goodman, Kenneth, and Goodman, Yetta. 1989. *The Whole Language Evaluation Book*. Portsmouth, NH: Heinemann.

Howes, Virgil. 1974. *Informal Teaching in the Open Classroom.* New York: Macmillan.

Johnson, David W.; Johnson, Roger T.; Holubec, Edythe Johnson; and Row, Patricia. 1984. *Circles of Learning.* Washington, DC: Association for Supervision and Curriculum Development.

Kendall, Frances E. 1983. *Diversity in the Classroom.* New York: Teachers College Press.

Lampert, Magdalene. "How Do Teachers Manage to Teach? Perspectives on Problems in Practice." *Harvard Educational Review,* 55(2), 178–194.

Marshall, Sybil. 1968. *An Experiment in Education.* Cambridge, England: Cambridge University Press.

Moffett, James. 1968. *A Student Centered Language Arts Curriculum.* Boston: Houghton Mifflin.

Postman, Neil, and Weingartner, Charles. 1969. *Teaching as a Subversive Activity.* New York: Delacorte.

Pratt, Caroline. 1948, 1970. *I Learn from Children.* New York: Simon & Schuster.

Ramsey, Patricia G. 1986. *Teaching and Learning in a Diverse World.* New York: Teachers College Press.

Wassermann, Selma. 1990. *Serious Players in the Primary Classroom.* New York: Teachers College Press.

Wassermann, Selma, and Ivany, J. W. George. 1989. *Teaching Elementary Science: Who's Afraid of Spiders?* New York: HarperCollins.

6 | Learning About Teaching from Writing Your Own Cases

Nancy Fusco's case

The classroom was crowded, noisy. The students were making *papier mâché* masks. Some were placing wet strips of paper on clay molds. Some were still shaping their molds and tearing strips of newspaper. Some were mixing batches of wheat paste. It was a productive time, and the children seemed happy, busy, seriously engaged. I surveyed the scene and felt pleased with myself. My first major art project with my class had gotten off to a very good start. I walked around the room observing, thinking that this had to be one of my very best teaching days in my short and tumultuous career in this combined fifth- and sixth-grade classroom.

"Ms. Fusco, Ms. Fusco," the intercom exploded with urgency. "Will you come to the office right away? There's an important phone call for you."

Damn, I thought. What can be more important than my being here with my students? I flicked the light switch on and off to get the students' attention. "I've got to go down to the office for a few minutes, so I'm leaving you on your own. I hope that you will behave responsibly." The children barely noticed as I slipped out of the door, so deep was their involvement in their tasks.

The call was from Mrs. Collins, Ned's mother. He had forgotten his money for the book club order, due today. Would I be good enough to advance Ned the money? Mrs. Collins would send it in tomorrow. "No problem," I said, while thinking, "Some emergency." I returned to the classroom to find the students still working on their masks. "This could take the rest of the morning," I thought, while I wondered if I should allow the art work to continue until then or to cut it off at 11:00, as I had originally planned.

"Better take care of Ned's book order first, before I forget," I thought, as my hand reached down to the bottom drawer of my desk where I had been keeping the money and the orders for the Arrow Book Club, to be sent in at the close of school today.

No manila envelope there, I groped further, pulled the drawer all the way out. Nothing but papers, assorted junk. "What the heck?" I thought. "Did I put it someplace else?" I was certain that I had put the envelope in the bottom drawer, but I searched the other drawers just to be sure. Maybe I had misplaced it? Maybe I had absent-mindedly put it elsewhere? The envelope with the money for the children's book orders was definitely gone. It had been there this morning, I knew, because I had collected money and book orders from Ricky and Margaret, and I remembered putting the envelope down into that bottom drawer. Hard as it was to believe, I had to conclude that one of the children had stolen it, probably while I was out of the room, while the rest of the class was busy with their masks.

My eyes traveled to where Kevin was working. He was wrapping long, wet shreds of newspaper around his clay form, seemingly oblivious to my gaze. I felt immediately guilt-ridden and angry. I had known from his former class records that Kevin had a long history of petty thievery. Why had I been so stupid as to have left the money in the drawer, unlocked and unprotected? Was Kevin the culprit this time? Was it my fault for being so cavalier about where I was keeping the money? Was there another explanation? And what should I do now? Seventy-six dollars was a lot for me to reimburse, yet who would be responsible for seeing that the children who had given me money would, in fact, receive the books that they had paid for?

I looked again at Kevin, his freckled face intent on lining up the wet paper strip with the shape of the mold, the picture of innocence. Suddenly I felt tired, defeated. How could Kevin, or any other child in my class, have done this to me? To the other children? My heart ached with an overpowering sense of betrayal.

Dave Liddle's case

I was a little nervous, but after all, it was the first time I had ever taught a case. My mentor teacher, Steve Faralkof, a strong advocate of teaching by the case method, had been using cases in his eleventh-grade social studies classes for the last two years and was impressed with the results he was getting from his students. He urged me, as his new student teacher, to try a case and offered to help me develop the skills I would need to conduct the class discussion effectively. I was intrigued and willing to give it a chance.

The day before, I had prepared the students by asking them to read for homework "The Case of Swallowed Pride," a case of one rural family's plight during the Great Depression of the 1930s. The next day, I began the class by arranging the students in groups of four, asking them to discuss the study questions appended to the case. I allowed forty minutes for this, almost half the class period. Following the students' work in their discussion groups, I called them together and began what I hoped would be a productive examination of the important issues in and around the Great Depression, as well as its impact on farm families in particular.

During the class discussion, I tried to use the discussion strategies suggested by my mentor teacher. Steve had told me that I must, above all:

Listen to each student's idea as he or she is stating it.

Try to paraphrase the student's idea in a nonjudgmental way, so that the student could hear it "played back" for his or her further examination.

Frame a thought-provoking question that required the student to examine his or her idea from another perspective.

Avoid using tough, challenging questions prematurely, as they tend to put students on the defensive and prevent deeper examination of the initial ideas.

The class discussion was slow in getting started. I opened the discussion by posing the first question from the study sheet, "What does the Great Depression mean to you?" To my disappointment, the students responded with cosmic silence. Steve, who was watching all this from the back of the room, smiled. He told me later that he had seen this happen many times, especially when students were unfamiliar with thinking their own ideas and had lingering fears from other classes about "giving the wrong answer." While Steve knew that the best strategy was to wait the students out, I did not have the confidence to wait for the students to break the silence.

My response to the silence was to ask the question again, and in the absence of a volunteer, I called on Malcolm, who was at that moment whispering a message into Brandon's ear.

"Whaddya say, man? I didn't hear you," Malcolm pulled my chain. The class snickered.

I tried to keep my tone neutral, my feelings in check, as I responded to Malcolm. "I asked you what the Great Depression meant to you, Malcolm. Do you have any ideas?" In spite of my attempt to be cool, I could not keep an edge out of my voice.

"Shoot, man. It mean poor. Poor like me." Again the class snickered. I felt I was losing it. I stopped to think about what Steve had told me and, in my anxiety, could not remember to "play Malcolm's idea back," indicating that I had heard it and was ready to work with him in examining the implications of that idea. Instead, I posed a tough, challenging question, unrelated to Malcolm's statement.

"Okay, Malcolm. What brought it about?"

Malcolm looked like he had been punched in the face. He sat back in his chair and twisted his body to the side, giving half his back to me. Then, as if talking to his friend Brendon, he said in a voice loud enough for me and the rest of the class to hear, "Why do you have to make me look stupid, man? I thought teachers were supposed to help you learn, not make you feel stupid."

I felt twenty-nine pairs of eyes fixing on me, as I wished the ground would open up and swallow me whole.

Helen Hunter's case

I heard her yelling even though the classroom door was shut, and when l opened it and entered, I saw her, hovering over Luis, who looked up at her, big black eyes filling with tears.

"Why did you do that? Answer me! Why did you do that, I said?"

The more the child retreated into his seat, the more strident her shouts became. "That is an ugly, disgusting thing to do. I won't have that happen in my class. Do you hear me? Don't you dare do that again." A red flush began at her neckline and mottled her face. It was as if she had seen Satan in this small, incontinent 6-year-old boy and was bent on exorcism. "Now get up and go and stand in the cloakroom until your pants are dry. l don't care if you have to stand there all day." Luis got up and went, like a wounded animal, to stand behind the partition that separated the instructional area from the storage area/cloakroom. My heart went out to him. I wanted to take him in my arms, cuddle him, and tell him, "There, there, little one. It's going to be all right." But I didn't dare.

l don't know how I was so unlucky as to have gotten a student teaching placement in Miss Bedol's class. Even though she had been teaching for 35 years, I could not imagine that I had anything to learn from watching her. She and I could not be further apart in what we wanted for children.

My student teaching supervisor was adamant that I would not be permitted a change of assignment. Miss Bedol was a senior teacher in the school. It was not politic for the Office of Student Teaching to suggest to the principal that anything was amiss about my placement with Miss Bedol. She was a strong union member, and the fallout of requesting a change of placement could have major repercussions for the college. My supervisor said, "Make the best of it. It's only for four months. Surely, there are *some* things you can learn from this well-organized, highly experienced teacher?"

I was indeed learning. l learned that if you did not allow 6-year-olds to go to the toilet when they asked for permission to do so, they were likely to wet their pants. I learned it was easy to brutalize 6-year-olds, because they had fewer resources to fight back with. And I was learning that I could stand by, mute with anger and fear, and watch all this happen, without taking a stand. What did that say about me as a person and as a future teacher?

Howie Fairbairn's case

"I've looked at your report cards, Howie, and I'm afraid I can't let them go out this way to the parents."

Tom Cunningham shifted the pile of blue cards from his desk, across to where I was sitting. He had been, for me, a supportive and open-minded principal, encouraging me to teach in my own way, my own style, which, I must admit, was a bit far out. I believed in open, humanistic, child-centered education, and my way often looked to outsiders like scrambled eggs. But *I* could see the structure in what others saw as chaos, and *I* knew how much the children were learning.

I was unenthusiastic about the district's adoption of written report cards for primary graders and distressed about having to give my second graders letter marks for their work. But I was determined that I would not allow the gains my students had made to be discounted by a less-than-good mark. I could not reconcile grading on a curve as a way of representing my students' efforts and growth. As a consequence, I felt I was able, legitimately, to give each of them a grade of A for their work in academic subjects.

Tom Cunningham had insisted on seeing all the report cards before they went out to parents. Now here he was, sitting across that big administrator's desk of his, telling me that he would not permit these cards to go home. It was not possible, he told me, for all the children to get A's. That's not how the system worked.

I sat there, my thumbs rubbing the edges of the pack of report cards, wishing I could make them disappear.

The classroom scenes described above have all been critical incidents in the lives of the four teachers involved. These incidents are not only the stuff of classroom life; they are more often important learning opportunities for the teachers themselves. For as teachers reflect on these critical incidents, examine them in their complexity, work to understand the roles of the various players, and free themselves from their own needs to either judge or to find the quick-fix solution, they learn much about the how and the what of teaching. They learn that classrooms and school events are rarely what they seem on the surface, and that knowing what questions to ask allows for a situation to reveal its deeper, more subtle meanings.

LEARNING TO REFLECT ON PRACTICE

It is easy, in the pressure-cooker atmosphere of a critical incident, to leap to quick, impulsive judgments and draw conclusions that respond only to the surface aspects of the situation. It is also easy to see that such judgments are unsatisfying as well as inappropriate. Impulsive judgments rarely take into account the more important variables of a situation; they often rest on assumptions that are unwarranted or false, leading to actions that are often misguided. In retrospect, we may wish that we had taken time to think before we acted. Our actions may have made us look foolish; trapped by pride, or fear of losing face, we may find ourselves sticking up for what we are sorry we did in the first place.

Developing habits of thinking about classroom events frees us from the need to judge and to act impulsively. We allow ourselves the time for reflection, time to make sense of what is happening at deeper levels and, consequently, to respond in more thoughtful, reasonable ways. Teachers who respond in these ways are often referred to as "reflective practitioners" (Schön, 1987).

In situations of uncertainty, in situations where children, colleagues, administrators, or parents behave in ways that are not immediately understood, reflective practitioners do not resort to simplistic explanations or judgmental labeling (e.g., "He's doing that because he's just lazy"). Rather, they are able to step back, size up, and make sense of what is happening, generate a working hypothesis that intelligently encompasses the data, and take the risk of acting on that hypothesis. The actions are thoughtfully and intelligently conceived, sometimes representing new and original strategies that clearly fit. These teachers are able to marry problem identification with problem solving.

In their problem-solving actions, such teachers are able to observe both themselves and the impact of their actions on the problem situation. They do this nondefensively, with an open attitude that allows for assessing the effect of their actions on the situation. They do not see their actions as ways to "fix" the problem once and for all, but rather as the most appropriate strategies in a situation that is "in play" and is likely to continue to unfold.

These teachers understand that while others may help them, they are ultimately responsible for educating themselves through this process. For teachers who are reflective practitioners, teaching is an examined act; and in their ability to take risks to deal with problems creatively, they grow as teachers.

At the other end of the spectrum are teachers who adhere strictly to predetermined sets of strategies and apply them regardless of the need to assess each situation thoughtfully, on its own terms. Rather than making intelligent assessments of complex situations, they see only what they wish to see and neglect to probe for deeper, more complex understanding. These teachers have neglected to see the problems in their complexity, and consequently they apply inappropriate strategies to deal with the situations. They are unaware of the mismatch between problem and action, chiefly because they have not learned to *apprehend*—to observe and understand what is going on. Their actions come out of convention, instead of what is appropriate to the situation. When the action does not work, these teachers are likely to blame others for their own inappropriate actions. When confronted with the inappropriateness of their actions, they respond defensively, unwilling to take a deeper look at how they themselves have misapplied strategies or misread the problem.

These teachers have, consequently, limited capability to learn from their own actions. They look for "packaged" solutions to problems, often looking to others for these solutions. If the solution does not work, they hold others to blame, instead of themselves. Teaching, for these teachers, is an "unexamined act." There is no art to what they do (Wassermann & Eggert, 1988).

How does a teacher learn to become a reflective practitioner? How do teachers learn to see events in their complexity? How do they learn to size up situations, suspend judgment, generate viable hypotheses, risk action, and nondefensively assess the impact of their actions on the event? And how do they learn to observe themselves in this process of learning to teach? In building habits of thinking about teaching lie the secrets of ongoing professional development and more effective classroom practice.

BUILDING HABITS OF THINKING: THE TEACHER AS CASE WRITER

There are many ways to make strawberry cheesecake, as there are many ways to build habits of thinking about teaching. Writing your own cases is one way. It is not the only way, but for those teachers and student teachers who have written their own cases, the benefits extend even beyond the claims made above.

Those of us who are willing to sit down and rethink the events in a critical incident through the lens of case writing must, through that action, engage in the process of meaning making. Writing gives us distance from the event and allows for new perspectives. We are thus able to see the event in new ways. New understandings and hitherto hidden meanings are uncovered. In the process, we learn to see ourselves more objectively and learn more about ourselves as teachers.

Writing up a case about a critical event is not the same as watching the event played back on a videotape, another means of self-examination. Writing offers more. Through the process of writing, the event is not merely played back, but re-created. In that re-creation, we are able to see ourselves in new ways. Teachers and student teachers who write their own cases build habits of thinking about teaching and strengthen themselves as reflective practitioners.

The act of writing up a critical incident is also cathartic. As one teacher put it, "Writing this case helped me to unload some of my feelings, feelings that I was not even in touch with at the time of the event. The writing process gave me a safe outlet for the expression of those feelings. The case helped me to know myself better as a teacher." Writing about ourselves is, of course, a primary vehicle for self-understanding.

Case writing may not be every teacher's cup of cocoa. Some balk at writing. "I'm no writer," they say. But one does not have to be, or aspire to be, a Hemingway to write a case. Cases are not essays or exams to be graded. They are means of recording events that have occurred, events in which you, the writer, have been a key player. If you can talk about that event on the telephone, or across the breakfast table, then it is likely that you are equally able to write it.

Those who shun writing for fear of being "not a good enough writer" may turn out to be pleasantly surprised. You only have to try it once to see that no one fails at writing one' s own case. You only have to try it once to see how case writing may work for you. If it does, you will have found a source of potential self-development that will endure for all of your teaching days.

Strategies for Writing Cases

For teachers and student teachers who would choose to write cases as a means of reflection-on-practice, there are strategies that may be helpful in increasing their power for meaning making and professional growth.

Choosing a critical incident. Classroom teaching is a hotbed of potential critical incidents, as any teacher is likely to tell you. Luis wet his pants. Daphne spilled paint on her shirt. Stewart has not done his homework. The hamster died. The film projector broke down in the middle of the movie. There is no more art paper. The report cards are due on Friday. The principal is coming to observe me tomorrow. Malcolm is standing on his desk (again) and hurling insults at the rest of the class. The windows have been painted shut, and the room is stifling. The class enrollment is up to 33. There are not enough books for all the children. Mrs. Bell does not want her son Adam to be in the Christmas pageant. If teachers were to tally all the events that are nettlesome, frustrating, and exhausting in a single school day, the score would likely be daunting. For those seeking a "critical incident" for case writing, there would be much to choose from.

Which, then, should be chosen? Which would have the greatest potential for self-discovery? For increased understanding? For professional growth? There are no hard-and-fast rules about choosing a critical incident, but some of the following criteria may profitably be applied in selecting what to write about:

- Did the incident have "emotional power" for you?
- Did the incident present a dilemma that you were uncertain about, with respect to how it might be resolved?
- Did the incident require you to make a difficult choice?
- Did the incident cause you to respond in a way that you feel unsatisfied with and are still thinking about?
- Did the incident have ethical or moral implications?

The chances are good that if your critical incident satisfies at least these criteria, your choice is likely to be highly productive in allowing for self-study, introspection, and deeper understanding of the event through case writing. The bottom-line criterion, however, is your consuming interest in the event, your feeling about wanting to write it up.

Describing the context. It is not essential that you begin your case by describing the events that led up to the incident. This is, however, one way to give background and to set the incident within a context. In describing the background events, think about the time when the situation first caught your attention. What happened then? How did the chain of events begin? What was the context in which the events occurred? What were your responses in the initial stages? How did your responses contribute to/exacerbate the events? What psychosocial factors entered into the situation? What physical factors? What educational factors? What historical factors? In writing this part of your narrative, you "set the scene" for what is to come. You also place your critical incident in the context in which it occurred, allowing for the event to be understood within that context.

Identifying the players in the incident. Every narrative is enriched by a group of players who assume active and contributory roles in the event. In writing your case, identify the key and subsidiary players. Who were the active players? Who were behind-the-scenes players? What roles did each play? What were each of their relationships with each other? With you?

As you examine each of the players' roles, consider the feelings of each. Consider, too, the motives, goals, and expectations of each. Do not forget to include yourself in the list of players, and do not forget to look at your role through the lenses of feelings, expectations, motives, goals, and personal values. Look. too, at some of the assumptions that you might have made. Where did these assumptions come from? How did your assumptions influence your actions?

Reviewing the critical incident and your response to it. As the events unfolded, a crisis occurred in which the cumulative events "peaked." What happened? What choices were open to you as you considered what to do? What risks were involved in making those choices? How did you respond? What feelings led you to that particular choice? What assumptions lay behind the choice? What were some perceived consequences of the choice? Who did you see as the "villains"?

What values do you hold that influenced your choice of action? What about the event still troubles you? What about your response to the event still troubles you? (Sometimes a teacher's response is "not to respond." If this was the case, examine your nonresponse through the same lenses.)

Examining the effects of your actions. Every action (or nonaction) a teacher takes results in a series of reactions. What were some reactions to the response you made? What was the impact of your response on the students? On the class-room climate? On the other players in the situation? What was the consequence of your action (or nonaction) on yourself? In what ways did what you did enhance/diminish your respect for yourself? How were you empowered (or dis-empowered) in your choice of action? What remains unresolved for you about this incident?

Revisiting the incident. As you revisit this incident, how do you see the events differently? How do you see the players differently? How do you see your own role differently? How do you see the risks differently? The consequences? If you had it to do again, what would you have done differently? What now allows you to consider a different choice of response? What insights about self-as-teacher were revealed to you in this process of self-examination?

As you consider translating critical incidents into a case narrative, keep in mind that the questions above are intended to serve as guidelines to your think-ing about the situation and about your role in the situation. They are not intended to be *the* questions to be answered in writing your case. The case writer is the final arbiter about how the case is to be constructed and what it should, finally, contain.

Reflection, Reconsideration, Rewriting

When you have completed the first draft of your case, put it away from you, in a safe place, for at least 48 hours, for "marinating." Then reread it and examine what you have written using the following self-editing guidelines:

1. What assumptions about people, places, events have you made? Are these as-sumptions valid? What changes need to be made as you reexamine your as-sumptions?
2. What attributions have you made to others? Where have you attributed mo-tives, causes, preferences, feelings, attitudes, authority, responsibility, and other human strengths and weaknesses to others? To what extent do these attribu-tions appear as "factual truths"? What changes need to be made as you re-examine the attributions you have made to others?
3. What "extreme" statements have you made? Where have you used terms that permit no exception, like *all, none, always, exactly the same, no difference, never*? Ask yourself about the extent to which these absolute terms are appropriate, and how and if they need to be modified.
4. What polarizations of possibilities have you made in the form of either/or statements? Where have you indicated a simple two-valued orientation (e.g., it is either good or bad; it is either right or wrong; they are either for or against) where perhaps shades of gray are more appropriate? Ask yourself about how

these either/or statements restrict your thinking and whether they need to be modified.

5. What value judgments have you made? Are these value judgments intended to be read as "factual truths"? Where did the judgments come from? Ask yourself about how your value judgments are reflective of your best thinking about the events in the case and how and if they need to be modified.

6. To what extent have you been able to go beyond the surface issues in the event and look to the deeper, more complex issues? What process has allowed you to do this or prevented you from doing this?

7. To what extent are you able to see yourself nondefensively as a key player in the incident? To what extent are you blaming others for what occurred? To what extent are you able to see the role you played in the process? To what extent are you able to "own" your own actions?

As you reflect on these questions in relation to your case narrative, you will want to make notes in the margins throughout the first draft of your case. You are the one in charge of editing your case—the only one to decide what needs to be changed and how the changes are to be made as you put your case into the next draft.

Extracting Meaning

It is experience that contributes most significantly to the process of maturing. But experience alone does not suffice to generate wisdom. One can experience marriage half a dozen times and still not benefit from the experience by making a wiser choice of mate. It is what we are able to make of the experience that allows for insight and enriches understanding. In the process of meaning making and extracting meaning from experience, we grow in our intellectual power, in our ability to understand, and in our wisdom and maturity.

Tools of reflection are brought to bear on meaning making; they enable us to move from trite and simplistic judgments into the examination of deeper and more complex factors within the experience. To questions such as "What's this all about?" we are best served by caution, by a willingness to suspend judgment. Because tough and critical-minded questions can often do much toward pointing to meaning, they should be encouraged rather than avoided.

Meanings are, of course, not set in stone, and there may be as many interpretations of an event as there are interpreters. There are, however, interpretations that are "more" or "less" appropriate. Interpretations are more appropriate when they are closely aligned with the data in the case; when value judgments, assumptions, and attributions are acknowledged; and when intuitive leaps beyond the data are taken with great caution. Interpretations are less appropriate when they go far beyond what the data support; when they are studded with unacknowledged value judgments, assumptions, and attributions; when intuitive leaps into the unknown are presented as factual truths.

The examination of self-in-the-process is perhaps the most challenging, as well as the most potentially fruitful, exercise for personal growth. Self-scrutiny is not for the faint of heart, but it is the stuff of which great teachers are made. There is nothing to it, except opening yourself to a nondefensive examination of who you are and what you are doing in the act called teaching—about as nonterrifying as bungee jumping. To do this, without self-reproach, is the key to healthful, professional growth. It is professional development worth a life-time of serious study.

Having now written your case narrative, and having subjected it to the scrutiny of reflection, reconsideration, and rewriting, it is time for you once more to put the case away and give yourself some more distance from it before you undertake the task of interpretation and analysis. If you can allow a week to pass between the editing and the interpretation/analysis stages of writing, this is to the good. When you return to read the case again, you can begin the deeper search for meaning.

Before you begin writing your interpretation and analysis, think about the following questions. You may want to write some notes in making your response to them.

1. What do you see as the central issues of this case? List them, and identify the issue that you see as most critical.
2. Which players did you write as "villains" and which as "heroes"? What feelings did you ascribe to each player? What motives? To what extent are these appraisals accurate?
3. To whom did you attribute "blame"? What other factors might explain the behavior of the "blamed" party?
4. What values were at stake for you in this case?
5. What feelings did this event promote in you? Which of your own emotional needs seemed to motivate your behavior?
6. What risks were involved for you in acting in a way that reflected your own values? What prevented you from acting on your values? What encouraged you to act on your values?
7. What did this incident teach you about yourself as a teacher? As a person?
8. What questions about children, about teaching, about administration, about yourself-as-teacher did this case raise for you? How will you go about gathering data that will inform these questions?

Use your notes as raw material and write, on a separate sheet of paper, your interpretation of your case. You may wish to glance at the interpretations below, written by those teachers whose cases opened the chapter, for reference.

Nancy Fusco's interpretation

I had made some assumptions—about the safety of the money in the bottom drawer of the desk. It means, very likely, that one or more children were involved in taking the money. It means that the children may have to lose their book orders, unless I find the money or find a way of replacing the money. I blamed Kevin at first, thinking that his history makes him guilty. Is Kevin the culprit? Impossible to know for sure, but he is suspect, based on his history.

What does this mean for me? I feel stupid, having been so careless about where I left the money. I trusted the children and feel disappointed, betrayed. I have given them much of myself, and this is how they repaid me? By stealing from me? Whew! Where is all this coming from? My own needs are getting in the way of my best professional judgment. I have expectations about how the children should have behaved and am disappointed, furious, when they let me down.

Writing this up gives me a clearer perspective on the events, as well as my role in them. I can see that an impulsive action—such as accusing Kevin face to face—would likely be highly inappropriate. What I've got to do is sit down, clear my head, unload some of my emotional baggage, and choose what I think will be an appropriate decision, in which the values I hold about teaching and about children are not violated.

David Liddle's interpretation

I was prepared. I worked hard. I wanted my first attempt at teaching a case to be successful. I didn't want to appear stupid or incompetent to the students or to my mentor teacher. I had a lot of self-esteem riding on this assignment. I was also very nervous.

I was too nervous to remember all the strategies to use in the class discussion. I lost it, and that's how I blew it. I became defensive, and that's how I blamed it all on Malcolm. Now I see how I put Malcolm on the spot and made him feel stupid. First, I deliberately called on him when I thought he wasn't listening. Second, I asked him a tough, challenging question that came out of my mouth before I had a chance to weigh its impact. Secretly, I wanted to "get" this student who was mouthing off to me in the class. I was mad, and I was unable to acknowledge my own feelings. When Malcolm suggested that I had made him look stupid, he was right. That was, sad to say, my intention.

In retrospect, I could have said something like, "You're right, Malcolm. That question is really challenging, and perhaps the class isn't quite ready for it yet. I think I was a bit premature in raising it so soon, so let's leave it for a bit, and perhaps you'll tell me more about your ideas about being poor. You said it's something that many of us in this classroom feel, too." If I had gone this route, if I had acknowledged my role in the situation, I would have owned some of my responsibility for the situation Malcolm was in.

For me, the issues in this case are about control. Who is in control, the teacher or the student? I felt that Malcolm was taking control from me, and I was afraid to let it happen, so I challenged him and put him down. Loss of control is a big issue for me, and one that I'm going to have to look at in my professional development. Two of the important questions I have to raise are how I'm going to learn those skills of conducting good classroom discussions and how I'm going to learn to be nondefensive when things go wrong in the classroom.

Helen Hunter's interpretation

The critical issue in this narrative is my fear. I was afraid of speaking up to Miss Bedol. I was afraid of telling her what was in my heart—that I thought she was a monster, and evil. I couldn't fathom a teacher who was so intent on hurting children. Yet I could not speak of this to her. First of all, who was I, a student teacher, to confront a senior teacher in this way? Second, I was afraid of the repercussions of such an action. I chose not to act; and in that way, I violated my own values about caring for children and treating them respectfully. I can see that sometimes teachers and especially student teachers are placed in situations where they must guard their feelings, where it is safer not to act. But I'm not sure that safety is the critical issue here.

I'm trying to see what I would have gained and what I would have lost if I had confronted Miss Bedol. I know that I would have made her an enemy. I also know that she would not have behaved differently with the children, that my confronting her would not have made a difference to how she was in class. So what would I have gained by speaking out? Perhaps my self-respect. At least I would have made my own feelings known and not stood by, and, by my silence, seem to be siding with the actions she had taken. I need to know more about Miss Bedol. What is it that causes a teacher like her to behave so hurtfully to students? Is she just mean? Or are there some underlying reasons I've yet to understand?

I must also place the Office of Student Teaching in the role of villain. They, I believe, have a responsibility to find the best placements for student teachers. Miss Bedol's class is definitely not the best placement. That they would not agree to finding an alternate placement for me is part of the bigger problem. They were likely also afraid, as I was, about the repercussions.

I will never forget this incident and what it meant to me to have to remain silent in the face of her treatment of children. I think of what someone wrote about evil being done when "good men remain silent" and I will always remember the pain of my silence.

Howie Fairbairn's interpretation

Critical for me in this incident was the issue of evaluation versus children's self-esteem. This, to me, was the number-one issue. That is, how do we as teachers make fair assessments of children's work, while at the same time promoting positive self-concepts? Is assessment more important than how children feel about themselves? Can we have both? Or are these mutually exclusive?

Another critical issue in this case was the power play between administrator and teacher. Who has the right to decide about the children's marks? If that right is taken away from the teacher, is the teacher being disempowered? How can the principal know which marks are fair?

At first, I was prepared to see Tom Cunningham as the villain in this case. On reflection, I just see him as a good man who is trying to do a good job. He has some values that are different from mine, and I must learn to respect that. The fact that he is the principal puts him into a situation where he can have the last word. I know that if I were prepared to take this issue to the Federation of Teachers, and call his action an infringement on a teacher's rights to choose, I might have a case. I have to decide what to do. Is my fight with Tom? Or can I find a way to reconcile his values about assessment with my values about assessment and self-esteem? I must get some distance from the emotionality of this case before I can apply professional wisdom and logic to my next actions.

CONCLUSION: SO YOU WANT TO BE A TEACHER?

The street was crowded with tourists and locals, the warm, summer evening a backdrop to the scene. People in shorts, eating ice cream cones, brushed by them as Bill Robbins, his wife, and his student teacher waited on the corner for the light to change. A young woman in her mid-20s, slim, chocolate ice cream dripping through her fingers, turned, walked back five steps and looked at him. "Mr. Robbins?" she asked. "It *is* you. You were my teacher. Do you remember me?"

He looked at her, his smile warm, a bit embarrassed. "Tell me your name," he said, his hand reaching out to touch her arm. "I can't remember."

"It's Marsha. It was a long time ago. Marsha Saba. Ten years, Mr. Robbins."

He looked at her, his smile broadened, but he did not remember. So many students, so many faces, so many years.

"It's okay if you don't remember. I remember you. You were the best teacher I ever had," she said, now shouting, as she turned to continue her walk, licking the ice cream from her fingers. Other passersby watching, smiling, were drawn into the scene.

His wife beamed at him. This was not a new sentiment for her. She had heard it before—indeed, in the 28 years of his teaching career, had heard it often.

"What do you do," his student teacher asked, "that makes them say that? How is it that they continue to remember you, to hold you in such high regard? What's the secret?"

He smiled again, sheepish, but full of pride. "I think they all know that I care about them," he began, his eyes looking down the street for the answer. "It's never them and me. It's always us. Partners in learning. Never adversaries. That's probably the main thing.

"I think they know, too, that I always expect them to give me the best they've got. But I think more than that, in all these years of teaching, I've never lost my enthusiasm for it. Kids know whether you're enthusiastic about what you're doing, whether you love teaching or are just marking time, doing a job. They can sense that right away about you. And you can't pretend enthusiasm. The phoniness sticks out right away."

"But isn't it impossible to teach the same subject year after year and still keep your enthusiasm? Don't you get bored? How do you do it?" the student teacher queried, thinking of his own future.

"Boring? Well, I guess it depends on how you teach it. I guess if you follow a formula-like approach, the teachers' manual kind of teaching—you know, if it's Thursday, it must be invertebrates—you're going to get bored pretty quickly. But if you know how to 'read' a class, to respond to what is there, and to create curriculum opportunities based on each class's differences, then it's like teaching a different subject each time. If you allow yourself to be responsive to students, instead of ruled by the textbook, each class will put its own spin on the curriculum, making it seem brand new each time. That's what keeps teaching alive, fresh, vital for me. And that's what keeps me alive and full of enthusiasm after so many years."

"That seems pretty risky," the student teacher mused. "You've got to be open to change, to roll with what comes each time, to make meanings out of all those new situations."

"Risk, Lawrence, is in the eye of the beholder. I think it's more risky to be stagnant, to do the same things day after day, year after year, to bore kids to death and to mummify yourself. I much prefer taking the risks that allow you to challenge yourself, to do what's required to grow on the job. You can't have growth without risk. And who wants a teacher who's not willing to take the risks to grow?

"A teacher makes choices, Lawrence," Bill Robbins continued. "The choices don't come from unlimited options, of course, but there are enough options available to define you and to shape you as a teacher. You become your choices. You know what you stand for. You are clear. You know the limits beyond which you are not going to compromise. You are unafraid to be who you are, unafraid to be open to looking at yourself, to growing on the job."

This time it was Lawrence Evans, the student teacher, who turned to look down the street, searching into his future, for what he would become, hoping that he would be able to keep his enthusiasm alive, that one day, his former student would tell him, "You know, you were the very best teacher I ever had."

REFERENCES

Schön, Donald. 1987. *Educating the Reflective Practitioner.* San Francisco: Jossey-Bass.

Wassermann, Selma, and Eggert, Wally. 1988. *Profiles of Teaching Competency* (revised form). Unpublished manuscript, Faculty of Education, Simon Fraser University, Vancouver, British Columbia.

About the Author

Selma Wassermann is a Professor in the Faculty of Education at Simon Fraser University, Vancouver, Canada. A recipient of the Excellence in Teaching Award at Simon Fraser University, she has published widely and is in much demand as a leader of teaching-for-thinking seminars and for case study teaching throughout the United States and Canada.